# angles on atypical psychology

# dedications

To Clare and Sam with love     *MJ*

To Charlie Woodcock, without whom I wouldn't be
writing psychology books     *DP*

It seems appropriate that this book should be dedicated
to my three lovely sisters, Penny, Ros and Kate who will
appreciate the joke. With lots of love to this wonderful trio
who are tirelessly supportive     *DD*

# angles on

## atypical psychology

## Matt Jarvis, Dave Putwain
## and Diana Dwyer

Series Editors: Matt Jarvis Julia Russell

Text © Matt Jarvis, Dave Putwain and Diana Dwyer 2002
Original illustrations © Nelson Thornes Ltd 2002

First published in 2002 by:
Nelson Thornes Ltd
Delta Place
27 Bath Road
CHELTENHAM
GL53 7TH
United Kingdom

. 03 04 05 06 / 10 9 8 7 6 5 4 3 2

A catalogue record for this book is available from the British Library

ISBN 0 7487 6812 2

Illustrations by Oxford Designers and Illustrators
Page make-up by Northern Phototypesetting Co. Ltd

Printed in Great Britain by Scotprint

# contents

# acknowledgements

We would like to thank all those who have worked with us on this book, including Rick, Carolyn, Fiona and Emily at Nelson Thornes, and Cara and Chris for their helpful comments on the manuscript. Thanks as well to all the teachers and lecturers who have provided us with such valuable feedback on the *Angles* series so far.

The authors and publishers would particularly like to acknowledge:

The Associated Press Ltd for the photo on page 200; Corbis for the photo on page 120; Corel (NT) for the photos on pages 101, 122, 181 (right) and 206; David Gifford/Science Photo Library for the photo on page 31; Format Photographers for the photos on pages 48 and 152; Sally and Richard Greenhill for the photo on page 201; The Hulton Archive for the photo (left) on page 181; The Hulton-Deutsch Collection for the photo on page 176; International Universities Press for the figures on pages 66 and 167; National Medical Slide Bank for the photo on page 32; Photodisc (NT) for the photos on pages 28, 72, 104 and 172; Rex for the photos on pages 85 and 159; Jean Reed for the photo on page 122; Robert Harding Picture Library for the photos on pages 19 and 152; Science and Society Picture Library for the photos on pages 91 and 116; Martin Sookias for the photos on pages 48 and 109; Stockpix (NT) for the photo on page 88; and The Wellcome Foundation for the photos on pages 39, 45 and 54.

Every effort has been made to contact copyright holders and we apologise if anyone has been overlooked.

# Coverage of examination board specifications

| Chapter | Topics covered | Edexcel | AQA A | AQA B |
|---|---|---|---|---|
| 1. Defining and Classifying Psychological Abnormality | Defining abnormality<br>Classification systems<br>Iatrogenesis and MPD<br>Stigmatisation<br>Cultural issues | Concept of abnormality<br>DSM system<br>Cultural factors in diagnosis | Defining abnormality<br>DSM and ICD systems<br>MPD<br>Culture-bound syndromes | What is abnormal?<br>DSM or ICD system |
| 2. The Biomedical Model | Genetics<br>Biochemistry<br>Drugs<br>ECT and TMS<br>Psychosurgery | The medical approach<br>One medical treatment | Biomedical approach<br>Drugs<br>ECT<br>Psychosurgery | Assumptions of medical approach<br>One medical treatment |
| 3. The Learning Approach | Conditioning<br>Social learning<br>Desensitisation<br>Flooding and implosion<br>Virtual reality therapy<br>Aversion<br>Token economies<br>Modelling | The behavioural approach<br>One behavioural therapy | One classical conditioning therapy<br>One operant conditioning therapy | Assumptions of the learning approach<br>One behavioural therapy |
| 4. The Cognitive Approach | Beck's theory<br>Cognitive neuropsychology<br>Cognitive therapy<br>REBT<br>EMDR | The cognitive approach<br>One cognitive therapy | Two cognitive therapies | Assumptions of the cognitive approach<br>One cognitive therapy |
| 5. The Psychodynamic Approach | Early experiences<br>Freudian theory<br>Attachment theory<br>Psychoanalysis and psychoanalytic therapy<br>Brief dynamic therapy | The psychodynamic approach<br>One dynamic therapy | Two dynamic therapies | Assumptions of the psychodynamic approach<br>One dynamic therapy |
| 6. The Humanistic Approach | Rogers' theory<br>Person-centred therapy<br>Gestalt therapy | The humanistic approach<br>One humanistic therapy | | Assumptions of the humanistic approach<br>One humanistic therapy |
| 7. The Social Approach | Social psychiatry<br>Labelling theory<br>Social constructionism<br>Social explanations of mental disorder<br>Community care<br>Community psychiatric nursing<br>Mental health support | The social approach<br>One social approach to treatment | | Labelling<br>Racism and sexism |

| Chapter | Topics covered | Edexcel | AQA A | AQA B |
|---------|----------------|---------|-------|-------|
| 8. Schizophrenia | Symptoms<br>Genetic factors<br>Dopamine hypothesis<br>Neurological factors<br>Cognitive theory<br>Psychodynamic theory<br>Alanen's theory<br>Communication patterns<br>Social drift vs causation | Symptoms<br>Biological factors<br>Psychological factors<br>Social factors | Clinical characteristics<br>Biological theories<br>Psychological theories | Symptoms and diagnosis<br>Biological theories<br>Psychological theories<br>Treatment<br>(see Chapters 2–7)<br>Sociocultural theories |
| 9. Depression | Symptoms and subtypes<br>Genetic factors<br>Biochemical factors<br>Neurological factors<br>Psychodynamic theories<br>Cognitive theory<br>The hopelessness model<br>Socio-economic status<br>Feminist perspectives | Symptoms<br>Biological factors<br>Psychological factors<br>Social factors –<br>two disorders | Clinical characteristics<br>Biological theories<br>Psychological theories | Unipolar, bipolar and SAD<br>Symptoms and diagnosis<br>Treatment |
| 10. Eating Disorders | Disorders and symptoms<br>Sociocultural approach<br>Feminist theory<br>Psychodynamic theory<br>Cognitive theory<br>Genetic factors<br>Biochemical factors<br>Neurological factors | Symptoms<br>Social factors<br>Psychological factors<br>Biological factors | Clinical characteristics<br>Psychological theories<br>Biological theories | Symptoms of both<br>anorexia and bulimia<br>Societal pressure<br>Family pressure<br>Cognitive factors<br>Biological factors<br>Treatment (see Chapters 2–7) |
| 11. Anxiety Disorders | Disorders and symptoms<br>Genetic factors<br>Biochemical factors<br>Neurological factors<br>Learning theory<br>Cognitive bias<br>Psychodynamic theory | Symptoms<br>Biological factors<br>Psychological factors | Symptoms of any<br>one disorder<br>Biological theories<br>Psychological theories | Symptoms of GAD,<br>agoraphobia, social phobia<br>and specific phobias.<br>OCD and PTSD<br>Biological explanations and<br>treatments (Chapter 2)<br>Psychological<br>explanations and<br>treatments, inc. learning,<br>cognitive, psychodynamic<br>and humanist (Chapters 3–7) |

# 1

# Defining and Classifying Psychological Abnormality

In this chapter we look at the various ways in which we can define human behaviour, emotion and thinking as 'atypical' or 'abnormal' and examine systems by which we can classify the range of psychological abnormalities into categories of mental disorder. We look in detail at the two most important systems for classification and diagnosis of mental disorder, the *Diagnostic and Statistical Manual of Mental Disorder*, produced by the American Psychiatric Association and the *International Classification of the Causes of Disease and Death*, produced by the World Health Organization. We will consider research into how useful these systems are, and look at the possible negative effects of receiving a psychiatric diagnosis. Finally, we will examine a range of cultural issues in the classification and diagnosis of mental disorder, including the importance of different cultural attitudes to mental disorder and the existence of culture-bound syndromes.

## Atypical or abnormal?

You may be wondering what the difference is between 'normal' and 'typical' or between 'abnormal' and 'atypical.' Why, in a book called *Angles on Atypical Psychology* have we chosen to begin with a chapter on *abnormality*? The terms mean roughly the same thing, but most of the time, we prefer to use 'atypical' because it is less of a 'loaded' term than 'abnormal' – it sounds less judgemental. However, in this chapter we are talking about people's judgements on what makes someone 'normal' or 'abnormal' and so it is important to use terms that make clear all the implications of such judgements. We therefore speak of normality and abnormality in this chapter.

# Who is abnormal?

Perhaps the most fundamental question we can consider in a discussion of atypical psychology is what precisely makes us think of a particular pattern of thinking, behaviour or emotion as abnormal? We can look here at four particularly important ways by which we might classify people as abnormal. As we shall see, none of these consistently distinguishes psychologically 'normal' and 'abnormal' people. We can also look at what we mean by 'ideal mental health' and consider whether deviation from this is a satisfactory way of defining abnormality.

## Statistically unusual people

The most literal way of defining something as atypical or abnormal is according to how often it occurs. According to this definition anything that occurs relatively rarely can be thought of as 'atypical'. This approach is most useful when dealing with human characteristics that can be reliably measured, for example intelligence, anxiety and depression. We know that in any measurable human characteristic, most people's scores will cluster around the average, and that as we move away from this average fewer and fewer people will attain that score. This is called the *normal distribution*. The normal distribution of IQ (intelligence quotient) is shown in Figure 1.1.

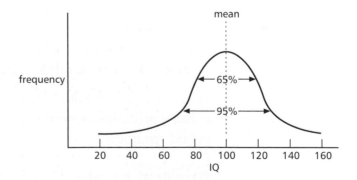

**Figure 1.1** The normal distribution of IQ scores across the population

The average IQ, according to tests on a cross-section of the population, is set at 100. The 85 and 115 scores are set as those between which 65% of people will fall and the 70 and 130 scores are set as those between which 95% of people will fall. If someone scores below 70 they fall in the bottom 2.5% of the population. This means that they meet one of the three criteria for diagnosis of *mental retardation* (the other two being onset of the low IQ before 18 years and the inability of the individual to meet the standards of their cultural group in communication, self-care, social skills, work, health or safety).

The limitations of the statistical infrequency approach to defining atypicality are as obvious as they are serious. IQ scores of 130+ are just as uncommon as those of below 70, but we wouldn't consider calling someone abnormal or giving them a diagnosis just because they were very bright! Neither would there be any advantage to giving someone a diagnosis of retardation based on their IQ score if they were living a happy and fulfilled life. Statistical infrequency *on its own* is thus not a sufficient criterion for defining behaviour as abnormal, although statistical measures, for example of IQ, depression or anxiety, may form part of the process of diagnosis.

## People whose behaviour deviates from social norms

Most of us tend to be at least a little wary of those whose behaviour does not conform to social norms. In some cases we might choose to define behaviour as abnormal just because it offends our sense of what is 'normal' or 'right' or 'moral'. There are behaviours that virtually all of us would agree are abnormal on moral grounds, and this is reflected in the diagnosis of *antisocial personality disorder*, commonly called *psychopathy*. The psychopath is impulsive, aggressive and irresponsible. According to the DSM-IV-TR one important symptom of antisocial personality disorder is 'failure to conform to social norms with respect to lawful behaviours as indicated by repeatedly performing acts that are grounds for arrest'.

Although we would generally agree that psychopaths are abnormal on the basis that they defy what we think of as important social norms, too much reliance on deviation from norms to define someone as abnormal can lead to the abuse of people's rights. Some particularly 'tragi-comic' examples of mental disorders were defined purely according to social convention in the nineteenth century (Masson, 1992; Gomm, 1996). Examples are shown in Table 1.1.

| Classification | Symptoms |
|---|---|
| Drapetomania | Slaves experienced an irrational desire to run away |
| Nymphomania | Middle class women were sexually attracted to working class men |
| Moral insanity | Women who inherited money spent it on themselves rather than on male relatives |

**Table 1.1** Examples of socially constructed nineteenth-century 'mental disorders'

Looking at the three examples in Table 1.1 it is clear that one reason for defining behaviour as abnormal (and hence unacceptable) is to maintain social control over a group (such as women or a minority ethnic group). In the nineteenth century, by being able to get women diagnosed with nymphomania or moral insanity (with the co-operation of male doctors), men were able to strictly control women's economic and sexual lives, in line with their own interests.

The classifications of drapetomania, nymphomania and moral insanity all appear quite ludicrous nowadays – *but only because social conventions have changed*. Whenever we define someone as abnormal because they breach a social norm, we place restrictions on their personal freedom. As well as raising these important ethical issues, defining atypicality by social deviation has important practical limitations. Social norms are culturally specific – they can differ significantly from one generation to the next and between different ethnic, regional and socio-economic groups. Imagine the response of people in Britain as recently as the early twentieth century to the idea of a modern rave or punk concert as entertainment, and you start to see just how much social conventions change from one generation to another (Figure 1.2).

**Figure 1.2** Cultural attitudes to what is normal change over time

## People in psychological distress

A quite different (and perhaps kinder) way of defining someone as psychologically abnormal is to consider how he or she is feeling. Certainly when people seek help for a psychological problem they usually do so, not because they have noticed that they are statistically unusual or socially deviant, but because they are suffering psychological distress. It is tempting to suggest that, rather than labelling unusual or non-conformist people as abnormal, we should focus our efforts towards helping those experiencing psychological suffering.

But how good a criterion is distress for defining psychological abnormality? Certainly, most mental disorders involve a degree of distress. In conditions like depression and anxiety, severe distress is perhaps the most important feature of the condition, and plays an important role in diagnosis. Moreover, it is important to know when people are experiencing distress because we can use psychological techniques to make them feel better, even in cases where their suffering does not add up to a diagnosis of a particular mental disorder.

However, a mental disorder is never diagnosed according to the individual's suffering alone. In the case of depression for example, a range of other symptoms accompanies depressed mood, including disruption to sleep and eating habits. Furthermore, there are some serious mental disorders in which the sufferer does not experience distress. In the case of antisocial personality disorder (or psychopathic disorder) for example, although the psychopath's behaviour may be of great concern to others, it does not normally bother the psychopath.

## People whose behaviour is maladaptive or dangerous

The terms *adaptive* and *maladaptive* come originally from evolutionary biology and refer to behaviours and characteristics that increase and decrease, respectively, the chances of an individual surviving or reproducing. One way of defining a person as abnormal is when their behaviour, thinking or emotional state reduces their chances of survival. Using the term 'maladaptive' a little more broadly we can also apply it to people whose behaviour, thinking or emotional state prevents them living a happy, fulfilled life. This can include any symptoms that prevent people keeping a job or having successful relationships.

Maladaptiveness in this broader sense forms an important part of diagnosis. For example, diagnosis of depression, anxiety disorders and schizophrenia usually requires that the everyday life of the individual is significantly affected by their symptoms. This is important as it gives us a relatively fair and objective way of identifying the point at which a person's individual characteristics become abnormal – whenever they start to interfere with their life. There may be cases, however, when someone's behaviour may appear maladaptive to others but is seen by the individual in terms of expressing themselves or making a political statement. People who take part in high-risk sports or political protest are technically behaving maladaptively as they are decreasing their chances of survival – but as a society we generally do not class these behaviours as abnormal, although we may think of them as irresponsible. If we were to class any behaviour that carried personal risk as abnormal we would significantly interfere with people's civil liberties. Thus, for example, boxing remains legal against the opinion of most doctors.

Maladaptiveness in the narrower sense of decreasing one's chances of survival becomes especially important when we start to consider the issue of whether to force someone to accept treatment against their will. Under the 1983 Mental Health Act, people can be detained against their will for a mental health problem only when their condition presents a significant risk to their own safety or that of others.

## 'Ideal mental health'

A different way of looking at normality and abnormality is not to look at what makes someone abnormal but rather at what we consider to be the characteristics of ideal mental health. In other words, what criteria does someone have to meet to be 'normal'? Jahoda (1958) suggested that we are in good mental health if we have no symptoms or distress, are rational and can introspect (look at ourselves) accurately, self-actualise (reach our potential), cope with stress, have a realistic view of the world, have good self-esteem and lack guilt, are independent and can successfully work, love and enjoy leisure. In one sense, Jahoda was well ahead of her time in these criteria, building in elements of psychological theory that were popular both before and after her time.

However, psychologists of different theoretical orientations would not necessarily consider these criteria for mental health equally important. Those favouring a biomedical model (see Chapter 2) would probably focus mostly on symptoms and distress, whereas those favouring a cognitive-behavioural approach (see Chapter 4) would be more likely to be interested in a person's rationality and ability to cope with stress. Humanistic psychologists (see Chapter 6) would be the most interested in self-esteem and self-actualisation, whilst psychodynamic psychologists (see Chapter 5) might be particularly interested in the ability to introspect and look at the world realistically.

Another problem of this approach lies in drawing the line between normality and abnormality. Do we have to meet all of Jahoda's criteria all the time before we are judged mentally healthy? Is it more important to meet all of them some of the time or some of them all the time? Thus, although Jahoda's concept of mental health is an ideal, we cannot use it on its own to identify abnormality. This is not to say that it is not important, however. In psychiatric diagnosis patients may be given a score of 1–100, known as their *global assessment of functioning*, representing their overall mental health (see p. 9 for an example).

## Conclusions: what is abnormality?

Although all the criteria above play a significant role in diagnosis of mental disorder, none of them on its own stands up very well as sufficient to define people's behaviour or experience as abnormal. In practice we use a mixture of criteria to decide who will benefit from being classified as abnormal: thus mental retardation, for example, is diagnosed when an individual's IQ is statistically unusually low *and* their behaviour is maladaptive.

A limitation with these ways of defining abnormality is *cultural relativism*. This means that what is statistically unusual or considered socially unacceptable or maladaptive varies from one culture to another. It is thus very difficult to make judgements about the 'normality' of someone from a culture other than your own. We revisit issues of culture and diagnosis on p. 18.

## interactive angles

Consider the three following case examples of potential abnormality. Match the case example to the criterion for defining them as abnormal.

**1** A woman seeks counselling because she is feeling so down.

**A.** Deviation from social norms.

**2** A psychologist is concerned about a schoolboy because his IQ is 64.

**B.** Personal distress.

**3** A man complaining about his late housing benefit gestures at staff with a stuffed lobster.

**C.** Statistically unusual.

## Systems for the classification and diagnosis of abnormality

There are a number of systems by which we can classify abnormal patterns of thinking, behaviour and emotion into mental disorders. These systems not only classify abnormality into mental disorders but also give guidelines on how to diagnose them. The two most widely used systems of classification and diagnosis are the Diagnostic and Statistical Manual of Mental Disorder (DSM), produced by the American Psychiatric Association, and the International Classification of the Causes of Disease and Death (ICD), produced by the World Health Organization. We can look at these in some detail.

### The DSM system

The American Psychiatric Association published the original DSM system in 1952. The current version of the DSM system is the fourth edition with *text revisions* (changes to the structure of the classification system rather than to the classifications themselves). DSM-IV (the fourth edition) was published in 1994, and DSM-IV-TR (fourth edition with text revisions) was published in 2000. DSM-IV contains over 200 distinct mental disorders.

Each successive version of the DSM has tightened up the criteria for diagnosing disorders: newer versions, for example, tend to specify how long symptoms are required to last for diagnosis. There have also been some changes in the nature of disorders identified by the DSM in line with changing social norms. Before the publication of DSM-III in 1980, homosexuality was classified as a mental disorder, but this classification has now been dropped. New disorders have also been identified since the earlier versions of DSM. For example, since DSM-III the category of eating disorders has included bulimia as well as anorexia and since DSM-IV it has included binge-eating disorders. The major categories of the DSM are shown in Box 1.1.

---

Clinical syndromes:
1 Disorders usually first diagnosed in infancy, childhood, or adolescence
2 Delirium, dementia, amnestic and other cognitive disorders
3 Substance-related disorders
4 Schizophrenia and other psychotic disorders
5 Mood disorders
6 Anxiety disorders
7 Somatoform disorders
8 Factitious disorder
9 Dissociative disorders
10 Sexual and gender identity disorders
11 Eating disorders
12 Sleep disorders
13 Impulse control disorders not elsewhere classified
14 Adjustment disorders

**Box 1.1** The major categories of DSM-IV-TR

---

Since the publication of DSM-III-R in 1987, diagnosis takes place on five different bases or *axes*. This approach is called *multiaxial diagnosis*. Although clinicians are not obliged to use all five axes when making a diagnosis, it is widely agreed that it is helpful to do so. The five axes of DSM-IV-TR are shown in Box 1.2.

Davison and Neale (1994) have provided a case example of a multiaxial diagnosis. A 45-year-old American construction worker named Alex was assessed after having been arrested for sexually assaulting a woman when he was drunk. He had been almost continually drunk since his daughter had been killed in an accident 4 years before, and he was now suffering liver damage. On investigation it turned out that Alex had a history of gang and domestic violence. He showed no concern or remorse. His multiaxial diagnosis was as follows:

- Axis I: alcohol dependence

- Axis II: antisocial personality disorder

- Axis III: liver damage

- Axis IV: arrest, death of child

- Axis V: 42.

You can see the advantages of multiaxial diagnosis from this case. Alex's current clinical condition of alcohol dependency is not sufficient to explain the complexity of his situation. From his history of violence and lack of remorse or concern at his current situation it appears that Alex also suffers from a long-standing personality problem. It is important to be aware of his liver damage as this may influence what treatments are safe for him. We would certainly also wish to take account of the death of Alex's daughter in planning any psychological treatment. The GAF score gives an idea of how urgent is Alex's need for treatment.

---

**Axis I: Clinical disorder** – the disorder or disorders from which the patient is suffering. In addition, other circumstances that may require intervention are noted here, including stress-related physical symptoms and a history of sexual abuse.

**Axis II: Personality disorders and retardation** – because these chronic conditions often go alongside axis I disorders they are looked at separately.

**Axis III: General medical conditions** – medical problems that are of relevance to the condition or its treatment.

**Axis IV: Psychosocial and environmental problems** – life problems that influence the psychological well-being of the individual, e.g. homelessness, unemployment

**Axis V: Global assessment of functioning (GAF)** – a score from 0 to 100 given to the individual to classify their overall functioning.

---

**Box 1.2** The five axes of the DSM-IV-TR

## The ICD system

The World Health Organization proposed the first draft of the ICD in 1948. It is currently in its tenth edition (ICD-10), which was published in 1992. One chapter of the ICD is devoted to mental disorders. Over time, successive versions of the ICD and the DSM have become more alike, and there was close consultation between the World Health Organization and the American Psychiatric Association when ICD-10 and DSM-IV were developed in the early 1990s. The 11 categories of mental disorder in ICD-10 (shown in Box 1.3) thus resemble fairly closely those of DSM-IV-TR.

**Includes:** disorders of psychological development

**Excludes:** symptoms, signs and abnormal clinical and laboratory findings, not elsewhere classified (R00–R99).

1  F00–F09  Organic, including symptomatic, mental disorders
2  F10–F19  Mental and behavioural disorders to psychoactive substance use
3  F20–F29  Schizophrenia, schizotypal and delusional disorders
4  F30–F39  Mood (affective) disorders
5  F40–F48  Neurotic, stress-related and somatoform disorders
6  F50–F59  Behavioural syndromes associated with physiological disturbances and physical factors
7  F60–F69  Disorders of adult personality and behaviour
8  F70–F79  Mental retardation
9  F80–F89  Disorders of psychological development
10  F90–F98  Behavioural and emotional disorders with onset usually occurring in childhood and adolescence
11  F99  Unspecified mental disorder

**Box 1.3** The 11 major categories of ICD-10

ICD-10 has fewer categories than DSM-IV-TR because each category tends to be slightly broader. There are occasional differences in the language used to describe disorders and groups of disorders. The biggest difference between the two systems is that ICD-10 is intended primarily as a *classification* system, although it includes details of what symptoms are required for diagnosis (Farmer and McGuffin, 1999). DSM-IV-TR, by contrast, is intended as a fully comprehensive manual for *diagnosis*, and so includes precise details of how to conduct diagnostic interviews and other tests. It also includes more precise diagnostic details, for example in the duration of symptoms required for diagnosis.

## Evaluation of diagnostic systems

For a system like ICD or DSM to work effectively it must satisfy two important criteria: reliability and validity. A system is *reliable* if those using it consistently make the same diagnoses. It is *valid* if the diagnoses identify something 'real' in the sense of being a distinct condition that has different symptoms from other conditions and which is likely to progress in a certain way and respond to one treatment rather than another.

### Reliability

The major way of assessing reliability of psychiatric diagnosis is by assessing the agreement with which different clinicians diagnose conditions in the same patients (this is known as *inter-rater reliability*). Studies of inter-rater reliability reveal that some diagnostic categories are much more reliable than others, and that procedures are more reliable for some types of patient than others. A recent study by Nicholls *et al.* (2000) shows that neither ICD-10 nor DSM-IV demonstrates good inter-rater reliability for the diagnosis of eating disorders in children: 81 patients aged 7–16 years with some eating problem were classified using ICD-10, DSM-IV and a system developed especially for children by Great Ormond Street Hospital. Over 50% of the children could not be diagnosed according to DSM criteria. Reliability was 0.64 (i.e. 64% agreement between raters), but this figure was inflated by the fact that most raters agreed that they couldn't make a diagnosis. Using ICD-10 criteria there was 0.36 reliability (36% agreement between raters). The Great Ormond Street system emerged as by far the best, having an inter-rater reliability of 0.88 (88% agreement). Some disorders have rather better inter-rater reliability. For instance, Pedersen *et al.* (2001) gave 10 Danish GPs one day's training in the use of ICD-10 criteria for diagnosing depression. Over the next 8 weeks they diagnosed a total of 116 patients with a depressive episode. In 71% of cases a psychiatrist agreed with the diagnosis. This suggests quite good inter-rater reliability for ICD-10 in the case of depression.

### Validity

Judging the validity of a system like DSM or ICD is rather more complex than judging reliability. The classic study by Rosenhan (1973) described below demonstrated how diagnosis could have good reliability but poor validity, as doctors consistently but wrongly diagnosed pseudopatients whose symptoms were faked.

## classic
## research

## situation affects clinical judgement

**Rosenhan, D.L. (1973) On being sane in insane places.** *Science,* 179, 250–258

**Aim:** Rosenhan was interested in how good diagnostic procedures were under DSM-II; specifically whether the diagnosis is really tied to the patient's symptoms or whether it is also affected by the environment in which the diagnosis takes place. The rationale for the procedure was that clinicians should be able to tell the difference between a patient suffering from a real mental disorder and a healthy 'pseudopatient' who, having reported a single symptom, then acts normally.

**Method:** Rosenhan himself and seven volunteers, five of whom were doctors or psychologists (a total of three women and five men), arrived at a range of hospitals reporting a single symptom, hearing voices saying 'empty', 'hollow' and 'thud'. Once admitted they then acted the role of model patients, co-operating with staff and seeking to be released as soon as possible. They recorded the responses of doctors and nurses when they spoke to them.

**Results:** All eight pseudopatients were admitted to hospital. The average stay was 19 days (the range being 7–52 days). In every case they were released with a diagnosis of schizophrenia in remission. In a number of the cases, real patients made comments to the effect that the pseudopatients had nothing wrong with them. However, in no case did doctors or nurses notice that there was nothing wrong (this is unsurprising given their lack of responsiveness to the patients). In response to questions, psychiatrists (71% of occasions) and nurses (88% of occasions) looked away and walked on without responding. Only on 4% of occasions did psychiatrists stop to talk to the pseudopatients, and the figure was even lower (0.5%) for nurses.

**Conclusions:** The study revealed two major weaknesses in the psychiatric system of the time. First, the environment has a major impact on the process of diagnosis, and in the hospital environment staff could not tell the mentally disordered from the mentally healthy. Second, once labelled with a condition like schizophrenia, patients find it very difficult to escape the label and be judged as 'normal'.

It is important to remember that Rosenhan's study took place 30 years ago, and that diagnostic procedures have improved in response. There have been major changes since the DSM-II, under which Rosenhan and his participants were diagnosed. The study should thus *not* be seen as an indictment of the current mental health system. Remember as well that the study showed extremely good reliability for the diagnosis of schizophrenia (100% agreement between psychiatrists seeing the same symptoms), and that in real life doctors are not normally confronted with people wishing to be admitted to psychiatric hospitals. The British author Ian McEwan recently used a different method to 'fake' a mental disorder and so test the validity of psychiatric classification.

**media watch**

The following extracts are taken from an article by Oliver Burkeman, published in *The Guardian*, 16 August 1999.

Few people, on the face of it, would seem so well acquainted with the strange place where imagination meets reality as the readers of the Royal College of Psychiatrists' *Psychiatric Bulletin*. As expert navigators of the wilder shores of delusion and hallucination, surely they of all people can be relied on to spot the difference between fact and fiction – to tell, for example, when they're being had? Well no, actually, as it turns out. Ian McEwan, the best-selling novelist, comes clean in this month's edition of the *Bulletin* about a literary sleight of hand perpetrated on the world of psychiatry that seems to have had several of its respected members comprehensively fooled.

The saga began in 1997 with the publication of McEwan's acclaimed novel *Enduring Love*, the story of a science journalist, Joe Rose, obsessively and violently stalked by a religious loner called Jed Parry. Joe diagnoses Jed's condition as a homoerotic manifestation of De Clerambault's Syndrome, a nightmarish state of erotomania named after the turn-of-the-century French psychiatrist who first identified it. It's a compelling, deeply disturbing tale – and one rendered even more haunting by the presence in the book's appendix of a case report reprinted from the *British Review of Psychiatry*. Only it isn't. The *British Review of Psychiatry* doesn't exist. McEwan decided to take the hoax a step further and submitted the appendix to the *British Journal of Psychiatry*.

It never made it into print but the novel was admiringly reviewed in the *Psychiatric Bulletin* by Ronan McIvor, a consultant psychiatrist. McIvor swallowed McEwan's jest whole, in a review that began with the fateful words: 'Based on a published case report....'

## Questions

**1** What does McEwan's hoax suggest about psychiatric diagnosis?

**2** What ethical issues are raised by hoaxes of this sort?

Another way of assessing the validity of diagnosis is to diagnose people using DSM and ICD and see to what extent the two diagnoses agree. This approach is known as *criterion validity*. Of course this only tells us if ICD is valid provided that DSM is also valid and vice versa, but it is useful in itself to be able to tell when the two systems agree and when they differ. Andrews *et al.* (1999) assessed 1500 people using DSM-IV and ICD-10 and found very good agreement on diagnoses of depression, substance dependence and generalised anxiety. Moderate agreement was found for other anxiety disorders but there was agreement only 35% of the time on post-traumatic stress, with ICD-10 identifying twice as many cases as DSM-IV. Overall, the agreement between the systems was 68%. Generally people were more likely to receive a diagnosis according to ICD-10 than according to DSM-IV. We would expect this because the criteria for diagnosis are tighter in DSM-IV, and it suggests that either they are too narrow in DSM-IV or too broad in ICD-10.

**for** and **against**

## reliability and validity of diagnosis

+ The reliability and validity of DSM and ICD systems have increased with each new version. ICD-10 and DSM-IV-TR are more reliable and valid than previous versions.

+ The inter-rater and test–retest reliability of some disorders are now very good.

– The reliability of some diagnoses is much lower.

– Inter-rater reliability for diagnosing childhood conditions using ICD-10 and DSM-IV is very poor.

+ Agreement on diagnosis using ICD-10 and DSM-IV is quite good for most conditions.

**where to now?**

**The following is a good source of further information concerning psychiatric diagnosis:**

**Davison, G.C. and Neale, J.M. (1994)** *Abnormal Psychology*. **New York: Wiley** – contains excellent sections on the criteria for defining behaviour as abnormal and the development of the DSM system.

**what's new?**

## iatrogenesis and dissociative identity disorder

One of the most fascinating questions facing contemporary psychologists is whether our procedures for assessing and diagnosing patients can actually *create* a mental disorder that wasn't present when the patient encountered the mental health system. This phenomenon of artificially creating a disorder is called *iatrogenesis*. Iatrogenesis has been particularly studied in relation to *dissociative identity disorder* (DID), formerly known as multiple personality disorder. According to DSM-IV-TR, DID should be diagnosed when a person has two or more separate identities or personalities, each of which has its own pattern of thinking and relating to the world, and each of which takes control of the individual at times. Typically, each personality cannot remember things that have happened when the others have been in control.

Shifts from one personality to another typically take place under stress. A classic case of DID is that of 'Eve'.

**The case of Eve** (Thigpen and Cleckley, 1957)
A 25 year-old woman, Eve White, was referred for treatment for severe headaches. She presented as serious, formal and demure, and talked freely about her current problem, her religious differences with her husband and their disagreement about the upbringing of their daughter. Following several months of therapy Eve's headaches improved. In one session her husband accompanied her, and he told the therapist that occasionally Eve forgot things and acted out of character. This was the first clue about Eve's condition. Later, Eve's husband called to report a bizarre scene in which he had returned home after a violent quarrel with Eve to find that she had no memory of the incident. She went on holiday to stay with her cousin, leaving on good terms but was then abusive by telephone to her husband and when he visited her. Eve later had no memory of this. During hypnosis Eve's therapist contacted her second personality, who called herself Eve Black. In contrast to Eve White, this personality was confident, crude and aggressive. Eve Black was always aware of Eve White, although Eve White had no knowledge of Eve Black. Usually Eve White was the dominant personality. However, Eve Black would take over on occasion, behaving in ways that would have horrified Eve White. Following the first occasion Eve Black was contactable without hypnosis. The EEG patterns and handwriting of the two personalities were independently judged by experts to be those of different people. Eve's headaches worsened again, and a third personality, called Jane, emerged. Jane was better adjusted than Eve White or Eve Black, but had no memory of events prior to her emergence. Neither Eve was aware of Jane. When the Jane personality fell in love her symptoms ceased entirely and she left therapy (as Jane) and married.

So how do psychologists explain cases like Eve? The traditional explanation for DID is that in response to prolonged trauma in childhood, we can respond by *dissociation*. This means that we cope with the trauma by splitting off part of our self, and withdrawing the rest of our self out of contact with the trauma. The resulting two or more selves then continue to co-exist as the individual gets older. Evidence to support this *psychodynamic* explanation (see Chapter 5 for a discussion) of DID comes from studies that have confirmed that most sufferers have indeed suffered severe childhood trauma. Lewis *et al.* (1997) looked at 12 cases of murder where the defendant manifested the symptoms of DID. In 11 cases (92%) there was substantial independent evidence to confirm a history of severe child abuse. In a survey of 75 female DID patients, Pearson (1997) found that most respondents had experienced childhood trauma, and those who had experienced both childhood and adult traumas were the most dissociated.

There is thus evidence that DID follows childhood trauma and is not iatrogenic in origin. However, there is also a conflicting body of evidence to suggest that DID can be produced artificially by psychological assessment procedures. Hypnosis, which is known to make patients more suggestible, may cause particular problems. Merskey (1992) reviewed published cases of DID and found that in every case, symptoms appeared following hypnosis. Although there have since been a number of indistinguishable published cases not involving hypnosis (Powell and Gee, 1999), there are other sources of evidence for an iatrogenic basis to DID. Nathan (1994) has pointed out that before 1990 there were fewer than 200 reported cases, but that by 1994 there were around 30 000. Unless there was a corresponding explosion of childhood trauma two decades previously – which seems unlikely – this figure suggests that some other process is at work. Moreover, virtually all the new cases have been found in USA and Canada, suggesting that the assessment techniques used in these countries are implicated. In addition, DID is usually found by clinicians who are actively looking for it rather than those who are theoretically neutral (Spanos, 1996). This is consistent with the idea that suggestion by the clinician may influence the patient to produce DID symptoms. Psychologists and other mental health professionals are divided on the issue of whether DID is iatrogenic or a childhood response to trauma. Cormier and Thelen (1998) surveyed American psychologists on their beliefs, and the majority believed DID to be a rare but genuine response to child abuse. In a different study, Pope *et al.* (1999) surveyed American psychiatrists about whether DID should remain included in DSM-IV. Only around one-quarter believed that there is strong evidence for the existence of DID and around one-third believed without reservation that it should remain in DSM-IV. Given the evidence linking DID to both childhood trauma and to iatrogenesis, it seems reasonable to suggest that the same symptoms *can* result from both sets of circumstances.

# The stigma of mental disorder

An important downside to receiving a psychiatric diagnosis is the risk of *social stigmatisation*. Stigmatisation occurs when we have an identifiable characteristic that predisposes people against us. People suffering from mental disorders attract considerable prejudice, and this can add significantly to the distress they already experience. To some commentators the social stigma of mental disorder constitutes sufficient reason not to diagnose mental disorder at all.

The media have been widely blamed for portraying negative stereotypes of people with mental disorders. This was investigated in a study by Philo *et al.*, (1994), in which the content of local and national media in Scotland was analysed for coverage of mental health issues during the month of April 1993. The results showed strong support for the role of the media in perpetuating negative stereotypes of people with mental disorders: 66% of all incidents (including factual and fictional cases) covered involved mental health issues involving accounts of violence. A further 13% showed people with mental health problems harming themselves. Overall only 18% of fictional and factual incidents were judged to give sympathetic coverage of mental health issues. The researchers then used questionnaires and interviews to try to get at viewers' responses to the coverage of mental health issues. With the exception of those who had personal experience of people with mental health problems, for example through family or work, viewers reported negative stereotyped views of the sufferers of mental disorder.

So how negative are people's perceptions of those suffering from mental disorder? Skinner et al. (1995) surveyed American college students on their attitudes to ex-psychiatric patients, ex-drug addicts and ex-convicts, asking for example about their social functioning, romantic relationships and work. Unfortunately, like the Scottish study by Philo et al., this study found that there was considerable stigma attached to mental disorder: ex-psychiatric patients were judged better than ex-convicts but worse than ex-drug addicts. A recent study by Corrigan et al. (2000) examined in more detail what factors led to stigmatisation, and how the nature of the stigma varied from one disorder to another. They asked 152 American university students about their beliefs regarding cocaine addiction, depression, psychotic disorders (such as schizophrenia) and retardation. Negative attitudes were related to beliefs about how controllable disorders were and to the likelihood of improvement. Cocaine addiction was judged to be the disorder in which patients had the greatest degree of control and retardation was judged to have the worst prospects for improvement. Thus both these conditions were found to carry stigmas, although the nature of the stigma was quite different in each case.

One of the saddest aspects of the stigma attached to mental disorder is the tendency of people with mental health problems to contribute to their own isolation by refusing to disclose personal and emotional experiences for fear of others' reactions. This phenomenon was investigated in a recent study conducted by MacDonald and Morley (2001).

# research now

## patients are afraid to tell people how they feel

**MacDonald, J. and Morley, I. (2001) Shame and non-disclosure: a study of the emotional isolation of people referred for psychotherapy.** *British Journal of Medical Psychology,* 74, 1–22

**Aim:** It is now well documented that there is social stigma surrounding the experience of psychological problems, and in particular of having a psychiatric diagnosis. However, there has been relatively little research into how sufferers of psychological problems respond to this stigma. The aim of this study was to find out whether outpatients would be reluctant to discuss their feelings with other people for fear of their response.

**Method:** 34 outpatients attending a clinic for psychotherapy were asked to complete an emotion diary for one week. In the diary participants noted any experiences that caused them to react with strong emotion, and whether they had disclosed their feelings to anyone. After a week the diaries were collected and participants were interviewed.

**Results:** In general the participants tended not to disclose their feelings. In 68% of cases incidents that aroused strong emotional responses were not disclosed to anyone. This contrasts with the results of studies using emotion diaries in the general population, which reveal that usually only about 10% of such incidents are not disclosed. Interviews revealed that the major reason for the reluctance of patients to disclose was fear of negative responses from others.

**Conclusion:** Patients receiving psychotherapy for a psychological problem are reluctant to disclose their emotional responses to everyday events for fear of being judged. This adds to the distress and isolation that frequently accompany mental health problems.

# Cultural issues in diagnosis

Culture is of great importance to psychiatric diagnosis in a number of ways. Culture is a set of beliefs, values and practices that characterises a group of people and varies between people from different parts of the world, between different ethnic and religious groups living in the same region, between socio-economic groups, between men and women and even between families. Most research has focused on differences between different national and ethnic groups.

## Cultural attitudes to mental disorder

Different cultural groups have different attitudes to psychological distress and mental disorder, and these attitudes can affect the processes of reporting symptoms and receiving a diagnosis. Particular disorders may have particular meanings to cultures. For instance, Kim and Berrios (2001) have identified the problems caused by the fact that in some Asian languages the terms for schizophrenia literally translate as 'the disease of the disorganised mind.' In Japan, the idea of a disorganised mind is so stigmatising that psychiatrists are reluctant to tell patients of their condition, and as a result only around 20% of people with schizophrenia are aware of it.

A recent study in Britain (Cinnerella and Loewenthal, 1999) examined the influence of religious and cultural influences on mental disorder, with particular regard to the symptoms and causes of depression and schizophrenia and the most effective strategies for tackling symptoms. A total of 52 participants (including white Catholics, Indian Hindus, black Christians, Muslim Pakistanis and Orthodox Jews) were given in-depth interviews in their own homes. Some important cultural attitudes emerged. Although all groups saw depression as the result of life events and other environmental factors there was a wide range of beliefs about the origins of schizophrenia. In all groups except the white Catholics there was a fear of being misunderstood by health professionals. Amongst the black Christian and Muslim Pakistani groups there was also a sense that depression and schizophrenia carried a social stigma. These two groups in particular believed in the power of prayer to relieve symptoms. Clearly these findings have important implications, as they suggest that certain communities in Britain are more reluctant to seek help for mental health problems than others.

## Culture and vulnerability to mental disorder

It seems that some cultural and ethnic groups are affected more by particular disorders than others. For example, Levav *et al.* (1997) compared the incidence of depression and alcoholism in American Jews, Catholics and Protestants. Overall the Jewish population had a higher rate of depression and a lower rate of alcohol abuse than the other groups. Interestingly, males accounted for the differences alone; Jewish men, but not women, were twice as likely to suffer depression and only half as likely to abuse alcohol as Catholics and Protestants (Figure 1.3). Whilst these differences could conceivably be explained by genetic predispositions in the Jewish and Christian populations, the most likely explanation is that some aspect of Jewish culture makes men more likely to respond to adversity with depression than with alcohol abuse. In Britain, Black and Irish people are significantly more likely than other groups to receive a diagnosis of schizophrenia. In these cases it seems probable that cultural bias in diagnosis, rather than genuinely greater frequency of schizophrenia, is the problem.

**Figure 1.3** In many societies, including Britain, it is common for men to abuse alcohol in response to stress or adversity

# Race discrimination in diagnosis and assessment

Littlewood and Lipsedge (1997) have suggested that the reason why Black and Irish people in Britain are more likely than others to receive a diagnosis of serious mental disorder has more to do with bias in the system than a genuine greater vulnerability in those groups. They describe the case of Calvin, a Jamaican man arrested following an argument with the police when a post-office clerk believed he was cashing a stolen postal order.

## interactive angles

Read the following description from a British prison psychiatrist of a Jamaican patient who is on remand, having been arrested for arguing with the police, who wrongly accused him of stealing a postal order.

*This man belongs to Rastafarian – a mystical Jamaican cult, the members of which think they are God-like. The man has ringlet hair, a straggly goatee beard and a type of turban. He appears eccentric in his appearance and very vague in answering questions. He is an irritable character and has got arrogant behaviour.*

## Questions

**1**  What cultural misunderstanding can you see in the psychiatrist's view of Calvin's religion?

**2**  In what other way does the psychiatrist describe Calvin in unflattering terms that relate to his ethnic or cultural group?

As always in psychology, we need to be aware of the limitations of case studies – we don't know how representative Calvin's case is of the treatment of minority groups in the mental health system. However, there is further evidence to suggest that mental health professionals perceive different ethnic and cultural groups rather differently. Stowell-Smith and McKeown (1999) performed a discourse analysis on the psychiatrists' reports on 18 black and 18 white male psychopaths from a range of maximum-security institutions. Discourse analysis is associated with the social constructionist approach to psychology (discussed on p. 118), and involves the *deconstruction* of written or verbal narrative in order to reveal the hidden assumptions in people's use of language. In this case discourse analysis revealed that the psychiatrists were much more likely to look at White patients' experiences of trauma and at their emotional state. Reports of black patients placed much more emphasis on the danger posed by the patients. This contrast suggests that the doctors saw white psychopaths more sympathetically.

## Culture-bound syndromes

Within the cultural traditions of some societies are beliefs in the existence of disorders with symptoms that do not fit neatly into the DSM and ICD systems. DSM-IV deals with this by the inclusion of a catch-all category of *culture-bound syndromes*. We have already seen examples of conditions that affect one culture more than another, so it is conceivable that there are conditions exclusive to a single culture. The alternative explanation for the apparent existence of culture-bound syndromes is that the conditions described by the DSM-IV and ICD-10 are experienced or interpreted differently in certain cultures. We look here at two possible culture-bound syndromes, *dhat* and *koro*.

### Dhat

*Dhat* is found in men from the Indian subcontinent. Its main symptoms are severe anxiety and an obsessive concern over the discharge of semen. This is accompanied by weakness and fatigue.

The existence of *dhat* is supported by a study by Chadda (1995), in which 50 patients reporting *dhat* were found to meet the criteria for mental disorder (unspecified) on the DSM-III-R (the fore-runner of DSM-IV). The fact that the patients appeared to be suffering sufficiently severe symptoms to warrant a psychiatric diagnosis yet did not meet the criteria for any existing DSM categories suggests that *dhat* is a disorder in its own right.

On the other hand, it may be that *dhat* is merely a more standard condition accompanied by the cultural belief that symptoms are associated with loss of semen. Many cultures, including those of India and neighbouring countries, share the belief in an association between semen, blood and energy. It has been suggested that *dhat* is simply a product of this cultural association such that when men discharge semen through ejaculation or in urine they expect to be weakened. Depressed patients experiencing loss of energy may *attribute* this symptom to any recent discharges of semen they might coincidentally have had. This association between *dhat* and depression is supported by a study by Mumford (1996), in which Pakistani men suffering from *dhat* were found to have key depressive symptoms including depressed mood and fatigue. Mumford suggests that we think of *dhat* as depression expressed in a culturally specific manner rather than as a distinct mental disorder.

## *Koro*

*Koro* is most commonly found in South Chinese men of Han origin, although cases crop up throughout South-east Asia. Occasionally *koro* has been diagnosed in women, and a small number of cases have been reported in Britain (Estcourt and Goh, 1998). Like *dhat*, *koro* involves sexual anxiety, but the symptoms are different. Sufferers of *koro* are plagued by the belief that their sex organs are shrinking and will disappear inside their abdomen, leading to death. The term *genital retraction syndrome* is thus also used to describe this syndrome.

Despite the occurrence of occasional cases outside China it appears that genital retraction syndrome is powerfully affected by cultural beliefs. Chowdhury (1996) looked at a range of circumstances in which *koro* has been reported and concluded that men who feel their penis shrink due to cold, wet or following ejaculation are likely to *interpret* this as genital retraction if *koro* is part of their cultural belief system. Cultural beliefs about *koro* thus prime people to panic if they feel the very normal sensation of their penis shrinking as its blood supply is reduced. In a case of genital retraction syndrome recorded by Oyebode *et al.* (1986) a penile plethysmograph (a pressure-sensitive penis ring attached to monitor in order to measure changes in size) was used to check whether the patient was accurate in his judgement of changes in his penis size, and confirmed that the patient was accurate in his assessment. This is important because it suggests that genital retraction syndrome is not a delusion, just a misinterpretation of a physiological event.

Bartholomew (1998) has attacked the diagnosis of *koro* as a mental disorder on the basis that, given the cultural beliefs of sufferers, their response to the sensation of a shrinking penis is quite rational. He maintains that there is little evidence to suggest that *koro* is associated with any other symptoms and therefore we should think of it as a social phenomenon, not as a problem of individual psychology. As Bartholomew says, *koro* is only classified as a disorder because its symptoms appear so bizarre from the perspective of European and American culture. There is, however, an argument for maintaining the classification of *koro* as a culture-bound syndrome if its symptoms can be relieved by conventional medicine. Hallak *et al.* (2000) report the case of a 56 year-old Asian man whose *koro* symptoms disappeared following anti-depressant medication. Although this suggests that *koro* may respond to drug treatment, we should be aware of the limitations of case studies. It may be that in this case the patient would have recovered anyway or, even if the drug treatment did help him he might not have been a typical case. One of the limitations of research into *koro* is that the vast majority of published studies have been case studies, and there is a lack of larger scale research.

# for and against

## the existence of culture-bound syndromes

**+** Conditions such as *dhat* and *koro* are sufficiently severe to warrant diagnosis but they do not appear to fit the symptoms of other disorders.

**+** There is a limited body of evidence to suggest that conditions like *dhat* and *koro* respond to drug treatments.

**–** If *koro* is merely the result of the rational interpretation of physiological symptoms according to cultural beliefs, then sufferers cannot be said to be suffering a disorder.

**–** The diagnosis of culture-bound syndromes may be racist because it 'medicalises' the cultural beliefs of people other than Americans and Europeans.

## where to now?

**The following are good sources of further information about cultural issues in diagnosis:**

▶ **Gross, R. *et al.* (2000) *Psychology: A New Introduction*. London: Hodder and Stoughton** – gives a very detailed chapter on culture-bound syndromes.

▶ **Littlewood, R. and Lipsedge, M. (1997) *Aliens and Alienists: Ethnic Minorities and Psychiatry*. London: Routledge** – a highly critical look at current mental health practices in Britain with regard to the treatment of different cultural groups.

## Conclusions

Drawing the line between normal and abnormal behaviour is a tricky business. Statistical rarity, social deviance, distress and maladaptiveness are all important criteria for defining behaviour as abnormal in systems of diagnosis, but there is no single criterion for abnormality that reliably distinguishes between people who we would and would not diagnose with a mental disorder. Whilst it is possible to define 'ideal mental health,' there are practical problems with applying this to the problem of identifying psychologically abnormal individuals. There are two particularly popular and sophisticated systems for the classification and diagnosis of mental disorder, the DSM-IV-TR and the ICD-10. Despite the sophistication of these systems there have been challenges to their reliability and validity. Moreover, having a psychiatric diagnosis carries a serious social stigma and we need to balance the costs and benefits of diagnosis. It is also important to consider issues of culture when thinking about diagnosis of mental disorder. Different cultural groups have different attitudes to mental disorder and some groups appear to be more vulnerable to certain disorders than others. There may even be some conditions that appear almost exclusively within certain cultural groups, although the existence of these culture-bound syndromes remains controversial.

what do you know?

1 Compare two or more criteria used for identifying psychological abnormality. How important is each criterion in the process of diagnosis?

2 (a) Describe the DSM system of classification.
(b) To what extent can we consider systems like DSM reliable and valid?

3 How much of a problem is the social stigma of mental disorder?

4 In what ways do we have to consider issues of culture in the diagnosis of mental disorder?

# 2

# The Biomedical Model

In this chapter we consider a model that explains mental disorders in the same terms as physical illnesses are explained; as being caused by the disruption or malfunction of biological processes. We consider the evidence for the role of genes and the biochemistry of the nervous system in mental disorder. Having looked at the role of biology in explaining the origin of mental disorder, we will then focus on some of the treatments such an approach offers. The rather controversial therapies of drugs, ECT and psychosurgery will be considered, together with the considerable changes that have occurred in the application of such treatments since they were first introduced. Finally, we will discuss a promising new alternative to ECT, Transcranial Magnetic Brain Stimulation.

## Assumptions of the approach

The biomedical model (or *disease* model) of psychopathology views psychological disorders as being caused by biological malfunction or disruption. Biomedical approaches to treatment are based on the idea that we can correct, or at least reduce, the effects of these malfunctions or disruption.

- Mental disorder can be understood as illness in the same way as physical conditions. It can thus be classified, diagnosed and treated by medical personnel in the same way as physical disease.

- The emphasis of the explanations is on the physiological aspects of mental disorder rather than its behavioural, thinking or emotional aspects. For example, the physiological approach would explain depression in terms of an imbalance of biochemical substances in the brain, such as serotonin, rather than in terms of low self-esteem, feelings of helplessness, irrational thinking and so on. This emphasis on physiology is, of course, on a theoretical level and does not suggest that medical practitioners are not also concerned with cognitive and emotional aspects of mental disorder.

- The symptoms of mental disorder can be understood in terms of malfunction of or disruption to biological systems. For example, this may involve the abnormal development of part of the nervous system or levels of neurotransmitters that are too high or too low. The underlying causes of these symptoms are also biological in origin, for example faulty genes or brain damage.

- Mental disorder can be treated by physiologically based approaches, including drugs, surgery and the application of electric shocks, magnetic fields and bright light.

The biomedical position is one with a very long history – indeed, the very language of psychopathology is grounded in the medical model, the most obvious example being that such conditions are often called mental *illnesses*. At one time all mental disorders were seen by some as being caused entirely by biological factors but most people now consider this position as untenable and recognise that most, if not all, psychological conditions (and some physical illnesses) are the result of a complex interaction of physiology and environment. There is considerable variability in the extent to which specific conditions can be explained in terms of biology, which is hardly surprising given the enormous range of clinical conditions that exist. In order to investigate the role of physical factors in the origins of mental illness, psychologists have pursued several avenues of research including the ones we will consider here, the role of *genes* and the *biochemistry* of the nervous system.

## The role of genes

*Behaviour genetics* is the study of individual differences in psychological characteristics that are attributable in part to differences in genetic makeup. Before we consider the effects that genes may have on abnormal behaviour, it is useful to briefly discuss how genes are inherited and the way in which they exert an effect.

Human beings have 46 chromosomes (23 pairs) in every cell of their bodies except in the ova (eggs) and sperm, in which there are 23, one of each pair. Via the egg and sperm, a child randomly inherits half its chromosomes from the mother and half from the father. Each chromosome is made up of thousands of *genes,* which are the carriers of the genetic information (DNA) that is passed from parent to child.

The total genetic makeup of an individual is known as the *genotype*. Genes contain the instructions for producing a physical body, which in turn have an effect on psychological characteristics. The observable physical and behavioural characteristics of an individual are known collectively as their *phenotype*. The phenotype is the result of both genetic and environmental influences. For example, two children may be born with a similarly high predisposition to suffer anxiety. If one then experiences a very stressful environment, he may become a very anxious adult and perhaps be prone to anxiety disorders such as phobias. The other may, in contrast, have a supportive and benign upbringing that results in a well-adjusted adult capable of coping well with anxiety provoking situations. Their genotypes are similar, but their phenotypes are very different.

It is also possible that the genotype can *produce* experiences that may result in a certain phenotype. By their influence on brain chemistry genes may, for example, have the *direct* influence of producing timidity in a baby boy. This may then have certain *indirect* consequences, for example, it may cause his mother to protect him and his peers to mock him. This in turn increases his timidity. The genotype has therefore had an *indirect* effect on the phenotype.

What is important to note is that psychopathological conditions are disorders of the phenotype, not the genotype. People do not, for example, inherit genes for such conditions as schizophrenia or an anxiety disorder. Rather, they inherit genes that make them *vulnerable* to the disorder. They inherit a genotype for the vulnerability, also known as the *diathesis*, but not the condition itself. This is expressed in the *diathesis-stress model*, which states that a combination of *both* genetic vulnerability *and* environmental stress produces mental disorders. Whether the genotype will eventually translate into the phenotype depends on many environmental factors. The potential effects that genes have on clinical syndromes (such as mental disorders) have been investigated by conducting *family studies*, *twin studies* and *adoption studies*. We will consider each in turn.

## Family studies

We share 50% of our genes with our parents and our siblings, and 25% with our aunts, uncles and grandparents. The knowledge of the extent to which genes within family members are shared provides a means of testing whether there is a genetic element to certain conditions. If the correlation between the degree of consanguinity (the amount of shared genetic material) and the prevalence of a disorder is high, then it is reasonable to assume that heredity is exerting an influence on the development of the particular mental disorder. For example, in Chapter 11 there is an account of a study by Hetterna *et al.* (2001), who analysed data on anxiety disorders from many family studies and found that, overall, individuals who were closely genetically related to a patient with an anxiety disorder were 4–6 times more likely than non-related others to develop an anxiety condition.

## Twin studies

One of the most useful ways of studying the contribution of heredity to any characteristic is to compare the degree of similarity between identical and non-identical twins. Identical twins, known as *monozygotic* (MZ) twins, have identical genetic makeup because they come from the same fertilised egg or zygote. Non-identical (fraternal) twins are referred to as *dizygotic* (DZ) twins because they come from two separate zygotes and are therefore no more genetically alike than ordinary brothers and sisters.

The degree to which twins are similar on any particular characteristic is known as the *concordance rate*. If the concordance rate for MZ twins is higher than that for DZ twins on a particular characteristic, then this indicates some heritability of that characteristic. Gottesman (1991) found a concordance rate for schizophrenia of 17% for DZ twins and a much higher rate of 48% for MZ twins (referred to in Chapter 8), strongly suggesting a hereditary element in schizophrenia. McGuffin *et al.* (1996), in a study of major depression (severe depression), found a concordance rate of 46% in MZ twins and 20% in DZ twins (Chapter 9). In contrast, Kendler *et al.* (1992) found the concordance rates for mild depression to be much more similar (49% for MZ and 42% for DZ twins). These two sets of data indicate a much larger hereditary element in major depression than in mild depression.

However, we do need to exercise some caution in the interpretation of data from twin studies. Although higher concordance rates for MZ than for DZ twins strongly implicate heredity, you can see from the example of schizophrenia that, whilst MZ twins have identical genetic material, on

**Figure 2.1** These twins are genetically identical but have nonetheless turned out quite different in many ways. This illustrates the importance of the environment

average half of the identical twins of people suffering schizophrenia do not develop the disorder. Therefore other factors (environment and experience) must also play a part. It is also possible that MZ twins, being identical, may be treated more similarly than DZ twins, especially if the DZ twins are not the same sex.

One of the problems of any comparison of concordance rates between people in the same family is that they share a similar environment, so it is never clear to what extent their shared experiences rather than heredity has contributed to a condition (Figure 2.1). One way to try to separate out the effects of heredity and environment is to look at individuals who were not raised in their biological families. We will therefore now turn our attention to adoption studies.

## Adoption studies

Comparison of the rates of any mental disorder between adopted children and both their biological and adoptive parents are another means of assessing the extent of heredity. The *Classic Research* section on p. 133 provides an account of an adoption study by Heston (1966), in which it was demonstrated that 10% of adopted children of mothers with schizophrenia developed the condition themselves. This is exactly the rate that would be expected in first-degree relatives raised by their biological mothers and far higher than the rate of 1% in the general population. Again, this strongly implicates heredity in this condition.

## Linkage analysis and molecular genetics

New techniques for studying inheritance of psychological characteristics come from the field of *molecular genetics*, which, as the name suggests, involves studying genes on the molecular level. Molecular geneticists use *linkage analysis* to try to ascertain the specific gene involved in a particular clinical condition. It uses as its starting point genes whose location on a certain chromosome and whose physical effects are already known, such as a gene that determines eye colour. Such genes are known as *genetic markers*. Blood samples are taken from members of families in which a particular mental illness is prevalent and used to ascertain the inheritance of the genetic markers. If the occurrence of the mental illness goes along with a particular genetic marker then it can be assumed that they are in a similar place on the same chromosome – in other words, that they are linked. A linkage analysis of the Old Order Amish (Egeland *et al.*, 1987) revealed evidence that bipolar disorder results from a dominant gene on the eleventh chromosome. These findings have not been replicated but research is ongoing. As yet, the work on linkage analysis is in the early stages but has progressed quite a long way in some areas such as Alzheimer's disease; it will doubtless prove to be of considerable value in the future.

## for and against

## the importance of genes

+ Evidence from twin, adoption and family studies all point to a role for genes in the development of mental disorder.

– There are sound reasons for questioning the validity of all these methods.

+ Molecular genetic studies have begun to show us which genes appear to be associated with mental disorder.

## where to now?

**The following are good sources of further information about behavioural genetics:**

▶ **Jarvis, M. *et al.* (2000) *Angles on Psychology*. Cheltenham: Nelson Thornes** – Chapter 1 contains a useful account of behavioural genetics research.

▶ *The Psychologist*, **March 2001** – a special edition devoted to papers on behavioural genetics. Although not exclusively concerned with psychopathology, it is relevant and interesting. The lead article by Plomin, a great enthusiast for the genetic approach, includes the use of twin studies and adoption studies with respect to autism. Other papers discuss the issue from various perspectives. Of particular interest is one by Steven Rose, a biologist who urges caution in applying genetic explanations to behaviour. All the articles are both thought provoking and readable and will be useful in various aspects of psychology.

## The biochemistry of the nervous system

The human nervous system is the most important system in the control of behaviour and the experience of mental events. At the centre of the nervous system is the brain, which manages all human capacities including learning, feeling emotions, relating to other people and perceiving the world. The nervous system is composed of billions of neurons, highly specialised nerve cells 'woven into a complex tapestry of connections and interconnections' (Dwyer and Scampion, 1996, p. 176).

Neurons are specially adapted to receive, process and/or transmit information to other cells. They communicate with each other (and with muscles and glands) both electrically and chemically. When a neuron is stimulated, a wave of electrical voltage called a nerve impulse passes down the axon to the terminal ending (see Figure 2.2). Between the nerve ending and the next cell there is a small gap called a *synapse*, across which electricity cannot pass. The impulse passes to the next neuron by means of chemicals called *neurotransmitters*, chemical messengers that cross the small distance across the synaptic gap and excite or inhibit the next neuron. When a neurotransmitter is released, some of it remains in the synapse and needs to be removed so that the synapse can return to its normal state. Some is broken down by enzymes while some of it is pumped back into the neuron from which it came, a process known as *reuptake*. If this process is faulty, then problems arise. As we shall see later in this chapter, and in Chapter 9, some therapeutic drugs operate by inhibiting the reuptake of certain neurotransmitters.

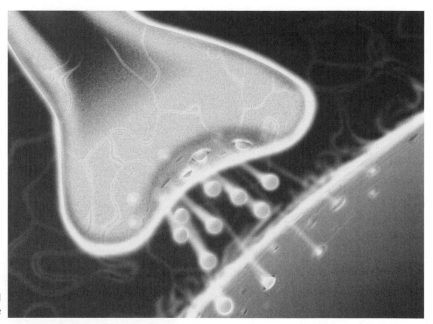

**Figure 2.2** A nerve cell and synapse

Neurotransmitters play a crucial role in many psychological processes, including mood and emotion. It is now clear that abnormalities in the production of neurotransmitters can contribute to psychopathological conditions. *Noradrenaline* (also called *norepinephrine*) has been associated with anxiety disorders, serotonin may be involved in some types of depression and eating disorders, and dopamine appears to be implicated in schizophrenia. Theories linking psychopathology to neurotransmitters often suggest that too little or too much of a particular neurotransmitter may be responsible for the condition. It is also possible that the receptors are at fault – if they are too numerous or too easily excited then this can have the same effect as too much transmitter being released. One of the theories of schizophrenia is that the hallucinations and delusions experienced are the result of an excess of dopamine receptors. The article below demonstrates how an understanding of brain structure can aid diagnosis of certain disorders.

# research
## now

## investigating schizophrenia and learning difficulties using magnetic resonance imaging (MRI)

**Sanderson, T.L., Best, J.J., Doody, G.A., Cunningham Owens, D.G. and Johnstone, E.C. (1999) Neuroanatomy of comorbid schizophrenia and learning disability: a controlled study.** *Lancet, 354, 1867–1870*

**Aim:** To investigate reasons for the relatively high frequency of schizophrenia in learning-disabled populations and to see whether the major presenting symptom is schizophrenia or learning disability.

**Method:** Three groups of patients and one group of normal controls were compared, each group matched on age and sex:

- 20 patients with learning disability

- 25 patients with schizophrenia

- 23 patients with both disorders

- 29 normal controls.

Each person was given a whole-brain scan; in addition, specific areas of the brain were scanned (see Figure 2.3).

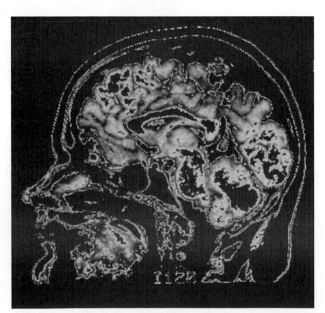

**Figure 2.3** MRI scans have allowed us to see in much more detail the structure of the brain. In some cases this has shown that mental disorder is linked to abnormal brain function or development

**Results:** The scans of the group with schizophrenia and the group with both learning difficulties and schizophrenia were very similar in terms of both general structure and the structure of the amygdala–hippocampus. The amygdala–hippocampus in both groups was significantly smaller than those in normal controls. The brains of the learning-disabled patients who did not have schizophrenia were smaller than those of the other three groups, but the amygdala–hippocampus was larger. Therefore the brain structure of people with both schizophrenia and learning difficulties resembles that of people with schizophrenia but not that of those with learning disability.

**Conclusions:** These results suggest that within the young learning-disabled population there is a group of people whose problems stem from a schizophrenic condition, but who have not been diagnosed as such. It is therefore possible that some individuals who are diagnosed with learning disabilities are actually suffering from schizophrenia, which has resulted in their cognitive deficits. If diagnosed, the schizophrenic condition may respond to treatment.

## Evaluation of biomedical explanations for mental disorder

A large and impressive body of research that demonstrates a link between biology and psychopathology has supported the biomedical model. This in turn has led to the development of drug therapies and other biological therapies (discussed in the next section), many of which have offered significant help in coping with abnormal psychological functioning.

However, there are several criticisms and limitations to the approach. First, the biomedical model is essentially a *reductionist* model because it reduces the explanation of psychopathology down to its most basic element (in this case to simple biology). The reductionist stance can result in the neglect of some of the most important psychological causes of behaviour and we may fail to see an individual as a whole person, regarding them rather as a body in which some part is malfunctioning. We may be able to explain a headache in terms of brain chemistry but that tells us little or nothing about the possible life stresses that may have given rise to that biological condition.

Second, although biological processes certainly do affect our behaviour, thoughts and emotions, it is not a one-way process. We are increasingly coming to recognise that our behaviour, thoughts and emotions affect our biology.

Third, much of the research into the biological causes of abnormality has been conducted on animals in which various conditions such as anxiety and helplessness have been induced by drugs, surgery or the way they have been conditioned. These procedures provide very little information about human functioning. Biological explanations based on such research are often incomplete or simply irrelevant to understanding human behaviour.

Fourth, evidence from family, twin and adoption studies indicating a link between genetics and clinical syndromes are open to other interpretations. The closer the genetic link, the more similar the environment is likely to be. Siblings not only have certain genes in common but are quite likely to have shared any potentially damaging experiences. We cannot therefore conclude that genes rather than environment were responsible for the abnormality. As mentioned earlier, there is a doubtless a complex interaction of environment and biology and concentration on one at the expense of the other is liable to lead us up blind alleys.

## for and against

### biomedical explanations

+ There is a large amount of empirical research to support biological explanations of mental disorders.

− The biomedical approach tends to neglect the role pf psychological factors in the aetiology (cause) of atypical behaviour.

− Our behaviour may affect our biology, therefore even when malfunctions of the brain or hormone imbalances occur they may be the consequence, not the cause, of abnormal behaviour.

## where to now?

**The following are good sources of further information on biomedical approaches:**

▶ **Murray, R., Hill, P. and McGuffin, P. (1996)** *The Essentials of Postgraduate Psychiatry.* **Cambridge: Cambridge University Press** – although a large and detailed book, this is not as intimidating as its name suggests, and has lots of good information on biomedical approaches to mental disorder.

▶ **Davison, G.C. and Neale, J.M. (2001)** *Abnormal Psychology*, **8th edition. New York: Wiley** – a standard undergraduate-level text with good general information on biomedical and other approaches to explaining mental disorder.

## Therapies based on the biomedical approach

The brain is an amazingly complex and delicate structure and has thus been difficult to study. Because the study of the brain has been limited by lack of technology (until modern imaging techniques such as PET and MRI scanning were developed), the development of biological treatments has lagged behind that of the psychological therapies. Often, drugs and other biological therapies have been introduced as the result of an accidental discovery rather than the result of systematic research into a particular condition. Nowadays, thorough research is conducted into biological therapies, which are very commonly used. In this section we will look at the three main biological therapies: drugs, electroconvulsive therapy (ECT) and psychosurgery.

## Drug therapies

The use of drugs to treat psychological disorders has a relatively short, controversial history. It started in the 1950s with the discovery of *psychotropic* drugs, drugs that act mainly on the brain and seem to alleviate the symptoms of various mental disorders. These were seen by some as a magic cure and were possibly over-prescribed without due appreciation of their side-effects, both physical and psychological. Over the years, research has led to a broadening of the range of available medication. Many new drugs have been introduced that do not have the same problems but controversy in many areas still rages.

There are four main classes of psychotropic drugs.

### Anti-anxiety drugs

*Anti-anxiety drugs* (also known as minor tranquillisers) help people to relax and reduce tension. An often-prescribed group of anti-anxiety drugs are the *benzodiazepines*, the trade names of two of which (Valium and Librium), have become household names. Although these drugs do reduce anxiety, they also induce both physical and psychological dependence, and in the 1960s this produced serious problems for those people, mainly women, who were prescribed them for years on end. Patients experienced such enormous problems with withdrawal symptoms that some people have literally continued taking them for a lifetime. Nowadays these drugs are more likely to be prescribed for very short periods, perhaps for 'one-off' anxiety-provoking situations.

### Antidepressants

*Antidepressant drugs* help elevate mood and lift depression. One of the most recent of these drugs is fluoxetine hydrochloride, more commonly known by its trade name of *Prozac*. Along with *Seroxat*, Prozac is one of a group of drugs in the SSRI (selective serotonin reuptake inhibitor) class, which was hailed as being entirely safe because people could not develop dependence on them or overdose. However, recently concerns have been expressed that the use of such drugs may actually increase suicide risk in the first few weeks of treatment (Harriman 2001). There is also concern that such drugs are being marketed for an ever-widening range of complaints, including premenstrual tension, and are far more often prescribed by GPs than by psychiatrists. Prozac is now so widely used and the prescribing of it so contentious that it has been the subject of several books and numerous newspaper articles.

### Antibipolar drugs

*Antibipolar drugs* are used to stabilise the mood of those people suffering from bipolar disorder (discussed in Chapter 9), in which mood swings between depression and mania. The most commonly used of these is lithium carbonate, which is estimated to help in 70–80% of cases. The doses, however, have to be carefully monitored or they may threaten a person's life. Despite this, lithium is often regarded as one of the success stories of drug therapy since, as Comer (1992) comments, 'Administered properly ... this and related drugs represent a true medical miracle for people who previously would have spent their lives on an emotional roller coaster' (p. 165).

### Antipsychotic drugs

*Antipsychotic drugs* are used in the treatment of psychotic conditions such as schizophrenia. The older class of drugs were the *phenothiazines*. A major problem with these drugs is the side-effects of movement disorders such as severe shaking, muscle tremors and spasms of involuntary jerky movements. An irreversible condition known as tardive dyskinesia affects 10–20% of all patients treated over a long period of time (Sweet *et al.*, 1995).

As with other classes. drugs first introduced in the 1950s have been superseded by more effective ones with fewer side-effects, for example *clozapine*. This can be effective in patients who do not respond to traditional antipsychotics (Kane *et al.*, 1998) and is actually more effective overall (Rosenhack *et al.*, 1999); it can, however, impair the immune system in a very small percentage of patients. Even more recently, two new antipsychotics have been introduced – *olanzapine* and *risperidone* – both having fewer side-effects but being as effective as the traditional antipsychotics (if not more so). The search for ever-more effective drugs with fewer side-effects is ongoing.

Although they are more effective than any other single form of treatment for schizophrenia, drugs alone are not sufficient treatment for most sufferers. Nevertheless, combined with psychotherapy they can help many patients with schizophrenia lead normal lives. Unfortunately, some patients do not respond to any antipsychotic drugs.

The following extracts are taken from an article by Sarah Boseley, published in *The Guardian*, 9 July 2001.

A group of psychiatrists has made a formal protest to the president of the profession's royal college against a drug company's sponsorship of a conference opening today.

They complain that the industry's marketing distorts the mental health agenda to the point where pills are seen as the answer to all ills.

In a letter to John Cox, President of the Royal College of Psychiatrists, the group says that money widely available for sponsoring meetings of doctors is an attempt to persuade psychiatry to go down the biomedical route and to ignore social circumstances that might be the true cause of the illness.

Two consultant psychiatrists, Pat Bracken and Phillip Thomas from the University of Bradford, members of the group that calls itself the Critical Psychiatry Network, will join mental health service users in demonstrating their concerns.

The group claims that 'biomedical frameworks' – the focus on drugs – increasingly dominate research and education in psychiatry, in spite of limited evidence as to how or whether the drugs work. Dr Bracken points to a paper in the journal *Ethical Human Sciences and Services* last year on the efficacy of the SSRI (selective serotonin reuptake inhibitor) class of antidepressant, which includes Prozac, which concluded that the drugs worked little better than dummy pills – 'there is a less than 10% difference in the antidepressant effect of drug versus placebo'.

Dr Bracken and colleagues feel the drive to find a medical cause of all mental illness ignores issues such as poverty, family breakdown, or other social or cultural problems. They call for the college to pull back from the increasingly close relationship with the pharmaceutical industry.

## Questions

1 What are the implications of drug companies funding research into therapies for certain disorders?

2 What factors are likely to be ignored if a biomedical approach is taken?

3 Why may it be tempting for state health services to concentrate on biomedical rather than psychological therapies?

4 What ethical concerns are expressed in this article?

# interactive
## angles

There has been considerable media coverage of the alleged side-effects of SSRIs, and about the allegations of dodgy practices on the part of drug companies. Carry out an Internet search, using a search engine such as Alta Vista or Google and key words like Prozac, Seroxat, drug companies, etc. Compile a list of arguments for and against the use of these drugs.

## Electroconvulsive therapy (ECT)

ECT is a procedure in which a very brief application of electricity is used to induce a seizure. It has a fearful reputation, dating back to a time when it was applied without anaesthetic or muscle relaxant and was almost certainly used to subdue troublesome patients; however, its modern application is very different. The patient is anaesthetised with a fast-acting barbiturate and given a muscle relaxant to temporarily paralyse the muscles so they do not contract during the seizure and cause broken bones. Electrodes are fitted to the head and a small electric current is passed through the brain for one second or less. The resulting seizure, monitored by an EEG machine, lasts from about 30 seconds to a minute and the patient regains consciousness about 15 minutes later. He or she usually experiences confusion, a headache and sometimes nausea and has no memory for events surrounding the treatment. These symptoms usually disappear within a few hours.

ECT is usually given 2–3 times a week for between 1 and 4 weeks, until the patient appears recovered, then two more treatments are administered to prevent relapse. No one knows how or why ECT works or what the electrically stimulated seizure does to the brain. It is thought that it acts by temporarily altering some of the brain's electrochemical processes (see p. 162 for a further discussion). ECT is still a very widely used form of treatment, mainly for people whose depression is so severe that they cannot wait 3 weeks or so for antidepressants to take effect (due to absolute desperation and suicide risk) or for whom these drugs are ineffective. It is also used for acute mania and certain forms of schizophrenia.

The use of ECT is still highly controversial. Much of this controversy surrounds its effectiveness, the severity and extent of the side-effects and the lack of knowledge of how it works. There is also concern that its use is viewed as a quick and easy solution to a problem better tackled by long-term psychotherapy. It is very difficult to be objective about the use of ECT because opinions about it are so extreme. Recent studies have tended to show good effectiveness, but some side-effects. Ng *et al.* (2000) administered ECT to the right hemispheres of 32 patients suffering from major depression (see p. 156 for a discussion of major depression). Depression scores decreased by around 50% following treatment, although memory was found to be seriously affected when tested immediately after a 6-week course of treatment (over 30% of personal memories were lost). However, most of this memory loss was made up within the next month, and overall the study was supportive of the value of ECT.

Papolos (1997) claims that ECT has a higher success rate for the treatment of severe depression than any form of treatment and that suicide attempts are relatively rare after ECT. In a recent follow-up of 58 depressed patients, Gagne *et al.* (2000) found that 93% of patients who continued to have ECT and take antidepressants following an episode of major depression remained free of symptoms 2 years later, as opposed to 52% of those who continued to take antidepressants alone. This suggests that ECT is helpful in preventing recurrence of depression. On the other hand, Youssef *et al.* (1999), in an article entitled 'Time to Abandon Electroconvulsion as a Treatment in Modern Psychiatry' claims that ECT is not superior to drugs, and that much of the improvement attributed to ECT is an effect of placebo or possibly anaesthesia. They argue that the treatment merely shortens the duration of an illness rather than improving the outcome. The controversy is ongoing. However there is now a new and exciting alternative to ECT that is painless and safe – transcranial magnetic brain stimulation.

## what's new?

# transcranial magnetic brain stimulation

Transcranial magnetic brain stimulation (TMS) is a non-invasive and painless method of brain stimulation (Figure 2.4), which may offer an alternative to ECT. The method involves the production of a magnetic field produced by a wire coil held outside the head. The magnetic field then induces an electric current in nearby regions of the brain. Unlike electricity, which is diffused by bone, high-intensity magnetic pulses pass readily through it, so when a magnetic current is passed through the skull, it is possible to focus on a more specific

**Figure 2.4** The TMS apparatus

area of the brain than is possible with ECT. Perhaps the most crucial difference between ECT and TMS is that the latter does not produce major motor seizures. It is therefore possible to avoid side-effects such as transient memory loss, and an anaesthetic is unnecessary. The treatment is usually administered daily for at least a week and is referred to as rTMS (repetitive TMS).

Research on rTMS gives cause for cautious optimism. George *et al.* (1995) conducted a pilot study of the effect of rTMS on six long-term depressed patients who had previously not responded to treatment. Two of them showed considerable improvement. One of the responders, a middle-aged woman, reported feeling well for the first time in 3 years. Pridmore *et al.* (2000) compared the effect of rTMS and ECT in patients suffering from major depression who had failed to respond to at least one course of medication. Although ECT was slightly better overall, the difference was not great. The researchers therefore concluded that rTMS has antidepressant effects of sufficiently useful proportions to make further research worth while. Klein (2000) similarly comments that preliminary evidence from studies of depressed individuals suggests that it might, in some cases, offer an alternative to ECT.

## Psychosurgery

Psychosurgery involves severing or otherwise disabling areas of the brain to treat mental illness. Psychosurgery has a notorious and gory history. It was first introduced by Moniz in 1936, at a time when there were no drugs to treat mental illness. An operation, known as a *frontal lobotomy* (or *transorbital lobotomy* depending on the precise technique used), was hailed as a solution to overcrowded and understaffed asylums and mental hospitals and performed on an estimated 50 000 people in the USA between 1938 and the mid-1950s. These early operations were performed with surgical knives, electrodes, suction, even ice picks, to cut or sweep out great portions of the frontal lobe. They often left patients extremely apathetic, intellectually impaired and with a changed personality. Many suffered complications such as seizures and paralysis and it was not unusual for them to die as a result of the operation. Despite this, Moniz was awarded the Nobel Prize for Medicine in 1949.

These serious irreversible effects led to a change in procedures and the introduction of a far more sensitive and precise operation. The introduction of drugs to treat psychoses also resulted in a drastic drop in the rate of operations. Modern psychosurgery involves the use of a computer-based process called *stereotactic magnetic resonance imaging* to guide a small electrode to the limbic system (a part of the brain concerned with emotion and autonomic body functions). An electric current is then passed through the electrode to burn a small lesion, about 1 cm in diameter.

A *cingulotomy* is the most common form of psychosurgery. It involves cutting the cingulate gyrus, a small section of the brain that connects the limbic system to the frontal lobes. This is performed to alleviate mental disorders such as major depression, bipolar disorder, chronic anxiety states and obsessive–compulsive disorder.

Psychosurgery is very rarely used now – fewer than 25 operations are carried out in the USA and Britain annually and only one or two in Australia. It is a treatment of last resort after all other forms of therapy, both biological and psychological, have been unsuccessful and is only performed with the patient's fully informed consent. However, there is no consensus among practitioners as to how long other therapies should be tried before resorting to psychosurgery. The estimated success rate is 50–67% for OCD and 55–78% for major depression and bipolar disorder, depending on the procedure used, with few if any adverse side-effects.

One valid criticism of psychosurgery is that there is a lack of theoretical knowledge on which the treatment is based. In other words, when it is successful we do not know why. Some knowledge is available, for example that electrical stimulation of some parts of the limbic system can affect anxiety levels and that abnormalities in glucose metabolism have been found in specific areas of the limbic system in patients with OCD. However, the exact nature of any dysfunction and its effect on emotion is not yet understood.

Considerable concern continues to be expressed about any procedure whose effects are irreversible. The organisation MIND (Darton, 2000) draws attention to an alternative procedure tried on four patients suffering from very severe OCD that had not responded to treatment. Electrodes were implanted in their brains and were used to stimulate a small area of the brain rather than destroy cells. Three of the four patients showed improvement. In one patient the anxiety and obsessional thinking were relieved when the stimulation was on but not when it was switched off. It is not clear how long the treatment continued but the study did indicate that long-term stimulation might be useful in the management of OCD.

## for and against

### biomedical treatments

**+** There is substantial evidence for the effectiveness of biomedical treatments in relieving the symptoms of mental disorder.

**–** Biomedical treatments sometimes have serious side-effects.

**–** There are concerns in some quarters that drugs may be over-used because of the importance of sponsorship by drug companies.

**+** Biomedical treatments are becoming increasingly safe and effective, and there are innovative new treatments such as TMS.

**where to**

**now?**

The following are good sources of further information on biomedical treatments:

▶ **Fancher, R.T. (1995)** *Cultures of Healing*. **New York: Freeman** – takes a very critical look at the biomedical model in general.

▶ **Glenmullen, J. (2001)** *Prozac Backlash*. **Touchstone Books** – argues the case against Prozac.

**Healy, D. (1993)** *Psychiatric Drugs Explained*. **Kings Lynn: Mosby** – a well-written guide to the use of psychotropic drugs.

▶ **Kramer, P. (1997)** *Listening to Prozac*. **London: Penguin** – puts the case in favour of Prozac use.

## Conclusions

It is important to note that even those people who recognise that biology may be the cause of a mental problem do not necessarily advocate biological intervention and feel that psychological methods are appropriate in some cases. Indeed, rarely are biological therapies advocated as the *only* means of treatment; sometimes such interventions are recommended to put the patient in a frame of mind in which they are receptive to psychological therapy. For example, in some cases of anxiety disorders and depression, drugs may be deemed necessary to bring the individual to a state in which they can benefit from psychological treatments. In other conditions, such as bipolar disorder and schizophrenia, it may be necessary for a patient to receive medication for life but these medications are likely to be fully effective only when used alongside psychological therapies.

The use of biological therapies implies that there is a direct relationship between biological dysfunction and mental dysfunction, but this is by no means always the case. For example, stress causes the release of adrenaline and noradrenaline in the bloodstream, which can then have an adverse effect on behaviour. Rather than taking medication to reduce the levels of these particular hormones, it is better to help the individual to reduce their level of stress, or to help them find ways of coping with situations so that they are no longer stressful.

Biological therapies provide an invaluable and sometimes life-saving tool in the treatment of mental disorder, and improvements in the existing methods and better alternatives are constantly being researched. However, it is unlikely (and probably undesirable) that biological treatments should ever be the only help that sufferers are given. A combination of appropriate somatic and psychological therapies is always likely to provide the most favourable outcomes.

1   Discuss ways in which the role of genetic factors in abnormal behaviour can be investigated.

2   What role may biochemical factors play in causing abnormal behaviour?

3   Discuss arguments for and against the biomedical approach to explaining atypical behaviour.

4   Describe and evaluate the use of **two** biomedical therapies for abnormal behaviour.

5   Evaluate the use of biological therapies in treating abnormal behaviour.

# 3

# The Learning Approach

what's
ahead?

In this chapter we will look at how the processes involved in learning have been used to explain the origins of mental disorders. We will consider how classical conditioning can lead to the association of fear and anxiety with everyday events or objects. In addition, we will consider how operant conditioning can result in maladaptive behaviours being, often unwittingly, reinforced and therefore encouraged. We will also look at how vicarious learning, by means of modelling and imitation, can result in inappropriate behaviours.

Having considered ways in which learning theory explains the origins of mental disorders, we will then focus on the therapies that this theoretical approach offers. This will include the traditional approaches such as systematic desensitisation, modelling and token economies and the more recently developed virtual reality exposure therapy.

## Assumptions of the approach

The learning or *behavioural* approach views abnormal behaviour as having developed in the same way as all other behaviour; as the result of learning processes. In essence, the symptoms of psychological disorders arise because an individual has learned self-defeating or ineffective ways of behaving.

- Mental disorders can be understood as patterns of learned maladaptive behaviour.

- The emphasis of the approach is on observable behaviour as opposed to physiology, emotion or thinking.

- The learning of maladaptive behaviour takes place by processes including classical and operant conditioning and social learning.

- Mental disorder can be treated by behavioural therapies, in which maladaptive behaviours can be unlearned and replaced with new and more adaptive behaviours.

## Classical conditioning

*Classical conditioning* was originally demonstrated by Pavlov, who conditioned dogs to salivate to the sound of a bell (see Figure 3.1). Dogs innately salivate to food; they do not need to learn to do this. The food is an unconditioned stimulus (UCS) and the response it elicits (salivation) is known as an unconditioned response (UCR) because no learning is involved. By pairing a bell with food, Pavlov conditioned dogs to salivate to the bell, even when no food was presented. The bell was the conditioned stimulus (CS) and the salivation to it was a conditioned (learned) response (CR). The dogs became excited when they heard the bell. The significance of this procedure was that an *emotional response* had been conditioned to a previously neutral stimulus.

**Figure 3.1** Pavlov's dogs

In the case of Pavlov's dogs the emotional response was a pleasant one, but any emotional response, including anxiety and fear, can become associated through learning with any neutral stimulus. This is important in the development of anxiety disorders (discussed in Chapter 11). Over time, if a stimulus is regularly coupled with an unpleasant experience this stimulus will elicit fear and dread, possibly throughout a lifetime. In the case of a very intense emotion it may require only one coupling for the fear to become well established. If, for example, a person was brutally assaulted in a certain side-street, then entering that street may produce the same emotional response that was associated with the assault. Likewise, the smell of the after-shave used by their rapist may trigger dreadful feelings in a victim after the event. The acquisition of a phobia by classical conditioning was demonstrated by Watson and Rayner (1920) when they conditioned the fear of a white rat in unfortunate Little Albert, the classic study described on p. 205.

Another area where classical conditioning is important in explaining mental health problems is in the *paraphilias* (or sexual fetishes). Studies have demonstrated that we can condition animals to respond sexually to neutral stimuli. Kippin (2000) classically conditioned ejaculation in rats to the smell of lemon or almond. The male rats were allowed to copulate with females bearing one of the two odours. Although the males initially showed no preference for copulating with a female bearing a particular smell, they subsequently displayed a preference to mate again with those bearing the smell that they had come to associate with ejaculation. It is believed that humans can acquire sexual fetishes by similar processes. A harmless example of such a conditioned response is shown below.

**media watch**

The following is taken from a letter to the problems page in the *News of the World*, January 2000.

**Question**: My boyfriend and I tried an experiment which I'd like to tell you about. For two months we made love every night with Barry White on continuous play on our CD player. Now whenever either of us hears that music we become sexually aroused.

**Answer**: A long-dead foreigner called Pavlov did much the same sort of experiment but used dogs, bells and food. Your research project sounds far more interesting and I suggest you apply for a grant to help you continue your studies.

**1** Explain this couple's experience in terms of classical conditioning.

**2** Give an example of how a more serious sexual fetish might be acquired by classical conditioning.

Whilst this is a harmless and even amusing account of a conditioned sexual response it is believed that similar processes can be involved in the development of more serious sexual fetishes including paedophilia.

# Operant conditioning

In *operant conditioning* animals and humans learn as a *consequence* of their actions. If they receive a reinforcement from the environment after making a particular response, this strengthens the response and increases the likelihood that it will recur. The work on the importance of reinforcement in shaping behaviour was pioneered by Thorndike (1911), who formulated the *law of effect*. This states that responses that lead to satisfying consequences will be strengthened while those that lead to unpleasant ones will be weakened. Skinner reformulated this law as the *principle of reinforcement*, a law which Skinner believed to be the foremost means of explaining and controlling human behaviour.

It is important to draw a distinction between two types of reinforcement, *positive reinforcement* and *negative reinforcement*. Positive reinforcement strengthens a response because the consequences are pleasant – a hungry pigeon will learn to press a lever to obtain food; a child will learn to say 'please' in order to be given a biscuit. Negative reinforcement involves strengthening a response by removal of an unpleasant (aversive) consequence – a child will clear up a mess in order to avoid a telling-off; a pigeon will learn to press a lever in order to avoid an electric shock. It is important to note that negative reinforcement is not the same as punishment; a response is being strengthened, *not* weakened, and it is *avoidance* of an unpleasant stimulus that influences behaviour, not the administration of something aversive. Negative reinforcement is a very powerful means of learning behaviour; from the perspective of abnormal psychology, it has a special significance because it involves anxiety. Learning to avoid adverse consequences can be extremely stressful, especially when the adverse consequences are very unpleasant and their administration is rather unpredictable. A child who tries to appease a vicious parent may become extremely fearful and anxious when trying to learn exactly what is necessary to avoid a beating.

The importance of reinforcement can be seen in the development of several types of problem behaviour. For example, aggression is often reinforced in children – if one child pushes another and snatches a toy from them, gaining the toy is a reinforcer and the aggressive response is strengthened. In this case reinforcement does not come from other people but there are many examples of the way in which unwanted behaviour is inadvertently reinforced. For example, a disruptive child gains attention, and even a telling off can be preferable to being ignored. Similarly, a severely depressed individual may receive a great deal of sympathy and understanding from concerned family members, meaning that their depressed behaviour is reinforced (Figure 3.2). A different way in which operant conditioning accounts for problem behaviour can be seen in substance abuse. The abuse of alcohol and other drugs may result from the fact that initially people feel good after taking them, so the drugs act as a positive reinforcer. Once the

**Figure 3.2** Too much sympathy may reinforce depression under some circumstances

habit is established, negative reinforcement is likely to maintain it, since not having the drug brings extremely unpleasant withdrawal symptoms, which are alleviated by further doses of the drug.

## Social (observational) learning

*Observational learning* is another influential form of learning, the importance of which was discussed by the *social learning theorists*. It involves learning through imitating other people. Children tend to copy the behaviour of significant people in their lives, especially parents, same-sex peers and influential media characters. In a series of experimental studies, Bandura (1965, 1973) demonstrated that children will copy an aggressive model, especially if the model is seen to be rewarded for the aggressive behaviour. Mineka *et al.* (1984) observed that young monkeys were initially unafraid of snakes, but will acquire fear of snakes if they witness older monkeys fleeing from one. Modelling, like operant and classical conditioning, also has important implications for treatment of psychological disorders.

## inter**active** angles

Musophobia is the irrational fear of mice.

## Questions

1  Explain how musophobia might be acquired through classical conditioning.

2  Explain how musophobia might be acquired through modelling.

## Evaluating the learning approach to explaining mental disorders

On the positive side, the learning approach has been heralded as a precise and objective way of regarding human behaviour. It has also been very useful in drawing our attention to the effects of conditioning (and hence certain early experiences) on behaviour. By using carefully controlled experimental procedures, it has offered a wealth of empirical evidence in support of the underlying theories. The research has also demonstrated the effectiveness of the application of these theories to changing behaviour.

However, the approach is not without shortcomings. First, although therapies based on the learning approach have been fairly successful in changing certain types of behaviour, this does not necessarily mean that faulty learning *caused* the problems in the first place. Davison and Neale (2001) use a common-sense example, provided by Rimland (1964), to illustrate this argument. The mood of a depressed person may well be improved by providing positive reinforcement every time they increase their activity level, but this is not evidence that their depression and apathy was originally caused by absence of rewards.

Second, one of the major problems with the behavioural account of humans is that it underestimates the complexity and flexibility of the human mind. A fundamental characteristic of humans is their ability to think and reason – we are not simply puppets with no free will or ability to critically consider our own behaviour. Some recognition of this has been made by the *cognitive-behavioural theorists* who have moved away from the very strict traditional behaviourist approach and now take account of the fact that people's behaviour is influenced by their own interpretation of a situation, by their hopes and expectations and by their capacity to take some control over their lives. Bandura (1974) stated that humans have a 'capacity for self-direction' and are not totally at the mercy of their environment. The cognitive-behavioural approach bridges the gap between the learning approach and the cognitive approach, which is considered in more detail in Chapter 4.

## for and against

## the learning model as an explanation for abnormal behaviour

**+** The basic concepts of the learning approach, such as strength of response, can easily be empirically tested, and have largely been supported by research.

**+** Clinicians have successfully used behavioural techniques to help change some problem behaviour.

**–** There is no strong evidence to suggest that most mental disorders are acquired as the result of faulty conditioning.

**–** The fact that clinical symptoms can be simulated under laboratory conditions does not necessarily mean that these symptoms are acquired in this way in ordinary life.

**–** The learning approach underestimates the complexity of humans and sees them as being entirely at the mercy of environmental influences; there is little consideration for freewill, consciousness or personality.

**The following are good sources of information about the learning approach:**

▶ **Davison, G.C. and Neale, J.M. (2001)** *Abnormal Psychology*, **8th edition. New York: Wiley** – good coverage of all the major theoretical approaches to explaining mental disorder.

▶ **Jarvis, M., Russell, J., Flanagan, C. and Dolan, L. (2000)** *Angles on Psychology*. **Cheltenham: Nelson Thornes** – gives a good general account of the learning approach to psychology.

# Behavioural therapies

Therapies based on the learning approach are collectively known as *behavioural* or *behaviour* therapies, although some researchers prefer to use the term *behaviour therapy* to refer to those based on classical conditioning and the term *behaviour modification* for those based on operant conditioning. The principle underlying such therapies is that since maladaptive behaviour is the product of unfortunate earlier conditioning it can be modified through reconditioning.

The focus of the therapy is on changing specific behaviours. This is in contrast to, for example, the psychodynamic approach, which concentrates on uncovering the contents of the unconscious mind; or the cognitive approach, which aims to alter thought processes. After examining the patient, the behaviour therapist outlines in advance the precise behaviours that need to be modified and the specific behaviours that need to be learnt. The faulty or maladaptive behaviour is reduced first and then adaptive behaviour, or behaviour incompatible with the unwanted behaviour, is encouraged. Although it is convenient to label these therapies according to the main technique used, bear in mind that a combination of such therapies would often be used, depending on the exact nature of the condition and the person receiving the therapy.

## Systematic desensitisation, flooding and implosion therapy

We discussed earlier the concept of extinction – if, after conditioning, Pavlov's dogs heard a bell ring but were given no food, the conditioned response of salivation would eventually disappear. However, in the case of some abnormal behaviours, especially phobias, extinction has no opportunity to occur. Consider a woman who is phobic of cats. She will do everything possible to avoid them. On seeing a cat, her anxiety level rises sharply and when she escapes it drops. In the language of learning theory, she has developed a *conditioned avoidance response* to all cats. Such a response is highly resistant to extinction because the avoidance response is *negatively reinforced* – avoiding the cat has led to escape from an extremely unpleasant feeling. So, in theoretical terms, classical conditioning has caused the problem (association of cats with fear) while operant conditioning maintains it by negative reinforcement. Behavioural therapies for phobias therefore concentrate on providing *exposure* to the feared object or situation and thus an environment in which extinction can occur. Systematic desensitisation does this gradually and provides an alterative, incompatible response; flooding, implosion therapy and virtual reality therapy do it rather more abruptly.

### Systematic desensitisation

Using the work of Mary Jones (1924), who recognised that one way to treat a phobia was to introduce an individual to the phobic object very gradually while inducing responses that are incompatible with fear, Wolpe (1958) devised a systematic programme for reducing anxiety before exposure. The procedure is composed of three stages:

1   The individual is given training in deep relaxation. This may involve the use of hypnosis or drugs.

2   He or she is asked to imagine situations that provoke anxiety and build up a hierarchy from least to most fear provoking. These situations create a scale of increasing levels of anxiety known as the subjective units of discomfort (SUD) scale.

3   The client is then asked to imagine the anxiety-provoking situations, starting with the least disturbing and moving gradually up the scale to the most disturbing. At all stages, the person is encouraged to relax and no advancement is made to the next stage until relaxation is achieved. Because it is impossible to be relaxed and anxious at the same time, the individual becomes gradually (systematically) desensitised to the frightening situation.

## classic research

# experimental desensitisation of a phobia

**Lang, P.J. and Lazovik, D.A. (1963) Experimental desensitisation of a phobia.** *Journal of Abnormal and Social Psychology*, 66, 519–525

**Aim:** The main aim of the study was to test the effectiveness of desensitisation in treating phobia of snakes. A secondary aim was to assess the validity of the criticism made of desensitisation by psychodynamic therapists – that because symptoms ultimately come from unconscious conflicts, one phobia, when removed, is likely to be replaced by another.

**Method:** The participants, all college students, were chosen from a group who all rated themselves on a questionnaire as having a fear of snakes that was 'intense'. They were interviewed by the researchers and if their fear was judged to be weak, they were not used as participants. Those who were chosen to take part in the study reported such disturbances as 'I feel sick to my stomach when I see them', or 'My palms get sweaty, I'm tense.' They also avoided being anywhere near a live snake and watching them on film or television. Even pictures in magazines upset most of them.

The assignment of participants to the control or experimental group was essentially random, although there was some attempt to balance participants roughly in terms of intensity of fear and motivation to participate in the study. There were 24 participants in all: the experimental group consisted of four men and nine women; the control group three men and eight women.

Participants were trained in deep muscle relaxation over a number of sessions. They also drew up a fear hierarchy, which was different for everyone but typically consisted of 'writing the word snake', 'seeing a caged snake in a zoo', 'accidentally treading on a dead snake'. They were given eleven 45-minute sessions of systematic desensitisation, during which they were hypnotised, instructed to relax deeply and then asked to imagine each step of the hierarchy in turn. Only when totally relaxed did they move up the hierarchy.

**Assessment:** The participant was told that there was a non-poisonous snake in a glass case in a nearby laboratory. He or she was encouraged to enter and describe their reactions. The snake was 15 feet from the entrance. The experimenter then walked to the case and removed the wire grid covering it, assuring the participant that the snake was harmless. The experimenter asked the participant to come to the cage and see what he was doing. If they refused, they were asked to come as close as possible. If they came to the cage they were asked to touch the snake (a 5-foot-long black one) after seeing the experimenter do it. If this was successful, he or she was invited to hold it. The participant was asked to rate their anxiety (on a 10-point scale) and the experimenter also estimated it on a 3-point scale.

**Results:** The treatment programme successfully reduced phobic behaviour in the experimental group, as shown by reduction in avoidance behaviour and subjective ratings of fear, although not with the entire group. None of the control group showed any change. The improvements were maintained 6 months later. There was no evidence at all that other symptoms had appeared to replace the phobic behaviour.

**Conclusion:** These findings are consistent with the learning theory of phobias but further research is required to see if it is the best explanation for why systematic desensitisation is effective. It would be especially useful to measure changes in muscle tension during the presentation of the fear hierarchy in order to evaluate the theory.

The researchers drew three main conclusions:

- It is not necessary to explore the reasons for the phobia or its 'unconscious meaning' in order to eliminate it.

- No symptom substitution occurred.

- In reducing phobic behaviour, it is not necessary to change basic attitudes, values or personality, but simply to change behaviour.

A rather different example is provided by Davison and Neale (2001), who discuss the case of a postman with a crippling fear of being criticised. He was asked to imagine situations such as saying 'good morning' to his boss, having someone complain about late mail and being criticised by his wife for buying the wrong bread. In the original programme devised by Wolpe the feared stimulus was imagined, but many behaviour therapists believe that exposure to real-life phobic situations (either instead of or in addition to using imagination) is essential to successful treatment and is far more effective than imagination alone (Craske *et al.*, 1992). For this reason, participants are often gradually introduced to the real object of their phobia rather than simply being asked to imagine it.

### Flooding and implosion

In flooding the client is exposed to the feared stimulus in its most disturbing form for a prolonged period of time. Implosion therapy is similar, except that the individual is asked to imagine and relive anxiety-provoking scenes. These therapies differ from systematic desensitisation in that, rather than trying to prevent fear occurring, they deliberately elicit a massive amount of anxiety. Both flooding and implosion therapy are based on the idea that a high level of autonomic arousal is impossible to sustain and that eventually the feelings of fear and panic subside. After many sessions in a safe therapeutic environment the maladaptive responses are extinguished.

A classic example of the use of flooding for phobias was that of an adolescent girl with a phobia of travelling in cars who was driven around for 4 hours until her initial hysterical response subsided and her fear disappeared (Wolpe, 1973). A typical way in which it would be used for obsessive–compulsive disorders would be to oblige a individual with hand-washing obsession to touch something they regarded as 'dirty', such as a newspaper, and then not wash their hands for several hours – until the anxiety had extinguished.

Stampfl (1975) (reported in Carson and Butcher, 1992) recounts an example of the use of implosion therapy with a young woman whose fear of going under water was so great that she wore a life jacket in the bath. She was required to imagine herself taking a bath in a 'bottomless' tub without a life jacket and sinking under water. This scene had to be repeated 14 times before treatment was complete but she was then able to take a bath without wearing a life jacket.

Like most therapies, these forms of behaviour therapy are far more effective in treating some conditions than others. Clinical and experimental evidence indicates that systematic desensitisation is effective in eliminating or at least reducing phobias (McGlynn, 1994). It has also been used in the treatment of obsessive–compulsive disorders (discussed in Chapter 11) but tends to be less successful, having about a 50% success rate (Sue and Sue, 1990). When used for such conditions, it is more effective when the symptoms are relatively recent (Foa and Tillmans, 1980); flooding, on the other hand, has been particularly effective in controlling obsessive–compulsive behaviour, more so than implosion therapy.

Marks (1976) maintains that in-vivo (real-life) exposure is more effective than in-vitro (imagined) exposure, no matter what the therapy. (As mentioned earlier, some therapists believe that systematic desensitisation is only really effective if carried out *in-vivo*.) Foa and Tillmanns (1980) also argue that real-life exposure plus imagined exposure is better than real-life exposure alone. Marks (1987) argues that flooding overall is more effective than systematic desensitisation.

From an ethical point of view, the main problems with flooding and implosion therapies, especially the former, is that they are very traumatic. If the client decides to discontinue treatment the therapy could even do more harm than good because escape from the fearful stimulus has been reinforced. A new form of exposure therapy is that of virtual reality.

## virtual reality exposure therapy

**Figure 3.3**  A virtual reality apparatus

One of the most recent developments in behaviour therapies is the use of a virtual reality (VR) environment in order to expose a participant to a realistic simulation of a particular situation. Virtual reality offers a realistic environment in which participants become active within a computer-generated three-dimensional virtual world. This gives the user a sense of *presence* or *immersion* in the virtual environment (Rothbaum *et al.*, 2000).

The most usual way to create a virtual reality environment is to use a head-mounted display consisting of a separate screen for each eye with optics, stereo earphones and a head-tracking device. Users then interact with a virtual world that changes in a natural way as they move their head and body (Figure 3.3).

Rothbaum *et al.* (1995) were the first researchers to conduct a controlled study using VR. They treated acrophobia (fear of heights) by exposing phobics to virtual footbridges of various heights and stability, outdoor balconies and a glass elevator that ascended 50 floors. The participants reported physical symptoms of anxiety such as sweating, 'butterflies', loss of balance and heart palpitations. All of the ten people treated showed a significant reduction in fear of heights and seven of them actually exposed themselves to heights in real-life even though this was not part of the treatment. No member of an untreated control group showed improvement.

The fear of flying is a phobia particularly suited to VR exposure therapy because of the difficulty and expense of using real aircrafts and flights. Moreover, it is a common fear, estimated to affect 10–25% of the population. Rothbaum *et al.* (2000) used VR exposure and standard exposure to treat fear of flying using eight sessions over 6 weeks. The study was very well controlled, with participants being randomly assigned to the treatment groups and standard measures being used so that replication was possible. DSM classification was used to ensure that participants were genuinely suffering from fear of flying and the same therapist delivered both treatments, thus eliminating potential therapist effects. After treatment participants were given a flight and their willingness to fly and anxiety during the flight was used as a measure of success. The VR exposure was very effective, with 93% of participants agreeing to fly, the same as the standard exposure group. Both treatment groups were better than the controls and gains were maintained at a 6-month follow-up.

Other studies of VR therapy include its use for spider phobia (Gilroy *et al.*, 2000), fear of driving (Wiederhold *et al.*, 1999) and claustrophobia (Botella *et al.*, 1999). Of particular significance is the finding that spider phobics are more inclined to seek treatment if it involves VR exposure than if they have to face real spiders. Thus VR exposure may prove valuable in increasing the number of phobics who seek therapy (Garcia-Palacios *et al.*, 2001).

Although it is a little premature to assess the effectiveness of VR exposure therapy, the signs are that it is very effective and that improvements are maintained.

## for and against

## use of virtual reality exposure therapy

+ It is less time-consuming than traditional methods such as systematic desensitisation.

+ It creates a more realistic environment than using imagination or computer graphics.

+ It is often more convenient, practical and inexpensive than *in-vivo* exposure.

− Its use is limited; it is unsuitable for use with some conditions. For example, it is not really suitable for coping with some social phobias, such as eating in public.

- Some people have suffered cybersickness after wearing the head-mounted displays for some time.

- The equipment required is complex, expensive and cumbersome (Rizzo *et al.*, 1998).

## Aversion therapy

Aversion therapy operates by using classical conditioning to pair an undesirable behaviour with an unpleasant (aversive) stimulus, so that the behaviour is eventually eliminated because it is no longer enjoyable. For example, an alcoholic would be asked to taste or even simply smell alcohol and then be given an emetic, causing violent sickness. A heavy smoker may be asked to puff away on their favourite cigarette while noxious choking fumes were poured into the room.

Although aversion therapy often uses classical conditioning, operant conditioning can also be used. For example, an alcoholic might be given an emetic (possibly in the form of an implant) that would operate only if he or she drank alcohol. The emetic works as a punishment for voluntary behaviour (in this case drinking). Some aversion programmes also use positive reinforcers for alternative, more appropriate behaviours – for example, when a smoker extinguishes a cigarette some fresh air is pumped into the room.

Aversive conditioning has been used to try to eliminate many inappropriate behaviours, including drug addiction and sexual disorders such as paedophilia, with varying degrees of success. There are, however, several problems associated with its use. First, because of the unpleasant nature of the treatment programmes, the drop-out rate tends to be high. Second, if the noxious stimuli are applied only in the laboratory, as is the usual practice, then any changes in behaviour are unlikely to generalise to real life: in fact, some people, having left the therapeutic situation, may feel that they can now have a drink or smoke a cigarette because there will be horrible consequences. Third, the participant may become anxious and resentful during the treatment. Fourth, and very importantly, there are serious ethical concerns over the use of aversion therapy. Many therapists feel that it is wrong to inflict pain and discomfort on people even if they have fully consented to it – and this is especially true when electric shocks are used as the noxious stimulus. Furthermore, concerns have been expressed that the treatment has a worrying potential for abuse or misuse. For this reason a procedure called *covert sensitisation* is occasionally used as a substitute for aversion therapy. In this case the client is asked to imagine unpleasant consequences of the maladaptive behaviour – so a smoker may imagine choking and/or being diagnosed with and suffering from lung cancer.

Aversion therapy is rarely used as a sole means of treatment because, although it may be effective in eliminating maladaptive behaviour, it is unlikely to have long-term benefits unless more appropriate behaviour is adopted. It is therefore more often used as a preliminary treatment in order to eliminate the inappropriate behaviour and set the scene for substituting a new behaviour that is more socially appropriate and which, because it is more satisfying, often provides its own reinforcement.

## Token economies

Token economies are based on the basic principles of operant conditioning, that behaviour which is reinforced is likely to be strengthened. When using a token economy the participant is rewarded for appropriate behaviour by the secondary reinforcers (namely tokens), which can be exchanged later for desirable items such as luxury food, television watching or additional recreational time (see Figure 3.4). In institutions, they may even be used for weekend passes. This system has been used with problem school children, juvenile delinquents and people suffering from developmental disability and schizophrenia.

Ayllon and Azrin (1968) used this system with female long-stay patients with schizophrenia in a psychiatric hospital, reinforcing behaviours such as neat appearance, hair brushing, bed making and performing other chores. It led not only to a marked improvement in behaviour but also to the important additional benefit of an increase in staff morale. One of the problems in many institutions (and in families for that matter) is that inappropriate behaviour is often unwittingly reinforced by the attention it receives. A token economy system focuses staff attention on rewarding appropriate behaviour while ignoring inappropriate actions (Menditto *et al.*, 1994). Recently the token economy system has been elaborated and extended for use with patients with schizophrenia. It is not claimed that such programmes will cure schizophrenia but their use does lead to a marked improvement in quality of life by resocialising patients and teaching basic self-care.

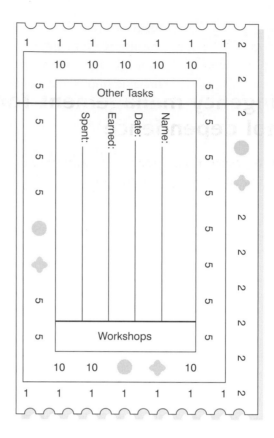

**Figure 3.4** An example of a token economy card

Token economy programmes have been very successful in a variety of settings but work best in institutions where the reinforcement programme can be carefully controlled. However, there are both practical and ethical problems involved. Sometimes the improvements in behaviour do not extend outside the setting in which they were implemented. Another problem is that this system is impracticable as a means of encouraging some complex behaviours such as developing language. Some people have criticised the token economy system as manipulative and inhumane, treating people as performing animals. However, others argue that in real life most people work for 'tokens' (in that they earn money) and it is part of everyday life to have our behaviour shaped by reinforcers. Moreover, as Carson and Butcher (1992) remark, the view of some lay people that token economy systems are the equivalent to expecting people in institutions to 'perform' for simple amenities is highly misjudged. Leaving them without the normal systems of rewards and punishments that operate in everyday life is liable to result in chronic social disability.

Modified use of token economy systems, all based on providing reinforcement but sometimes combined with punishment for unwanted or inappropriate behaviour, are common in many therapeutic settings.

# research now

## contingency management for treatment of alcohol dependence

**Petry, N.M., Martin, B, Cooney, J.L. and Kranzler, H.R. (2000) Give them prizes, and they will come: contingency management for treatment of alcohol dependence.** *Journal of Counselling and Clinical Psychology,* 68(5), 250–257

**Aim:** To evaluate the effectiveness of a contingency management (CM) procedure that involves giving the opportunity to win prizes as reinforcers.

**Method:** 42 alcohol-dependent males, diagnosed using DSM-IV, were randomly assigned to receive standard treatment (ST) or standard treatment plus contingency management (CM).

*Standard treatment* consisted of 4 weeks of an intensive outpatient day programme followed by aftercare. The intensive day programme consisted of 5-hour sessions, 5 days a week, focusing on factors such as life skills training, relapse prevention and coping skills training. During this time, participants were required to provide breath alcohol samples daily. In addition, once a week they were interviewed about any alcohol or drug use in the past week and provided a urine sample.

During the 4 weeks of aftercare, participants provided breath and urine samples weekly.

Those in the *contingency management* group received this standard treatment but every time they provided a negative breath test they also earned the right to draw a slip of paper from a bowl. If they provided five consecutive negative breath tests, they were given five bonus draws.

75% of the slips were 'winning' ones with small, medium or large prizes. The majority (90%) were small prizes of $1 tokens (for use in certain shops); 9% were medium prizes of objects worth $20 and there was a single large prize (choice of a handheld TV, a boom box or five medium prizes).

Participants in this group also earned draws for completing other steps in their treatment programmes, such as becoming active in Alcoholics Anonymous. In keeping with the principles of a behavioural programme, the precise behaviours that would constitute these steps were clearly laid down and specific verification obtained.

**Results:** The reinforcement system was very effective in retaining the participants in treatment and in reducing the number who relapsed.

Of the CM participants 84% stayed in treatment for the 8-week period, compared with 22% of the standard treatment ($p < 0.001$). By the end of this period 69% of the CM and only 39% of the ST group were still abstinent ($p < 0.05$).

**Conclusion:** The contingency management programme was demonstrated to be effective in the treatment of alcohol abuse. It can be used in addition to standard treatment procedures in order to increase the success of such a programme.

# Modelling

The fact that people learn through imitating the behaviour of others has been used in therapy in a variety of contexts, including the teaching of simple skills to individuals with learning difficulties (such as feeding oneself), as a means of demonstrating social skills, and in the treatment of phobias. Films have also been used to help people with sexual problems to overcome their inhibitions with sexual behaviour (McMullen and Rosen, 1979).

In a similar vein, *role play* may be used by a therapist to demonstrate how certain situations may be tackled, such as asking an employer for a day's leave or asking someone for a date. Marder *et al.* (1996) have successfully used this technique to teach patients suffering from schizophrenia (see Chapter 8) how to effectively manage social situations. It may also be used in assertiveness training for shy and submissive people who have serious problems in expressing their feelings.

Marks (1986) suggests that modelling is most effective if the following criteria are met:

- The demonstrator is similar to the patient.

- He or she is coping rather than perfect.

- He or she receives a reward for the behaviour.

- The modelled behaviour is in manageable, short components.

- The participant is asked to imitate the model's behaviour immediately after witnessing it.

- Feedback is provided immediately, telling the participant how they are doing.

- Praise is provided for good performance.

Modelling is part of learning in everyday life – from a very early age we copy our parents, older siblings and peers. It is therefore a relatively easy and painless method to use in therapy and has become a useful technique for treatment of many conditions. It is especially useful in the treatment of interpersonal problems for which the therapeutic alternatives are more limited than in other types of conditions.

## behavioural therapies

**+** There is a large body of evidence to suggest that behavioural therapies are successful in tackling the symptoms of mental disorder.

**+** There is no doubt that behavioural therapies can improve a patient's quality of life.

**–** There is a question whether altering someone's behaviour is really a cure, and there may be cases where doing so may simply mask the underlying problem.

**–** There are serious ethical issues to be considered in the use of behavioural therapies.

# where to now?

The following are good sources of information about behavioural therapies:

▶ **Davey, G.C.L. (ed.) (1997)** *Phobias: A Handbook of Therapy Research and Treatment.* **Chichester: Wiley.**

▶ **Davison, G.L. and Neale, J.M. (2001)** *Abnormal Psychology***, 8th edition. New York: Wiley** – offers an in-depth discussion of several issues mentioned in this chapter, including the use of virtual reality as a therapeutic tool (page 47); the use of modelling and role play in assertiveness training (page 50); and the use of behaviour therapy for hospitalised patients with schizophrenia (page 306).

▶ **Fonagy, P. (1996)** *What Works with Whom? A Critical Review of Psychotherapy Research.* **London: Guilford Press** – this book provides a fairly recent report on the effectiveness and appropriateness of therapies, including behavioural ones.

▶ **Paul, G.L. and Menditto, A.A. (1992) Effectiveness of inpatient treatment programs for mentally ill adults in public facilities.** *Applied and Preventative Psychology Current Scientific Perspectives***, 1, 41–63** – a useful discussion of the use of token economy and other related techniques for the treatment of people in institutional care.

## Conclusions

Having considered the contributions and limitations of the learning approach to the understanding of atypical behaviour and of the individual therapies, we will now consider the efficacy of behavioural therapy overall. Behaviour therapy is a very popular method of treatment that has several advantages. The therapy has a widely accepted theoretical basis: the principles of learning on which it is based have been demonstrated in many studies to have scientific validity. At the beginning of therapy, a list is drawn up of the precise behavioural changes that are required, making it possible to measure the therapy's effectiveness precisely. It is also a very economical method of treatment because most programmes require only a short period of treatment.

Like all therapeutic methods, behaviour therapy works better with some conditions than others. Since these therapies operate by defining what precise behaviours need to be changed, the more vague and ill-defined the symptoms the patient presents with, the less appropriate behaviour therapy is likely to be. On the other hand, it is effective in treating anxiety-based disorders such as simple phobias, obsessive–compulsive disorders and post-traumatic stress disorder (Smith *et al.*, 1980). In addition, although behaviour therapy cannot cure psychoses such as schizophrenia, the work of Paul and Menditto (1992) has demonstrated the considerable benefits that some of the behavioural programmes have brought to people suffering from these conditions – and, indeed, to those who share their environment. Operant techniques based on systematically rewarding desirable behaviours and extinguishing undesirable ones have been particularly successful in the treatment of a wide range of childhood problems including bed-wetting, extreme social withdrawal and severely disruptive behaviour (Kazdin and Weisz, 1998).

Some critics of behavioural therapy point to the fact that in treating specific behaviours it provides clients with little insight into the causes of their symptoms or the associated psychological disorder from which they are suffering. Psychodynamic therapists maintain that in some cases behaviour therapy may treat the symptoms rather than the causes of mental disorder and is therefore of limited value. However, as Costello *et al.* (1995) point out, the therapist invariably offers more than simply a means of specific behaviour change; encouragement and counselling are an integral part of the treatment. Indeed, the very reason for the effectiveness of behaviour therapy may be that it involves discovering the source of the anxiety underlying a patient's problems (Goldfried and Davison, 1994). This introduces a rather different criticism – that the success of behaviour therapy may depend at least partly on the attention and interest of the therapist rather than on the strict application of learning principles. Nevertheless, it is fair to say that, although therapies based on learning principles can never be a 'cure-all', they do offer a practical and effective treatment for a wide variety of conditions and, for this reason, are here to stay.

1   Describe and evaluate classical conditioning as an explanation of mental disorders.

2   Outline two psychological therapies based on the learning approach.

3   Discuss the effectiveness and appropriateness of behavioural therapies.

# 4

# The Cognitive Approach

what's
ahead?

The cognitive approach has been the dominant force in psychology since the early 1970s. The essence of this approach is to study internal mental processes such as perception, attention, memory and problem solving. Although these processes cannot be directly observed (we cannot open up someone's brain and 'see' their memory) they can be inferred from experimental tasks (e.g. we can work out what is going on in memory, from how well people remember things). In this chapter we take a look at how the cognitive approach has been applied in the study of psychopathology, to explain the development of mental disorders such as depression, and the link between cognition and brain function (the *cognitive–neuropsychological approach*). The later part of the chapter looks at how the cognitive approach has been used to develop therapeutic techniques for mental disorders and the effectiveness of the cognitive and cognitive–behavioural therapies.

## Assumptions of the cognitive approach

The cognitive approach to the study of mental disorders developed in the late 1960s and early 1970s following the so-called 'cognitive revolution' in psychology. Dissatisfied with the limitations of learning approaches (see Chapter 3), psychologists began to study internal mental processes such as perception, attention, memory and problem solving using the experimental method. The cognitive paradigm has now become the dominant approach in psychology (Richards, 1996) and as a direct consequence cognitive explanations and treatments for mental disorders have become dominant over other psychological approaches. The cognitive approach makes a number of implicit assumptions about the study of mental disorders:

- Rather than aiming to provide complete explanations for mental disorders, the cognitive approach focuses on explaining specific symptoms. For example, cognitive theories of schizophrenia focus on explaining symptoms such as thought insertion (see p. 143) rather than the totality of the disorder.

- The emphasis in the cognitive approach is on the role of cognitive processes, for example memory and thinking, in mental disorder. These cognitive factors are believed to play a direct causal role in certain mental disorders. For example, irrational beliefs about personal vulnerability are believed to put people at risk of anxiety. In other disorders such as schizophrenia, cognitive factors may not be the cause of the disorder but are the results of neurological factors (remember that brain function will affect cognitive function and vice versa).

- If symptoms of mental disorders are linked to cognitive factors, then it should be possible to treat these symptoms by targeting these cognitive factors. This is the basis behind the cognitive therapies developed by Aaron Beck and Albert Ellis.

## Beck's cognitive theory of emotional disorders

Beck (1976) proposed a cognitive theory to explain mental disorders characterised by cognitive content, including depression, anxiety disorders and eating disorders. The starting point of Beck's theory is that people react differently to unpleasant or *aversive* situations. For example, some people will develop depression following an unrelenting succession of tragedies, but not all people. Beck argued that it is necessary to consider internal mental processes in order to explain why some people develop a disorder and why others do not. As Figure 4.1 (overleaf) shows, aversive life events combined with a certain set of cognitive processes might interact to produce an emotional disorder. Essentially, Beck's view is that cognition precedes an emotional response, so that a disorder characterised by emotional content is caused (in part) by cognitive processes.

Beck believed that dysfunctional beliefs are formed early in childhood through the acquisition of certain types of *schemas* (packets of information about different aspects of the world), and that different disorders are characterised by different types of schemas. For example, depression is characterised by what Beck calls a *cognitive triad* of negative schemas: negative views of one's self, one's personal world and one's future (see p. 167 for a fuller account). In contrast, anxiety is characterised by *vulnerability schemas*, perception of a physical and psychological threat to oneself. A key point in Beck's theory is that an individual who has acquired these schemas will not necessarily develop an emotional disorder. Some kind of critical life event is required to activate these schemas. For example, someone who has acquired a cognitive triad will not necessarily develop depression; only if they experience a situation similar to the one in which the negative schemas were initially acquired are the schemas likely to be activated, leading to a negative world view that in turn predisposes the individual to depression.

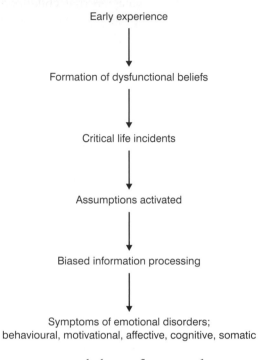

Early experience

↓

Formation of dysfunctional beliefs

↓

Critical life incidents

↓

Assumptions activated

↓

Biased information processing

↓

Symptoms of emotional disorders;
behavioural, motivational, affective, cognitive, somatic

**Figure 4.1** Beck's cognitive theory of emotional disorders (Beck, 1976)

Once schemas are activated they influence information processing so that only information consistent with that schema is processed and other information tends to be disregarded. For example, once a cognitive triad is activated the individual will only process information consistent with their negative view of their self, their world and their future It is this biased information processing which gives rise to the symptoms of the emotional disorder. Because the individual is only processing information consistent with their dysfunctional beliefs, it reinforces their distorted view of the world and confirms their belief that they were right all along.

There is no doubt that Beck's theory has been enormously influential in establishing the cognitive approach as the dominant approach in clinical psychology, and his ideas were eagerly taken up by clinical psychologists in the UK as they attempted to forge an identity separate from the psychiatric profession (Parker *et al.*, 1995). However, evidence for Beck's therapy is mixed and a number of important criticisms have been made of his theory. The key to finding evidence for Beck's theory is to show that cognitive processes are *causing* the emotional disturbance. This can be difficult in practice, as somebody with an emotional disorder who goes to a clinical psychologist already has the disorder, and it is not possible to measure their cognitive processes before the onset of the disorder. Nonetheless there are two potential routes to take: use experimental tasks to try to measure differences in cognitive processes between participants with and without an emotional disorder or to evaluate Beck's therapy (to tell whether an emotional disorder can be treated by changing cognition).

Research has also supported Beck's notion of biased information processing in depression, at least in cases of major depression (see p. 168). It is also accepted that childhood life events are associated with adult depression (Brown and Harris, 1978; Eley and Stevenson, 2000). This is consistent with Beck's ideas (as it is with other explanations such as that of Freud, see p. 165), but does not directly support cognitive theory unless it can be demonstrated that the early experience actually does lead to dysfunctional beliefs, which then put an individual at risk of developing an emotional disorder later in life.

The effectiveness of Beck's cognitive therapy as a treatment is well documented (see the Butler and Beck study later in the chapter), but this does not demonstrate the validity of Beck's theory (Oie and Free, 1995) – just because Beck's therapy works, his theory is not necessarily correct. Eysenck (1997) is highly critical of the way schematic processing is used in Beck's theory: it is not well defined and may account to little more than a belief. More importantly, the existence of schemas in Beck's theory is established through the use of circular reasoning – the existence of a schema is inferred from certain responses (on experimental tasks for example), and that schema is then used to explain the information processing biases producing that response. Such an approach is not scientific and there is no way of independently verifying the existence of such hypothetical cognitive structures. For social constructionists the cognitive approach is overly reductionist and mechanistic, having difficulty in explaining people who hold contradictory beliefs, or who think dynamically rather than rationally (Parker *et al.*, 1995).

## for and against

### Beck's theory

**+** Research has supported Beck's view that depressed participants show biases in information processing.

**+** Research has supported Beck's view that, in depression at least, cognitive factors do appear to play a causal role.

**–** Beck's cognitive therapy is effective in treating a wide range of emotional disorders, but this does not necessarily mean that Beck's theory is correct.

**–** Concepts such as schemas are not well defined and are established through circular reasoning.

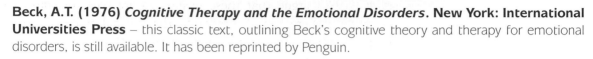

**The following is a good source of further information on the cognitive approach:**

▶ **Beck, A.T. (1976)** *Cognitive Therapy and the Emotional Disorders*. **New York: International Universities Press** – this classic text, outlining Beck's cognitive theory and therapy for emotional disorders, is still available. It has been reprinted by Penguin.

## The cognitive neuropsychological approach

The cognitive neuropsychological approach is based on the relationship between cognitive function and brain function. Brain function has a profound affect on cognitive function and any changes in brain function often manifest as changes in cognitive function. The use of patients with brain damage has become one of the key methods in advancing knowledge about cognitive function (Eysenck and Keane, 2000). For example, in the area of memory, the famous case study of H.M. (Blakemore, 1988) who had difficulty forming new long-term memories following surgery to remove his hippocampus, has been cited as the single strongest piece of evidence for the distinction between short-term and long-term memory.

In psychological disorders, there remains the possibility that cognitive symptoms might be manifestations of an underlying change in brain function, although this is not the case for all psychological disorders. For example, Beck's theory (outlined above) is probably a 'pure' cognitive theory in that disorders such as depression and phobias are (partly) caused by cognitive factors themselves. In other disorders such as schizophrenia and post-traumatic stress disorder (PTSD) it seems likely that cognitive symptoms are themselves caused by changes in brain function. Therefore a cognitive theory for some disorders (e.g. depression) may be causal, and for other disorders (e.g. schizophrenia) may be more explanatory than causal. Frith (1992) strongly points out that, even though a cognitive theory of schizophrenia may not be causal, it may still be the best theory of schizophrenia. This is partly because cognitive theories tend to work with symptoms rather than disorders and therefore avoid problems of changing diagnostic criteria, and partly because cognition can be mapped onto brain function.

Scott and Stradling (2001) developed a cognitive–neuropsychological model for PTSD (see Chapter 11) by combining cognitive theory with an understanding of how the brain deals with emotionally traumatic stimuli. An influential cognitive theory of PTSD was proposed by Brewin *et al.* (1996) based on the theory of cue-dependent forgetting. The main feature that distinguishes PTSD from other anxiety disorders such as phobias is the force by which the person re-experiences the traumatic event, complete with the full sensory and emotional range present at the original event. It is almost as if the person is back in the original traumatic event. Often these experiences are triggered by sights, sounds or smells that are seemingly insignificant but related to the traumatic event. For example, someone with PTSD following a particularly traumatic car crash may experience a 'flashback' triggered by the smell of petrol. Brewin *et al.* (1996) argue that these flashbacks are types of cue-dependent memories, where stimuli similar to the original traumatic event may trigger sensory and emotional aspects of the memory. These cue-dependent memories operate on two levels: verbally accessible memories such as the ability to recount the traumatic experience and situationally accessible memories. These are the non-verbal, sensory and emotional memories, associated with flashbacks.

Scott and Stradling (2001) argue that Brewin's cognitive theory of PTSD maps very neatly onto work carried out into the neurobiology of PTSD by LeDoux (1998). LeDoux has found that emotionally traumatic memories are located in an area of the brain called the amygdala. Memories activated by the amygdala are non-conscious emotional memories lacking information about time and space. When stimuli such as a loud bang trigger the 'alarm' in the amygdala, corrective information is sent from the hippocampus, the site of most recent verbal memories coded in time and space, to switch off the alarm. However, people with PTSD have a smaller hippocampus than those without PTSD (Yehouda, 1998), so when their amygdala is triggered by sensory stimuli (such as a loud bang) the hippocampus cannot turn the alarm off. The amygdala continues to sound alarm, reproducing the original physical state that accompanied the trauma (sweating, palpitations, etc.) together with the non-conscious sensory memories of the trauma, but not located at the original time of the traumatic event (i.e. the trauma that occurred in the past is re-experienced in the present). Such a mechanism represents the flashbacks experienced by people with PTSD.

## for and against

## the cognitive–neuropsychological approach

+ Neuropsychological evidence about brain function can be used to test cognitive theories of mental disorders.

− Cognitive–neuropsychological theories of mental disorders are somewhat speculative, as they involve mapping one type of explanation (neuropsychological) onto another (cognitive).

− Neuropsychological evidence is often of a very complex nature, with many contradictory findings.

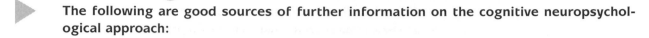

## where to now?

▶ The following are good sources of further information on the cognitive neuropsychological approach:

▶ **Frith, C.D. (1992)** *The Cognitive Neuropsychology of Schizophrenia*. **Hove: Psychology Press** – a landmark text tracing the history of neurological research into schizophrenia, and how such a body of findings can be incorporated within the cognitive approach.

**Scott, M.J. and Stradling, S.G. (2001)** *Counselling for Post-Traumatic Stress Disorder*. **London: Sage** – this extremely accessible text outlines both cognitive and neurological correlates for PTSD, going on to suggest how a synthesis of the two approaches can be used in cognitive therapy for PTSD.

# Cognitive and cognitive–behavioural therapies

Cognitive therapy refers to those therapeutic techniques aiming to change or modify a person's thoughts or beliefs. This is in part based on the belief in *cognitive primacy*, the idea that thinking occurs before, and leads to, emotion and behaviour. For example, in Beck's theory outlined above certain negative schema (the cognitive triad) can result in depression. Based on this theory, the way to treat depression is to target these negative schemas and dysfunctional beliefs. Sometimes cognitive therapists will set clients behavioural tasks (sometimes referred to as *homework*) in order to dispute dysfunctional beliefs. For example, a therapist might ask a depressed client to plan an evening out to the cinema to counter their belief that life is always dull. These therapies are thus sometimes referred to as cognitive–behavioural therapies. The two terms are used interchangeably and do not refer to different techniques or therapies. This section will consider the techniques employed by two of the most well known cognitive therapies (Beck's cognitive restructuring and Ellis's rational emotive therapy), along with the evidence for these therapies.

## Cognitive restructuring (Aaron Beck)

The goal of Beck's cognitive therapy is to reduce symptoms of emotional disorders by challenging and reversing these dysfunctional beliefs and attitudes, a process referred to as cognitive restructuring. Beck *et al.* (1979) break down this type of therapy into six distinct stages (see Box 4.1). This process is firmly rooted in the *metacognitive process* – the ability to reflect on and modify thinking patterns. Without this kind of executive control it would not be possible to identify and change dysfunctional beliefs and biased ways of thinking.

---

1 Explaining the cognitive rationale and purpose of therapy.
2 Teaching the client to monitor automatic thoughts.
3 Using behavioural techniques to challenge negative thoughts.
4 Responding to negative thoughts.
5 Identifying dysfunctional beliefs.
6 Termination of therapy.

---

**Box 4.1** The procedural sequence of cognitive therapy (Beck *et al.*, 1979)

Automatic thoughts can be described as 'the things we tell or picture to ourselves as we go about our daily business' (Davison and Neale, 1994, p. 566). They can be likened to a running dialogue we have with ourselves and represent the first step in identifying dysfunctional beliefs. Clients are taught to identify and to monitor automatic thoughts when they are feeling depressed or anxious by considering the types of questions listed in Box 4.2. The therapist then teaches the client to challenge beliefs using available evidence from the client's life and personal circumstances.

---

1 What went through your mind?
2 What are you thinking about yourself?
3 What are you thinking about others?
4 What are you thinking about your future?

---

**Box 4.2** How to identify automatic thoughts (Gilbert, 1997)

For example, if a client held the dysfunctional belief 'If I do not finish all of my work I am incompetent and a failure', one way of challenging this belief would be for the therapist to point out biases in such a belief (e.g. 'all-or-nothing' thinking). The client could then keep a record of times when they might not have finished all the work they had planned but still managed to have positive experiences in other areas of life. This evidence could be used to challenge their belief that they are always a failure.

Another method of challenging beliefs is to set the client behavioural tasks that counter their dysfunctional beliefs. For example, a therapist could 'timetable' uplifting events (e.g. going out to the cinema with friends) to challenge a depressed patient's view that life is always miserable (see Figure 4.2, overleaf). This technique can be a powerful method of providing evidence to counter the dysfunctional belief.

**Figure 4.2** Cognitive therapists may schedule enjoyable events in their client's week

The second phase of therapy is to use dysfunctional beliefs to identify stable cognitive patterns (or core beliefs) that are more subtle and which correspond to the vulnerability schema(s) acquired in early life (as described in Beck's theory). For example, a depressed person may hold a core belief that everything they do results in failure. This is dealt with using the techniques described above: thought monitoring, disputing negative thoughts and behaving in ways counter to the dysfunctional beliefs. In addition, the client is encouraged to identify more healthy or flexible core beliefs and plan 'experiments' to test out these new core beliefs in everyday life. The outcome of these experiments can be used to provide further evidence to challenge dysfunctional beliefs.

### The effectiveness of Beck's cognitive therapy

Butler and Beck (2001) carried out a meta-analysis (a method of combining data from many studies) comparing 9138 participants in 325 studies across a range of disorders and therapies. The success of therapy is worked out using relapse rates and a statistical formula called effect size. Roughly speaking, an effect size of 0.2–0.5 is not very effective, 0.5–0.8 is medium and anything above 0.8 is really good. Table 4.1 shows Beck's cognitive therapy to be an effective therapy for a wide range of disorders and Table 4.2 shows that it has a much lower relapse rate in depression for cognitive therapy than antidepressant medication.

| Disorders | Mean effect size |
|---|---|
| Adult depression | 0.9 |
| Adolescent depression | 0.9 |
| Generalised anxiety disorder | 0.9 |
| Panic disorder | 0.9 |
| Social phobia | 0.9 |
| Marital distress | 0.62 |
| Anger | 0.62 |
| Childhood somatic disorders | 0.62 |
| Chronic pain | 0.62 |
| Bulimia | 1.62 |

**Table 4.1** The efficacy of cognitive therapy (Butler and Beck, 2001)

| Therapy | Relapse rate |
|---------|--------------|
| Cognitive therapy | 29.5% |
| Anti-depressant medication | 60% |

**Table 4.2** Relapse rates for depression (Butler and Beck, 2001)

While this research shows just how effective Beck's cognitive therapy can be, the methodology of meta-analytic studies has been criticised by Guthrie (2000) as they only use *efficacy studies*. Efficacy studies assess the success of therapies in well controlled situations, but only use participants with *monosymptomatic* conditions, meaning that they fit the diagnostic criteria for one disorder exactly and show no symptoms of other disorders. This type of participant may not be representative of clients referred to a clinical or counselling psychologist in the community. Such individuals are less likely to have a 'pure' condition; for example, they may also be abusing alcohol. So a question mark hangs over whether cognitive therapy will be as successful with clients without a 'pure' disorder.

A more general problem with evidence-based outcome studies is that, although they show cognitive therapy to be an effective treatment, they do not shed any light on *why* cognitive therapy works. There are many ingredients to cognitive therapy and the outcome study does not allow us to assess which mechanism is causing the improvement leaving a number of questions unanswered. There is a possibility that the success of cognitive therapy may not even be due to cognitive restructuring.

## Rational–emotive behaviour therapy

Ellis (1962) proposed that we have two basic goals: to feel relatively happy and to be free of pain. These are, however, preferences and not necessities. In Ellis' view, rationality consists of thinking in ways that contribute to the attainment of these goals, irrationality consists of thinking in ways that block their attainment. Thus a rational outlook to life consists of striking a balance between short-term and long-term goals. Ellis (1991) proposed three key ideas behind rational–emotive behaviour therapy – REBT (see Box 4.3)

---

1 Thought and emotion are closely related.

2 Thought and emotion are so closely related that they usually accompany each other in a circular cause-and-effect relationship, and in certain respects are the same thing, so that one's thinking becomes one's emotion and one's emotion becomes one's thinking.

3 Thought and emotion take the form of self-talk – sentences that we keep saying to ourselves eventually become thoughts and emotions; thus a person's self-statements are capable of both generating and modifying their emotions.

---

**Box 4.3** The key ideas behind REBT

REBT is not a theory of *no* emotions, but one of *appropriate* emotions. It may be appropriate for someone in an alien and difficult world to be fearful, cautious and vigilant so that they take steps necessary for realistic protection. Anxiety, however, is seen as an inappropriate emotion based on irrational thinking and may block appropriate behaviour. Thus emotions are appropriate when they are accompanied by rational beliefs, and are functional in the sense that they do not block the possibility of effective action and attainment of goals.

Ellis's emphasis is much more on how people sustain their irrationality than on how they develop it. He considers that psychology has focused on how people originally become illogical, but not on how people maintain their illogical behaviour or what they should do to change it. REBT operates within an ABC framework:

- A is the *activating event*: a fact or event or the behaviour or attitude of another person.

- B is the *beliefs* we hold about A.

- C is the *cognitive*, emotional or behavioural consequence of A.

Ellis considers that humans largely control their own emotional destinies through the beliefs held at B. Thus the emotional and behavioural consequences of the various activating events in our lives are controlled by our belief systems and we are capable of learning to control and modify our belief systems (and hence their consequences). Table 4.3 shows the ABC model applied to understanding the effects of failing an exam.

| A | Activating event | Failing exam |
|---|---|---|
| B | Beliefs | 'I should have passed.'<br>'I am a failure.'<br>'I can't bear not passing.' |
| C | Consequences | Depression |

**Table 4.3** Ellis's ABC model (Palmer and Dryden, 1995)

The existence of this type of irrational belief prevents people exhibiting *stoicism* (the ability to withstand the effects of adverse events). Ellis proposed that the most efficient way of helping someone to feel better was to change their irrational beliefs and make them more stoical. Abrams and Ellis (1996) identify two types of irrational belief that cause particular problems when we encounter adversity: *musturbation* is the tendency to think that we *must* be perfect and successful at all times, *I-can't-stand-it-itis* is the belief that it is a disaster whenever something does not go smoothly. Musturbation makes us too sensitive to failure and I-can't-stand-it-itis makes even minor problems seem disastrous.

## Changing to rational beliefs

The major objective of REBT is to substitute rational and functional beliefs for irrational and dysfunctional beliefs at stage B. This can be cognitive, through helping the client to identify their *shoulds* and *musts* or behavioural through homework assignments (similar to those of Beck) and self-reinforcement. The ABC model is expanded:

- *D* is *disputing* irrational beliefs.

- *E* is the *effects* of successfully disputing irrational beliefs. These can be cognitive (rational beliefs), emotional (appropriate feelings) or behavioural (desirable behaviour).

## The effectiveness of REBT

In a meta-analysis of 31 outcome studies Engels *et al.* (1993) found that REBT was more effective for treating anxiety-based disorders than systematic desensitisation or therapies in which REBT was combined with some form of behavioural therapy. Table 4.4 shows all forms of therapy are effective (remember, an effect size of 0.8 or more demonstrates a highly effective treatment), particularly REBT. For a brief outline of measuring the effectiveness of therapy using effect size, see the discussion of Beck's cognitive therapy above.

| Therapy | Mean effect size |
|---|---|
| REBT | 1.62 |
| Combination therapy | 1.42 |
| Systematic desensitisation | 1.35 |

**Table 4.4** The effectiveness of REBT (Engels *et al.*, 1993)

Further evidence for the effectiveness of REBT comes from a review of 89 outcome studies by Silverman *et al.* (1992). They showed that REBT was more effective than, or at least equal to, other types of therapy (such as systematic desensitisation) for a wide range of disorders including depression, anxiety disorders, sexual dysfunction, type A behaviour, anger, self-esteem, stress and alcohol abuse. It was also equal to person-centred therapy for clients with a variety of symptoms not specific to any particular disorder.

- 49 studies showed REBT to be the most effective treatment.

- In 40 studies there was no difference between REBT and other therapies.

- No studies showed any treatment to be more effective than REBT.

While these reviews seem to be leading to the conclusion that REBT is without doubt a highly effective treatment, Solomon and Haaga (1995) discuss whether results of such studies can be generalised to routine clinical practice (this is an issue for all therapy outcome research – see the discussion of Beck's cognitive therapy above). Owing to various methodological difficulties in outcome studies, such as the lack of an equivalent control group and only using short-term follow-ups, the effectiveness of REBT may have been seriously underestimated. This problem, however, is offset by another, which is that REBT outcome studies tend to be conducted by highly trained therapists who are proponents of REBT and who are likely to be better at delivering REBT than the non-specialist. Solomon and Haaga argue that these factors will probably balance each other out in a meta-analysis, but more research is required.

## Discussion of the effectiveness of cognitive–behavioural therapy

Most contemporary practitioners of cognitive–behavioural therapy (CBT) freely mix techniques from Beck's cognitive therapy, Ellis' REBT and other more recently developed approaches. Thus most studies have evaluated the success of this 'mixed CBT', and a very large number now support the effectiveness of CBT.

An exciting recent development has been in the application of CBT to treat schizophrenia and related conditions. Until recently it was widely believed that this type of disorder was not treatable by psychological therapies, but there is now research to show that in some patients symptoms can be alleviated by CBT.

## research now

# CBT can help some patients with schizophrenia

**Chadwick, P., Sambrooke, S., Rasch, S. and Davies, E. (2000) Challenging the omnipotence of voices: group cognitive behaviour therapy for voices.** *Behaviour Research and Therapy,* 38, 993–1003

**Aim:** Until recently it was widely believed that schizophrenia did not respond to psychological therapies and could be treated only by biomedical means such as drugs. The aim of the study was to test the relatively new idea that CBT can be helpful in tackling the symptoms of schizophrenia. More specifically, the effectiveness of CBT conducted in groups was examined.

**Method:** Twenty-two participants with a diagnosis of schizophrenia, characterised by the symptom of hearing voices, were assessed with regard to their cognitive and emotional symptoms. Depression and anxiety were measured, as were beliefs in the power and control of voices. They took part in eight sessions of group CBT, in which therapists focused on challenging patients' beliefs about their voices. At the end of the course of treatment patients were re-assessed.

**Results:** The major finding was that participants experienced a significant reduction in negative beliefs about the power of their voices and the extent to which they were controlled by them. No reduction in anxiety or depression was reported, although patients felt they had benefited from the groups and the behaviour of some was visibly less affected by their schizophrenia.

**Conclusion:** CBT is effective in tackling the cognitive aspects of schizophrenia, and it appears that improvements in this area have a positive effect on patients' general functioning and quality of life.

Despite the positive findings of most research, and the exciting range of conditions to which CBT can be applied, some researchers have reservations about the zeal with which clinical psychology has embraced the approach. Harrington *et al.* (1998) have pointed out that some key reviews have ignored studies that have shown CBT in a less positive light. In a minority of instances CBT has been found to be distinctly inferior to alternative therapeutic approaches. For example, in a study of alcohol dependency (Sandahl *et al.*, 1998) found that at 15-month follow-up the number of patients abstaining from alcohol was significantly higher after psychodynamic therapy (see Chapter 5 for a discussion) than following CBT. Concerns have also been raised about the kind of research on which our understanding of the effectiveness of CBT is based; most studies have focused on the short-term benefits on *monosymptomatic* patients (those showing symptoms of only one condition). We thus know relatively little about long-term effects of CBT or its effects on patients with a broad range of symptoms.

## eye movement desensitisation and reprocessing (EMDR)

EMDR is a controversial treatment, originally designed as a therapy for PTSD by Shapiro (1989). The therapy involves exposure to the traumatic stimuli while the client follows an object moving horizontally back and forth (either by the therapist moving their hand back and forth – does this sound similar to hypnosis? – or by a more sophisticated device using a moving light). The use of EMDR has produced heated debate, partially because Shapiro claims it is so effective and partially due to a lack of understanding about how it might work.

Shapiro has suggested a cognitive–neuropsychological basis for EMDR, where eye movements trigger a physiological mechanism, promoting an information processing system to restructure memory. Hence traumatic memories of the sort experienced in a PTSD flashback can be successfully re-integrated into their original time and place. Shapiro has gone on to suggest that EMDR could be used to treat pain, delusions, ritual abuse, phobias, generalised anxiety, schizophrenia, eating disorders and many other conditions (Shapiro, 1995); a grand claim indeed, and one which is not always supported.

Renfrey and Spates (1994) compared PTSD patients in groups treated with and without eye movements and found that symptom reduction was similar in both groups. In a review of several EMDR outcome studies, Lohr *et al.* (1998) conclude that eye movements are not necessary for a reduction of PTSD symptoms. Finger tapping has been shown to have the same therapeutic effect as eye movements (Wilson *et al.*, 1996). If, as these studies suggest, the therapeutic effectiveness of EMDR is not due to eye movement, then it seems the crucial component of this therapy is the exposure to traumatic memories in a safe environment. Senior (2001) recommends that the treatment should be re-named.

## Conclusions

The cognitive approach was taken up enthusiastically by clinical psychologists in the UK in the 1970s as they attempted to forge a separate identity from psychiatry (Parker *et al.*, 1995). The cognitive approach has now become the dominant force in clinical psychology resulting in an enormous amount of research into cognitive factors and mental disorders. There are now cognitive theories for virtually every disorder, more than this chapter has the scope to deal with, which have also formed the basis of many treatment programmes for offenders. The growth of cognitive psychology in clinical psychology has resulted in a dramatic increase in the use of cognitive-based therapies for mental disorders. Cognitive therapies have been shown to be extremely effective in reducing symptoms for a wide range of disorders, and for many therapists and clinical psychologists cognitive-based approaches are now the therapy of choice.

1   Describe the cognitive approach to the study of mental disorders. Include both assumptions and cognitive theories in your answer.

2   Evaluate the cognitive approach to the study of mental disorders. You could compare the advantages of taking a cognitive approach with other approaches, or consider evidence to support cognitive theories.

3   Are cognitive therapies effective? Support your answer with evidence from outcome studies.

# 5

# The Psychodynamic Approach

what's
ahead?

The psychodynamic approach is one of the older psychological models still used to understand and treat mental disorder. You may already have studied the work of Sigmund Freud, who developed the psychodynamic approach in the late nineteenth and early twentieth centuries. Freud and later psychodynamic theorists were interested in the ways in which childhood experiences, particularly those involving relationships with parents, affect psychological well-being in later life. In this chapter, having looked at the general assumptions of the psychodynamic approach, we take a look at some of Freud's ideas on mental health and examine them in the light of contemporary research. We also consider the more recent attachment perspective on mental health. The remainder of this chapter will be spent looking at psychodynamic therapies and evaluating their usefulness in tackling mental disorder.

## Assumptions of the approach

General assumptions of the psychodynamic approach to psychology can be found in Jarvis *et al.* (2000), p. 132. Here, we are interested more specifically in the assumptions made when taking a psychodynamic approach to understanding psychological distress and mental health problems.

- The quality of our early relationships, particularly those with parents, is of critical importance for our mental health in later childhood and adulthood.

- Early traumatic experiences, in particular those that cause disruption to our early relationships, are associated with later mental health problems.

- Our early experiences are retained in the *unconscious mind* and affect our later feelings, motives and relationships. By 'the unconscious mind' we mean those aspects of mental functioning of which we are not normally aware.

- Whereas the biomedical model treats mental disorder as physical illness, and learning and cognitive models see it in terms of acquired patterns of maladaptive behaviour and thinking, the psychodynamic model views mental disorder as emotional responses to trauma, unmet needs or unsatisfied instincts.

When considering the psychodynamic approach to mental health, it is important to make a distinction between these broad principles and specific psychodynamic theories. These theories, for example Freudian and attachment theories, are attempts to explain the reasons *why* these broad psychodynamic principles appear to hold true. The distinction is important because it is quite possible to work in mental health taking a psychodynamic approach without accepting the details of any particular theory. In this chapter we will explore both general psychodynamic principles and Freudian theory. We also look at a modern psychodynamic perspective on mental health, that of attachment theory.

## Early experience and later mental disorder

Before looking in some detail at Freudian and attachment perspectives on mental disorder it is worth first considering whether the broad psycho-dynamic assumptions about the impact of early relationships and trauma hold true – if not, there is little point in taking the theory seriously! To understand the ways in which early trauma can affect our adult functioning, let us begin with a case study from Lemma-Wright (1995), shown in Box 5.1.

Alex was the older of two young adult sisters. One weekend Alex organised a sea boat trip to celebrate her sister's birthday. The trip went well, but Alex suffered a panic attack on the boat. Alex had always loved her sister dearly, but she had also resented her a little, believing that her family had always doted on her, while ignoring Alex. On one occasion as a child, Alex had become so angry with her sister for being the centre of attention that she dragged her into the sea, frightening her badly. As an adult, Alex frequently felt obliged to organise her sister's life and to help her out of financial difficulties. She had no idea why she suffered the panic attack until a few days later when she had a dream in which she had a fight with a friend (who reminded her of her sister) and wished her dead. It then became apparent to Alex that the boat trip, in which she had once again taken her sister into the sea, had stirred up guilty memories of the time she had dragged her into the sea.

**Box 5.1** The case of Alex (adapted from Lemma-Wright, 1995)

We can understand Alex's problem by referring to the psychodynamic assumptions about the origins of mental disorder. Her difficulties began with her poor relationship with her parents, which in turn resulted in the traumatic experience of dragging her sister into the sea. The guilt resulting from this experience remained in Alex's unconscious mind, influencing her to look after her sister as an adult. When Alex organised the boat trip for her sister, this triggered the memory of the traumatic event in their childhood and the resulting flood of anxiety led her to have a panic attack. In this case Alex's condition, which might be diagnosed as *panic disorder* (see Chapter 11, which deals with anxiety disorders), can be explained as an emotional response to early trauma.

So do early experiences like trauma and poor parental relationships always lead to later psychological problems? The answer is no; there is no single early event that dooms an individual to later pathology. Moreover, other factors like our genetic make-up (Chapter 2) and learning experiences (Chapter 3) are also implicated in causing mental disorder. However, it *is* true to say that early trauma and poor early relationships greatly increase the probability of later psychological problems.

Research firmly supports the association between early trauma and poor early relationships and the incidence of later mental health problems. In chapters 8–11, which deal with specific mental disorders, we can examine in detail the links between childhood events and relationships and each of these conditions. For example, early loss experiences are associated with depression (see p. 165), early threatening experiences with anxiety (see p. 211) and poor whole-family relationships with schizophrenia (see p. 145). In no case can these disorders be explained entirely by these factors, but it does appear that they play a role.

# Freudian theory and psychopathology

For a more detailed general account of Freudian theory, see Jarvis *et al.* (2000). In this book we are just concerned with how Freud explained mental disorder. Freud's more specific ideas about particular disorders are examined in the relevant chapters. The aim of this section is to examine in more general terms how Freud's understanding of the mind helped him explain mental disorder. We can look in particular at Freud's hydraulic model of the mind and the controversial idea of psychosexuality. For further useful details of Freudian theory of mental disorder see in particular p. 165, where the role of early loss experiences in depression is discussed, and p. 211, where we look at Freud's view of anxiety.

## Freud's hydraulic model of the mind

Freud got the idea of the hydraulic model from literature, where phrases like 'to cry oneself out' and 'to blow off steam' were commonly used to describe emotional responses. These phrases suggest that the mind is a system in which psychic (mental) energy behaves in much the same way as physical energy. Freud believed that, like other forms of energy, psychic energy could be discharged or transformed but not destroyed. Trauma and the inability to express instincts resulted in a build up of psychic energy that led to the symptoms of mental disorder. One of the aims of psychodynamic therapy is *catharsis*, the release of accumulated psychic energy. Breuer and Freud (1896) explained the classic case study of Anna O in terms of dammed energy and her treatment in terms of catharsis.

# classic research

## the case of Anna O

**Breuer, J. and Freud, S. (1896)** *Studies on Hysteria. The Complete Works of Sigmund Freud, Volume II.* London: Hogarth

**Aim:** The aim of the case was primarily the treatment of Anna's symptoms. However, the case also served as a valuable demonstration of the usefulness of Freud's theory and therapy, which was just becoming well known.

**Case history:** Anna O was a 21-year-old, highly intellectual woman. Her symptoms developed when she was nursing her father through a long illness. During the first 5 months of his illness Anna devoted herself to caring for her father. Her own health deteriorated and she suffered weakness, anaemia and lack of interest in food. She became bed-ridden, meaning that she was unable to continue to nurse her father. It was at this point that her hysterical symptoms manifested themselves. She suffered a range of symptoms, including headaches, a narrowing of the visual field, deafness, paralysis of the neck, and lack of sensation in the limbs. Towards the end of the period before her father died in April 1881 she also suffered speech-related symptoms, forgetting words, then becoming mute for two weeks.

The shock of Anna's father's death worsened her symptoms. She began to suffer new symptoms including prosopagnosia (inability to recognise faces). During this period Anna also had symptoms of dissociation, displaying two personalities. One personality was anxious and depressed but fully aware of what was happening. The second was irrational and aggressive, throwing pillows and tearing buttons from her nightdress. Breuer had Anna removed to a country sanatorium, where she began what she called her 'talking cure.' This is the first recorded reference to the term and marks the birth of psychodynamic therapy. Breuer noted that when allowed to speak unchecked Anna tended to speak of events before the development of her symptoms, and that she would frequently link events to her symptoms. For example, she made an association between her deafness and a childhood incident where Anna's brother had caught her listening at her parent's door one night. During this process the symptoms would often worsen; however, following the focus on each symptom it would disappear.

**Interpretation:** Freud explained Anna's symptoms and treatment in terms of his hydraulic model. Her frustrated intellectual abilities had led to a build-up of psychic energy. The trauma of her father's illness had triggered a process where this energy was converted into symptoms. The process of catharsis that resulted when Anna talked to Breuer released the psychic energy and so lessened her symptoms.

Some psychologists find the hydraulic model a useful metaphor for explaining why the effects of early events can be experienced in the form of symptoms some time later. However, it is simply a metaphor, and modern studies of the brain have revealed that there is no actual build-up and discharge of any form of energy (Miller, 1999). Thus the hydraulic model describes effectively how people *experience* psychological distress but not literally what is happening to them. Psychologists are divided on the issue of whether metaphors like this are useful. From a psychodynamic point of view it is most important to understand how people experience psychological distress, and metaphors are a useful tool for this. However, more hard-nosed scientists say that the hydraulic model is unsupported and outdated, and would suggest that metaphors like this are misleading rather than helpful.

## Psychosexuality

Freud's view of psychosexuality is the most socially sensitive and controversial aspect of his theory. In his early work Freud proposed *seduction theory*, in which he emphasised the role of childhood sexual abuse in causing psychological problems. He famously put it thus: 'whatever case and whatever symptom we take as our starting point, *in the end we infallibly come to the realm of sexual experience*' (Freud, 1896, p. 193). The term 'sexual experience' is quite broad and describes a range of sexual traumas. Recall the case of Anna O, whose deafness in early adulthood was linked to her listening at her parents' bedroom door as a child. However, Freud identified sexual abuse as the major cause of psychopathology.

Contemporary research supports Freud's early view that childhood sexual abuse (CSA) is common and very harmful. In a review of studies Finkelhor (1994) found that the ranges of reported rates of CSA were 7–36% in women and 3–29% in men. Of the mental disorders examined in detail in this book, sexual abuse is associated with increased risk of anxiety disorders (Christo, 1997), depression (Stoppard, 2000), eating disorders (Schmidt *et al.*, 1997) and multiple personality disorder (Kluft, 1993). Some of these associations are extremely strong. Although this whole area is surrounded by controversy and no statistics can be taken as fact, some research has suggested that up to half of those suffering from eating disorders have been sexually abused, as have the majority of sufferers of multiple disorder (Crowe, 1997).

# media watch

## Connolly on the couch

These extracts are taken from an interview with the comedian Billy Connolly.

When Connolly's father returned from the Second World War to live in their overcrowded flat, he came home drunk most nights to share a sofabed with his son. For a period of about five years, Connolly says, his father, a fierce Catholic, 'interfered with him' – a secret he did not share with anyone until the day of his father's death, when he broke down and told his wife.

Billy Connolly has never told jokes; he has just let off steam and has fabulously enjoyed the process of doing it. Talking about the source of his humour, he says: 'I don't know why I'm funny. But there are reasons for my attitudes. People ask why I'm still angry when I'm loaded. And I don't know. But I like my anger. I find it comforting.'

From *The Observer Magazine* 23 September 2001

**Figure 5.1** Comedian Billy Connolly

## Questions

1 What lasting consequences of sexual abuse can you pick out of these extracts?

2 Explain Connolly's humour using Freud's hydraulic model.

Unfortunately, Freud shifted the emphasis of his work on psychosexuality away from sexual abuse towards the role of sexual fantasy. Freud believed that some of children's reports of CSA were actually sexual fantasies of their own, and that symptoms resulted from the repression of the sexual instinct, and in some cases the shameful memories of these fantasies. This has been interpreted by some writers, for example Masson (1984), as the deliberate abandonment of sexually abused children in order to escape the controversy his seduction theory had generated. Whatever Freud's motives, it is generally agreed that his shift away from seduction theory was a serious error.

Freud believed that one fantasy shared by all children took place in the *Oedipus complex*. This is a three-way family dynamic in which children in their phallic stage (3–6 years) develop a powerful attachment to the opposite-sex parent and see the same-sex parent as a rival. On an unconscious level they want to kill the same-sex parent and have sex with the opposite-sex parent (although they do not have an adult understanding of either death or sex). A classic case study of the Oedipus complex, Little Hans (Freud, 1909) is discussed in our later discussion of phobias (p. 209).

## Discussion of Freud's contributions

Although Freud is one of the most heavily criticised of all psychologists (Masling and Bornstein, 1996), some of his ideas remain useful in understanding the links between childhood experience and later psychopathology. Freud's observations that depression often followed an early experience of loss (p. 210), and that a variety of problems typically follow sexual abuse are well supported by contemporary research. His development of the 'talking cure,' which underlies modern psychological therapies, is one of the greatest ever contributions to psychology.

Brilliant as Freud was, we should not lose sight of the limitations of his theory. He was operating at a time when we knew almost nothing about the workings of the brain, and modern neuroscience has found no evidence of any biological process that might be related to 'dammed psychic energy' or its release. Freud's notion of psychosexuality (with the exception of seduction theory) now seems dated and irrelevant, and there is firm evidence that, even if the Oedipus complex exists, it is not a key determinant of mental health. If it were we would expect children of single and gay parents (who presumably do not have the opportunity to develop an Oedipus complex) to suffer serious mental health problems but this is not the case (see Jarvis, 2001 for a discussion).

## for and against

### Freudian theory

+ Some aspects of Freudian theory, for example seduction theory and the importance of early loss experiences, are supported by contemporary research.

– Freud's later emphasis on sexual fantasy is not supported by research, and it is widely agreed that his theoretical move away from seduction theory has been very unhelpful in understanding the effects of CSA.

+ Freud developed the 'talking cure', which still underlies modern psychological therapies.

– Freud's hydraulic model of the mind is not supported by contemporary research.

## where to now?

The following are good sources of further information about Freud's theory of psychopathology:

▶ **Bateman, A. and Holmes, J. (1995)** *Introduction to Psychoanalysis*. **London: Routledge** – an excellent account of a range of psychodynamic theories, including explanations of mental disorder.

▶ **Jarvis, M.** *Psychodynamic Psychology: Classical theory and Contemporary Research*. **London: Thomson Learning (in press)** – a state-of-the-art account of psychodynamic ideas, with a particular emphasis on up-to-date studies.

# Attachment theory and psychopathology

There have been numerous psychodynamic theories since that of Freud, many of which have added to our understanding of the links between early experience and psychopathology. One theory currently receiving a lot of attention is *attachment theory*. For a fuller general account of attachment theory, see Jarvis (2001). To summarise briefly, Bowlby (1958, 1969) proposed that humans have evolved the instinct to form childhood attachments to other humans in order to maximise the probability of surviving to adulthood. Of critical importance is the first attachment we form as babies to our primary carer, as this informs our understanding of relationships and hence the quality of all our future attachments. A wealth of research supports the idea that the quality of the first relationship is associated with adult friendships, romantic relationships, parenting ability and functioning at work. Research also suggests that the quality of a child's first attachment may be an important factor in their later mental health.

## Attachment types

Ainsworth and Wittig (1969) developed a procedure for classifying children into different attachment types. This procedure, called the *strange situation*, involved assessing children's responses to being left with their primary carer, left alone, left with a stranger and then being reunited with the primary carer. Three attachment types were initially identified using the strange situation (shown in Box 5.2).

**Type A insecure avoidant**: play independently. Not concerned when the primary carer leaves or returns.

**Type B secure**: play independently but return regularly to see the primary carer. Show some distress at being left and are pleased to be reunited with the primary carer.

**Type C insecure resistant**: explore less than others when the primary carer is present. Get very distressed at being left alone or with a stranger but are not easily comforted when the primary carer returns.

**Box 5.2** Attachment types identified by the strange situation (adapted from Ainsworth and Wittig, 1969)

A fourth category of attachment was added by Main and Solomon (1986). This is the type D (also called type AC) or disorganised attachment. Type Ds display a mixture of behaviours associated with types A and C, and may display fear towards their primary carer and prefer the company of the stranger.

There are believed to be two major determinants of attachment type, temperament and maternal sensitivity. The term 'temperament' refers to those aspects of the personality that are under the control of genes. Children who are born with a relatively unsociable temperament are most likely to end up with type A attachments, and those born particularly irritable are the most likely to end up type Cs. *Maternal sensitivity* is, however, probably the more important factor, and a large body of research

**Figure 5.2** Research suggests that this child will be less vulnerable to mental disorder because he has a good attachment to his mother

has shown that type B (secure) attachments are achieved by high-quality infant–primary carer interaction, specifically the skill with which the primary carer picks up and responds to signals from the baby (Figure 5.2). Highly controlling or rejecting parenting is associated with type A attachment and inconsistent parenting with type C attachment. Type D attachment is associated with mental disorder in the primary carer and with neglect and/or abuse of the child.

Although the strange situation remains a popular test of attachment in infants and young children it is obviously unsuitable for classifying attachment in adults. The most popular assessment tool for adults is the adult attachment interview (AAI). This is a 60-minute semi-structured interview that examines attachment-related experiences recalled from childhood. Adults are classified as one of four attachment types (shown in Box 5.3).

---

**Attachment type and vulnerability to mental disorder**

**Dismissing**: minimise the importance of attachment relationships. Have poor recall of childhood memories. Corresponds to type A in Ainsworth's classification.

**Autonomous**: value attachment relationships and have a realistic view of them. Have good access to childhood memories. Corresponds to type B in Ainsworth's classification.

**Preoccupied**: worry a lot about attachment relationships and are unable to discuss them rationally. Corresponds to Ainsworth's type C.

**Unresolved**: are unable to come to terms with an attachment-related trauma. Corresponds to Main and Solomon's type D.

---

**Box 5.3** Attachment types identified by the AAI

## Attachment type and mental disorder

Studies have shown that insecure attachment; in particular the disorganised (or unresolved) category, is associated with increased vulnerability to a variety of mental disorders. Rosenstein and Horowitz (1996) classified depressed adolescents in a psychiatric hospital according to three of the AAI categories (dismissing, autonomous and preoccupied): 69% were classified as preoccupied, suggesting that type C attachments are predictive of depression. Looking at a large sample of mixed adult psychiatric in-patients, and classifying them using all four AAI categories Fonagy *et al.* (1996) found that most patients suffering depression, anxiety disorder, eating disorders and substance abuse disorders were classified as unresolved. Even schizophrenia, which is usually attributed to biological rather than psychodynamic phenomena, is associated with insecure attachment. Tyrrell and Dozier (1997) found that 44% of their sample of people with schizophrenia were classified as unresolved according to the AAI.

Although there are very clear links between attachment type as measured by the AAI and a range of mental disorders, it is not necessarily the case that attachment type directly leads to the disorder. It may be that people suffering from mental disorder have distorted childhood memories and distorted perceptions of their relationships with attachment figures. If our genetic make-up is implicated in the development of mental disorder (see Chapter 3), infants may show signs of their later disorder from birth and hence have difficulty forming secure attachments. This would mean that insecure attachment is *associated* with mental disorder but not directly involved in its development. However, if this were the case we would expect that conditions like bipolar depression (which appears to be largely under genetic control) would be most strongly associated with insecure attachment and conditions less under genetic control (such as unipolar depression) would be less strongly associated with attachment. Actually the reverse is true (Dozier *et al.*, 1999), suggesting that genetic make-up and attachment operate independently.

### Reasons for the attachment–psychopathology link

Although it is clear that insecure attachment, in particular unresolved or disorganised attachment, is associated strongly with a range of mental disorders, it is not obvious why this should be. Bowlby (1980) suggested that the link operates through *internal working models*. These are the mental representations of relationships that we carry away from our relationship with our primary carer. If our internal working model includes loss, because our primary carer has left or died, then our internal working model will be dominated by expectations of loss, predisposing us to depression. If, on the other hand, we were abused or witnessed domestic violence our internal working model would be likely to be dominated by fear of or for others, and we will be vulnerable to anxiety conditions.

## for and against

## the attachment theory of psychopathology

**+** There is sound evidence to suggest that insecurely attached people are more likely to suffer from a range of mental disorders.

**−** The vast majority of studies are retrospective, assessing attachment in adulthood, after a disorder has already developed. Patients may report their attachments to be insecure as a result of their condition.

**+** The small number of longitudinal studies that have traced children from infancy to the development of mental disorder supports a link between insecure attachment and pathology. More longitudinal studies are currently being conducted.

**−** It is difficult to disentangle the effect of attachment on psychopathology from the effects of genetic make-up on both attachment and pathology.

## where to now?

The following is a good source of further information about attachment and mental disorder:

▶ **Cassidy, J. and Shaver, P.R. (1999)** *Handbook of Attachment*. **New York: Guilford Press** – a state-of-the-art guide to attachment theory and research. Contains some chapters devoted to the relationship between attachment and psychopathology.

# Psychodynamic approaches to therapy

**Figure 5.3** Traditionally, patients in psychodynamic therapy lie on a couch, while the therapist sits behind

The psychodynamic approach to psychological therapy originated with the case of Anna O (p. 83). Initially, in line with Freud's hydraulic model of the mind, the aim of the therapy was catharsis. Catharsis remains an important part of therapy. We can isolate catharsis from other therapeutic factors in order to test its importance by asking patients to write about traumatic or unhappy experiences (this is called *scriptotherapy*). In a recent review of studies of scriptotherapy, Smyth and Greenberg (2000) concluded that scriptotherapy reliably reduced psychological and physiological symptoms, supporting its usefulness in therapy.

Freud and later psychodynamic therapists added further *interpretive* techniques that aim to give patients *insight* into the origins of their symptoms. Psychodynamic therapies thus focus on the personal history of the patient, viewing their current emotional state, behaviour and relationships as products of their earlier experiences. For this reason, there is an emphasis in therapy sessions on discussion of the patient's past, and the therapist may make connections between present and past events or direct the patient to introspect further on childhood issues. However, a basic principle of psychodynamic therapy is that if allowed to *free associate* (to speak without direction) patients frequently return to childhood events and relationships. This means that psychodynamic therapists frequently do not need to direct patients to think about these things.

## Interpretation and insight

A distinguishing feature of the psychodynamic therapies is the use of interpretation to give the patient insight into the origins of their feelings and behaviour. The most important way in which insight can be achieved is by the interpretation of *transference*. Transference occurs when the patient relates to the therapist as if they were a significant figure from their past. For example, someone who has childhood memories of harsh parents may become very angry towards the therapist, transferring on to them the anger that they have carried towards their parents since childhood. By feeding back an interpretation of this transference of anger to the patient the therapist can give an insight into how their past relationships affect their current relationships, for example becoming unreasonably angry with people. One way in which therapists aid the development of transference is to minimise the details of their own lives and personality that are available to patients. This means that they maintain a 'blank screen' to patients, showing little emotion and not normally disclosing details of their own lives or their feelings towards the patient.

Interpretations can also be made of the patient's use of psychological defences. For example, a patient who consistently denies the importance of a problem may have this fed back to them as an interpretation of their use of denial as a defence. *Resistance* can also be interpreted. Freud (1912) placed great emphasis on the resistance of the patient to change, and described therapy as a battle to overcome resistance. According to Freud resistance can manifest itself in a number of ways, including the use of psychological defences and establishing a negative transference towards the therapist. Resistance may also manifest as silence and missing sessions. These are thus all open to interpretation. A good question to ask at this point might be whether insight really helps patients. This has been addressed in a study by Kivlighan *et al.* (2000).

# research now

## does insight really help?

**Kivlighan, D.M., Multon, K.D. and Patton, M.J. (2000) Insight and symptom reduction in time-limited psychoanalytic counselling.** *Journal of Counselling Psychology*, 47, 50–58

**Aim:** The major aim of all varieties of psychodynamic therapy is to give patients insight into their feelings, interpersonal behaviour and, when possible, their origins. However, there has been very little research to test the assumption that these insights actually make patients feel better. The aim of this study was to see whether new insights are followed by a reduction in symptoms.

**Method:** The participants were 12 psychodynamic counsellors and their patients. Patients and counsellors rated the severity of patients' symptoms before and after each of 20 sessions. Patients also completed a questionnaire called the Important Events Questionnaire (IEQ) to assess their insight after each session. Three independent judges rated patient insight from the IEQ. Changes in insight and symptom severity were tracked across the 20 sessions.

**Results:** Over the course of the 20 sessions there was a steady increase in insight and a steady reduction in the severity of symptoms, showing that psychodynamic counselling is associated with both increased insight and a reduction in symptoms. By looking at the sessions where key insights were gained and the points where symptoms declined it was possible to see whether the two variables seemed to have a cause-and-effect relationship. Immediately after each major new insight as measured on the IEQ, the severity of symptoms declined significantly, suggesting that the insight led to the decline in symptoms.

**Conclusion:** Psychodynamic counselling 'works' in that it is associated with increased insight and reduced symptom severity. Results also suggest that the insight actually led to the symptom reduction. This finding provides very strong support for the rationale underlying psychodynamic therapy, that insight into psychological problems helps to reduce their impact.

We can see then that insight as well as catharsis is implicated in the benefits of psychodynamic therapies. One way of assessing what factors are helpful is to survey patients. Mahon and Kempler (1995) asked patients who had just completed group psychoanalytic psychotherapy what factors they had found most helpful. Insight came out top with catharsis second. More general factors such as encouragement were reported as least helpful.

So what of transference? Remember that transference has traditionally been regarded as the single most important therapeutic factor in the psychodynamic approach to therapy. Research into transference has found rather mixed results. In a review of research, Henry (1994) report that, in general, research has found a negative rather than positive relationship between frequency of transference interpretations and the outcome of the therapy. However, Crits-Christoph *et al.* (1988) found a positive correlation between outcome and patients' agreement with transference interpretation. The lesson from these studies is clear; use transference interpretation sparingly and get it right!

## Varieties of psychodynamic therapy

Psychology texts often speak of *psychoanalysis* when discussing psychodynamic therapies. Actually this is a little misleading as classical psychoanalysis is relatively rare and in decline, while other forms of psychodynamic therapy are increasing in popularity. A range of psychodynamic therapies is shown in Box 5.4 below.

**Classical psychoanalysis:** a very intensive and long-term therapy. Takes place five times per week and typically lasts for several years. Sessions are particularly tightly boundaried and normally last exactly 50 minutes. Analytic technique is usually limited to the traditional use of free association and interpretation, particularly of the transference relationship. The patient often lies on a couch, as opposed to sitting facing the therapist.

**Psychoanalytic (or psychodynamic) psychotherapy:** a slightly less intensive but still usually long-term therapy. Sessions take place between one and three times per week and therapy typically lasts 1–5 years. Analytic technique approximates to that of classical psychoanalysis, but adherence to orthodox technique is often less strict and may occasionally include humour and information giving.

**Group psychoanalytic therapy**: applies the principles of psychodynamic therapy to working with groups, typically of 6–12 patients. There are most commonly two therapists, often paired as a male–female dyad to enact maternal and paternal transference. Technique depends on theoretical model. In *group analysis,* insight comes mainly from interaction with other group members (analysis *by* the group), whilst in the Bion model of group therapy the group is seen as adopting the behaviour of a single individual and is collectively interpreted by the therapists (analysis *of* the group).

**Brief dynamic therapy**: there is a variety of subtly differing brief approaches to psychodynamic therapy. As in long-term therapies, emphasis is placed on the interpersonal functioning and affective state of the patient, although in order to speed up the process therapy is typically more confrontational and patients are explicitly educated about their relationships rather than waiting for the development of a transference relationship.

**Box 5.4** Varieties of psychodynamic therapy (adapted from Jarvis, 2003)

Being long-term and intensive, psychoanalysis and psychoanalytic psychotherapy are expensive and disruptive to the lives of patients. In some cases this expense and disruption may be unnecessary. Some of Freud's cases showed very rapid improvement, for example the composer Gustav Mahler was treated successfully in only four sessions in 1908. However, for some decades virtually all psychodynamic treatment was long-term. Recently, some psychodynamic therapists have returned to the idea of brief dynamic therapy (BDT), and this is growing in popularity. Molnos (1995) has suggested that some features of long-term psychodynamic therapies, for example the use of free association and the therapist's 'blank screen', artificially lengthen the process. By focusing the therapy on particular issues, directing patients to introspect on particular events and educating them about their interpersonal behaviour rather than waiting for a transference relationship to develop, the processes of catharsis and insight in psychodynamic therapy can be greatly speeded up.

# The effectiveness of psychodynamic therapies

Early psychodynamic therapists did not systematically evaluate the effectiveness of their work, but psychologists became interested in outcome research. An early review by Eysenck (1952) brought attention to what he termed the 'outcome problem'.

## The Eysenck review

Hans Eysenck (1952) published a review of early outcome studies into psychodynamic approaches to therapy. Eysenck concluded that, based on this early research there was no evidence that psychodynamic psychotherapy increased the probability of a reduction in symptoms: patients in both no-treatment and therapy conditions both had on average a rate of improvement of around 66%. Although Eysenck's review is still sometimes talked about uncritically in psychology texts, there are some fairly serious flaws in its methodology (Bergin and Garfield, 1978). Eysenck included flawed studies that showed poor outcomes for therapy conditions whilst discounting the results of better studies that found better outcomes. He also used much tougher criteria for improvement in therapy conditions than in no treatment conditions and did not take account of the time taken for symptoms to disappear. This means that a lack of symptoms two years later in a no-treatment condition were counted as the same outcome as the disappearance of symptoms in therapy after a few weeks. Bergin and Garfield (1978) reanalysed Eysenck's data and concluded that the real rate of improvement without treatment was 30–43%, compared with an 83% success rate for psychodynamic therapies. Eysenck, however, remained a critic of psychodynamic therapies and maintained until his death (in 1997) that there is no evidence for the effectiveness of psychodynamic therapy.

## Contemporary outcome research

The backdrop to modern outcome research has changed considerably since Eysenck's original work. Nowadays, public health care organisations such as the National Health Service are expected to provide psychological therapies that are supported by outcome research. The development of this new ethos since the early 1990s has stimulated a new wave of psychodynamic outcome research. The findings of this new wave of research are unequivocally positive, and the latest findings suggest that psychodynamic therapies are at least as effective as other psychological treatments.

### Psychoanalysis and psychoanalytic psychotherapy

These are distinguished by their long duration and intensiveness. A major research issue is the extent of differences between classical psychoanalysis and the slightly less intensive and long-term psychoanalytic psychotherapy. This, as well as the general effectiveness of psychoanalytic treatments, has been addressed in a recent series of Swedish studies. Sandell *et al.* (1999) studied outcomes for 756 patients receiving state-funded psychoanalysis or psychoanalytic psychotherapy and found strong support for the effectiveness of long-term psychodynamic therapies and for the difference between the two therapies. Psychoanalysis was defined by having 4–5 sessions per week, in contrast to psychotherapy, which took place once or twice a week. Therapy continued for up to 3 years. At the end of treatment there were substantial gains in both the psychotherapy and psychoanalysis conditions, but no difference between the two groups. However, at 3-year follow-up the psychoanalysis group was rated as having significantly fewer symptoms. It seems that, unlike the psychotherapy group, the psychoanalysis group continued to improve after the end of the treatment. This is a highly significant study, being the first to demonstrate that classical psychoanalysis really is different from psychoanalytic psychotherapy.

Many researchers believe that the best outcome studies are *randomised control trials* (RCTs). These involve randomly allocating participants to conditions. This is difficult to do with psychoanalytic psychotherapy and psychoanalysis because the treatment takes place over a long period. If we were evaluating a four-week programme of a brief therapy we could simply randomly assign half our participants to a control group and leave them for 4 weeks, compare their states of mind with those who have had therapy and then give them the therapy. However, it would be grossly unethical to leave people for several years without treatment just to compare them with a treated group! Some psychologists are reluctant to accept the results of studies in which participants have not been randomly allocated because of the risk that patient variables will affect the results. Occasionally, however, the opportunity presents itself to randomly allocate participants to conditions in the study of long-term therapy, for example in situations where *no* patients would normally have access to therapy. Bateman and Fonagy (1999) took advantage of this in a study of the effectiveness of psychoanalytic psychotherapy in treating borderline personality disorder.

## research now

## a randomised control trial of psychoanalytic psychotherapy

**Bateman, A. and Fonagy, P. (1999) Effectiveness of partial hospitalisation in the treatment of borderline personality disorder: a randomised control trial.** *American Journal of Psychiatry,* 156, 1563–1569

**Aim:** Borderline personality disorder is a psychiatric condition characterised by difficulty with relationships, suicidal and self-harming behaviour and drug abuse. The borderline personality is notoriously hard to treat. The aim of this study was to see whether patients given psychoanalytic therapy would show greater improvements than those receiving standard hospital care.

**Method:** 38 patients were diagnosed as having borderline personality disorder using standard psychiatric criteria. They were randomly allocated to one of two conditions. One group was admitted as full-time psychiatric in-patients and remained in hospital for the course of the study. The other group spent part of the time as in-patients but the rest of the time living at home and attending individual and group psychoanalytic psychotherapy. This treatment lasted 18 months. Improvement in each group was assessed by looking at the incidence of drug use, depression, self-harming, anxiety, and suicide attempts. How often the patients needed to be readmitted after treatment was also compared.

**Results:** The group undergoing psychoanalytic therapy did significantly better on all the measures of outcome than did those in standard psychiatric in-patient care. The therapy group generally showed substantial improvement, whereas in general those in the standard treatment condition did not.

**Conclusion:** Long-term psychoanalytic psychotherapy is effective in treating borderline personality disorder. Significantly, it was more effective than standard in-patient care and resulted in fewer re-admissions to hospital. This is important because one of the questions asked about long-term psychotherapy is whether it justifies its high cost. Clearly in this case it did because it reduced the need for more expensive in-patient treatment.

## Brief dynamic therapy

Because of its brevity, BDT lends itself to randomised control trials and there is a large body of evidence to support its effectiveness. In one recent study Guthrie *et al.* (2001) tested the effect of four sessions of BDT with 119 patients following attempted suicide by poisoning. A control group received standard treatment (referral back to their GP). Six months later the BDT group had significantly lower suicidal thinking than the controls and they were significantly less likely to have made further suicide attempts. In another recent study patients suffering depression were allocated to either standard treatment with antidepressants or an experimental condition of antidepressants plus BDT. The experimental group reported the combined treatment to be more acceptable than medication alone, dropout was significantly lower and symptoms were further reduced.

Meta-analyses have been conducted on BDT, and most researchers have concluded that its effectiveness is equivalent to that of CBT (Chapter 5) and behavioural therapies (Chapter 4). Crits-Christoph (1992), in his meta-analysis of the results of 11 published studies into the efficacy of BDT, concluded that BDT was highly effective compared with no treatment and on a par with other major therapeutic orientations. More recently, Leichsenring (2001) carried out a meta-analysis of the results of six studies in order to compare the usefulness of BDT, CBT and behavioural therapy for treating depression. No differences emerged between the three treatments in the alleviation of depression.

## for and
## against

## the effectiveness of psychodynamic therapies

— Early studies found no evidence that psychodynamic treatments had any effect on patients.

+ Recent studies have found much more positive results, showing that psychodynamic therapies are at least as effective as other psychological treatments.

— There are few randomised control trials of long-term psychodynamic therapies.

+ There are, however, plenty of such trials for BDT, and other types of study of long-term therapy. The few randomised control trials of long-term therapies have shown very good results.

## where to
## now?

**The following are good sources of further information about psychodynamic therapies:**

▶ **Jarvis, M. *Psychodynamic Psychology: Classical Theory and Contemporary Research*. London: Thomson Learning (in press)** – contains detailed chapters on both the process and outcome of psychodynamic therapies.

▶ **Malan, D. (1995) *Individual Psychotherapy and the Science of Psychodynamics*. London: Butterworth-Heinemann** – an excellent guide to psychodynamic therapy, illustrated throughout with extremely useful case examples.

## Conclusions

Broadly, research has supported the general assumptions of the psychodynamic approach to understanding mental disorder. Factors such as early trauma and poor early relationships increase the probability of suffering a variety of psychological problems. A number of psychodynamic theories aim to explain these findings. Some of Freud's ideas still have some support and others remain useful metaphors to help understand the experience of psychological distress. However, others now appear outdated, and Freud has been extensively criticised for his theoretical shift away from the effects of sexual abuse towards an emphasis on sexual fantasy.

A more modern psychodynamic approach is that of attachment theory, which emphasises the importance of a child's first attachment for their later mental health. Attachment researchers have uncovered very strong links between quality of attachment and later mental health problems, including those that are widely believed to have a largely genetic origin, for example schizophrenia.

Psychodynamic approaches to therapy include long-term intensive treatment such as psychoanalysis and shorter and less intensive brief dynamic therapy. These all work on broadly similar principles, aiming to achieve catharsis and insight, although the ways in which these aims are achieved vary between short and long-term therapies. There is now a substantial body of evidence to support the effectiveness of both short and long-term psychodynamic therapies in treating a variety of psychological problems.

what do you know?

1 Compare and contrast Freudian and attachment theories of mental disorder. Which is better supported by research?

2 What factors make psychodynamic therapy helpful?

3 Discuss Eysenck's conclusion that there is no evidence for the effectiveness of psychodynamic therapies in the light of contemporary research.

# 6

# The Humanistic Approach

what's
ahead?

Humanistic psychology is deliberately constructed so as to be able to understand human nature using simple principles and a minimum of theory. This is therefore the shortest chapter in the book! Humanistic psychologists reject both psychiatric diagnosis and complex theories like those favoured by psychodynamic and cognitive therapists, relying instead on a number of basic assumptions about human nature. In this chapter we look at the assumptions underlying the humanistic approach and study in some detail the theory of Carl Rogers. We then consider two humanistic approaches to psychological therapy, Rogers' person-centred approach and Fritz Perls' gestalt model, and evaluate their usefulness in tackling psychological distress.

## Assumptions of the approach

Humanistic psychology emerged in the 1930s and 1940s. It aimed to be a 'third force' in psychology, the field at the time being dominated by learning theory and Freudian psychoanalysis. The assumptions of humanistic psychology concerning the origins of mental disorder are not dissimilar to those of the psychodynamic approach, although humanistic psychologists adopt a rather different view of human nature.

- People have a basic tendency to grow and fulfil their potential. Psychological problems result when external forces prevent us achieving this growth.

- Diagnosis of mental disorder is unhelpful, and the symptoms a person displays can be better understood as their individual response to the blockage of their growth.

- There is a strong association between mental health and a healthy self-image. Our self-image is affected by our treatment by others.

- Like the psychodynamic approach, humanistic psychology is primarily concerned with emotion rather than cognition or behaviour.

- People can make their own life choices, and under the right circumstances will make the best choices for them. The aim of humanistic therapies is to help people make the right life-choices and so fulfil their human potential.

In contrast to the psychodynamic approach, which emphasises the potential for things to go wrong in children's development (in particular what parents can do wrong), the humanistic model puts its emphasis on the potential of the individual to achieve and become the best person they can. This is a highly optimistic (some would say naive) view of human nature. The divergence of humanistic psychologists from other psychological perspectives is actually more philosophical than psychological. Self-image is considered important in both Freudian and cognitive theory, and the humanistic emphasis on emotion is shared by the psychodynamic model. In one sense therefore the humanistic model is not a theoretical perspective in the same way as learning, psychodynamic and cognitive models are, but rather a philosophical position.

# Carl Rogers' theory

In the field of mental health Carl Rogers has been the most influential of the humanistic psychologists. He proposed that understanding healthy psychological development depends on two ideas, the actualising tendency and the self-concept.

## The actualising tendency

Rogers (1959) believed that humans are primarily motivated by the need to *actualise* – to fulfil their potential and achieve the best level of 'human-beingness' they can. The relationship between the environment and the ability to actualise can be understood using the analogy of a flower, which will only grow to its full potential if the conditions are right. Just as a flower is constrained by the availability of environmental variables such as light, water and nutrients, so people flourish and reach their potential only if their environment is good enough. An unconscious process of *valuing* guides us towards choosing behaviours that will help us fulfil our potential. This valuing process can, however, be prevented from operating by the use of strict social rules and by a poor self-concept. Rogers believed that people are inherently good and creative but that they can become destructive when their valuing process is interfered with.

**Figure 6.1** Some humanistic therapists compare human development to that of a flower

## The self-concept

Rogers noticed that in therapy patients would often make reference to themselves, saying things like 'I'm not being my real self' or 'I wonder who I really am.' Rogers began to place great importance on this emphasis on the 'self' and how people thought of themselves. Rogers (1961) proposed that the most important aspect of the self-concept is *self-esteem*. Self-esteem means essentially how much we like ourselves. Rogers believed that we hold in our mind an image of our self as we currently are and an image of our ideal-self, what we would like to be. If these two self-images are *congruent* (the same), we will experience a good level of self-esteem.

The development of congruence and the resulting healthy self-esteem depends on receiving *unconditional positive regard* from others in the form of acceptance, love and affection. Without unconditional positive regard we cannot self-actualise. Some children lack unconditional positive regard from their families in childhood. Harsh, inattentive parenting or parenting that involves *conditional love* (love that is only available if the child conforms to certain conditions) is likely to lead to low self-esteem in adulthood, and such individuals are vulnerable to mental disorder, especially depression.

There is considerable support for the central ideas of Rogers' theory, that self-esteem is crucial to our well-being and that unconditional positive regard in parenting is important for the development of high self-esteem. In a classic study Coopersmith (1967) demonstrated both the importance of self-esteem for development and the importance of unconditional positive regard in development of self-esteem.

## classic
## research

# it's important to like ourselves!

**Coopersmith, S. (1967) *The Antecedents of Self-esteem*. San Francisco, CA: Freeman**

**Aim:** Coopersmith was interested in the importance of self-esteem in child development. He aimed to learn about both what effects having high or low self-esteem might have on a child and about what factors might determine a child's individual level of self-esteem.

**Method:** Coopersmith studied several hundred 9–10-year-old white, middle-class boys (Coopersmith, 1968). He used four measures to establish the self-esteem of each boy: a psychometric test called the Self Esteem Inventory, teachers' estimates of how well the boys reacted to failure, a test called the Thematic Apperception Test (in which pictures are presented and participants say what they think is happening) and assessment of their confidence in an unfamiliar situation. On the basis of these measures, Coopersmith divided the boys into groups of high, middle and low self-esteem. He then looked at the characteristics of the boys in each group, including their confidence, ability to take criticism, popularity and academic success. Coopersmith also went on to investigate the types of upbringing the children had had, using questionnaires and in-depth interviews with both the boys and their mothers.

**Results:** Distinct differences emerged between the groups. Boys with high self-esteem were most expressive and active. They were the most successful and confident group, both academically and socially. The middle group were the most conforming. Children with low self-esteem were the lowest achievers and tended to underrate themselves. They were the most socially isolated group, self-conscious and sensitive to criticism. Coopersmith found that parenting style was very significant. Children with high self-esteem had plenty of positive regard from parents, but also had firm boundaries on acceptable behaviour. Low self-esteem appeared to follow harsh or unloving parenting or lack of behavioural restrictions. Coopersmith followed up the boys into adulthood and found that the high-esteem group remained more successful in terms of work and relationships.

**Conclusion:** The Coopersmith study clearly supports Rogers' ideas, both that self-esteem is important for healthy psychological development and that positive regard from parents is a major factor in the development of self-esteem. However, Coopersmith also found that firm boundaries in behaviour laid down by parents predicted high self-esteem and this is perhaps less in keeping with Rogers' ideas.

Numerous studies have supported the link between parenting style, self-esteem and mental health. Lau and Pun (1999) looked at the relationship between parents' evaluations of children in 974 families and the self-esteem of the children, who were aged 8–13 years. Where parents had positive views of their children, the children tended to have higher self-esteem. This was especially the case where the positive parental attitude was shared by both parents. In another study Burnett (1999) collected information from 269 Australian primary school children regarding their self-concept and the frequency of positive and negative comments from teachers. It was found that positive comments from teachers were associated with improved self-concept, which was in turn associated with greater achievement (see Figure 6.2). This supports the view that achievement (actualisation) is dependent on self-esteem, which is in turn dependent on positive regard from others.

You can see how Rogers' emphasis is not on what goes wrong in human development to cause psychopathology, but rather what are the necessary ingredients to healthy development. In the main Rogers did not explore in detail the mechanisms by which failure to meet the optimum conditions for psychological growth actually led to mental disorder, but emphasised the broad humanistic principles instead.

**Figure 6.2** Children's self-esteem can be powerfully affected by positive comments from teachers

## for and against

# Rogers' explanation of mental health

➕ There is ample support for the link between parenting style and self-esteem, and for the importance of self-esteem in mental health.

➖ Other theories can explain these links as neatly as Rogers' can.

➕ Rogers' emphasis on the causes of mental health complements the emphasis in other theories on the origins of mental disorder.

➖ Rogers did not explain in the same detail as alternative theories exactly how parenting, self-esteem and mental health are linked.

## where to now?

**The following are good sources of further information about humanistic psychology, and in particular the ideas of Carl Rogers:**

▶ **Merry, T. (1995)** *Invitation to Person-centred Psychology*. **London: Whurr** – an interesting introduction to humanistic psychology, answering key questions about human nature from a humanistic perspective.

▶ **Thorne, B. (1992)** *Carl Rogers*. **London: Sage** – a general introduction to the ideas and techniques of Carl Rogers.

# Humanistic approaches to therapy

Although humanistic therapies are broadly informed by the assumptions of humanistic psychology, they are quite distinct from one another in their techniques – much more so than are different psychodynamic or cognitive therapies.

## Person-centred therapy

A patient who Rogers saw at the Rochester Society for the Prevention of Cruelty to Children may have particularly influenced his ideas about therapy. She was the mother of a delinquent boy who Rogers was seeing for therapy. Rogers made interpretations about her behaviour towards her son based on psychodynamic theory. However, the woman consistently rejected all interpretations. She asked if Rogers took on adults for counselling. When he said that he did she began to tell him (for the first time) about her problems and how these had affected her son. Rogers became convinced by this incident of the importance of allowing patients to talk freely, and this was the idea behind his person-centred therapy (or *counselling* – unlike practitioners of other models Rogerians do not distinguish between the two).

One major difference between humanistic counsellors and other therapists is that they refer to those in therapy as 'clients' as opposed 'patients'. This reflects the fact that they see the therapist and client as equal partners rather than as an expert treating a patient. Humanistic counsellors do encourage clients to focus on and explore feelings, but, unlike psychodynamic therapists they are *completely* non-directive, refraining from asking clients to focus on or explain things they have said. Rogerians do not offer interpretations but merely encourage the client to keep on talking in the belief that they would eventually find their own answers. One reason why Rogers rejected interpretation was that he believed that, although symptoms did arise from past experience, it was more useful for the client to focus on the present and future than on the past.

### The core conditions for personal growth

Rogers worked towards personal fulfilment in his clients. Rather than just liberating them from the effects of their past experience, as psychodynamic therapists do, Rogerians try to help their clients to achieve personal growth and eventually to self-actualise. Rogers (1961) suggested three *core conditions*, which facilitate clients in their personal growth.

- **Empathy** – the ability to understand what the client is feeling. An important part of the task of the person-centred counsellor is to follow precisely what the client is feeling and to communicate to them that the therapist understands what they are feeling.

- **Congruence** – also called genuineness. This means that, unlike the psychodynamic therapist who generally maintains a 'blank screen' and reveals little of their own personality in therapy, the Rogerian is keen to allow the client to experience them as they really are.

- **Unconditional positive regard** – Rogers believed that for people to grow and fulfil their potential it is important that they are valued as themselves. The person-centred counsellor is thus careful to always maintain a positive attitude to the client, even if they are disgusted by their actions.

As Mearns and Thorne (1988) point out, we cannot understand person-centred counselling by its techniques alone. As humanistic psychology is primarily a philosophical system the person-centred counsellor is distinguished by their positive and optimistic view of human nature. The philosophy that people are essentially good, and that ultimately knows what is right for them, are the essential ingredients of successful person-centred work. Mearns and Thorne sum up person-centred therapy as 'all about loving.' Because person-centred counsellors place so much emphasis on genuineness and on being led by the client, it is not possible to have the same strict boundaries of time and technique as is practised in psychodynamic therapy. If they judged it appropriate, a person-centred counsellor might diverge considerably from orthodox counselling techniques.

# inter**active**
## angles

Match the three instances in Table 6.1 below to the therapeutic technique being employed.

| Technique | Scenario |
| --- | --- |
| Empathy | The therapist looks unfazed when a client tells them they are cutting themselves. |
| Congruence | The therapist tells a bereaved client that they too have lost a loved-one. |
| Unconditional positive regard | The therapist smiles when the client recalls a happy event and frowns when they recall an unhappy one. |

**Table 6.1** Therapeutic techniques

## Spirituality

The person-centred tradition is unique in psychology in that, with its emphasis on 'growth' it is easily compatible with the idea of *spirituality*. Although not all person-centred therapists are religious, and although you certainly do not have to be religious to practise or benefit from person-centred therapy, there has been a long association between this style of therapy and the Church. One of the main factors in deciding what you think of person-centred therapy may be how comfortable you are with ideas like *personal growth* and *spirituality*. To some people these will be essential aspects of life; to others they will be meaningless. One effect humanistic psychology has had on the field of psychopathology in general is to have recognised the spiritual dimension. This reflected in the publication of the DSM-IV in 1994, when for the first time, the category *Religious or spiritual problem* was included as a diagnostic category.

### Discussion of person-centred therapy

The common-sense ideas behind person-centred counselling are immensely appealing to many people, and this approach now dominates the counselling field. One reason for the popularity of the person-centred approach is its simplicity. Rogerian ideas are relatively easy to understand (though not to practise) so much less academic study is needed for trainees than for those studying cognitive or psychodynamic therapy. Rogers and his followers have also brought home to psychologists the importance of truly listening to clients. Myers (2000) performed a qualitative study on the impact of being listened to on five female clients in person-centred therapy. Each client's experience was quite distinct, but in each case it could be seen that the experience of counselling in some gave them an experience they had not had in previous relationships.

Person-centred counselling is undoubtedly helpful for many clients. Greenberg *et al.* (1994) reviewed the results of 37 outcome studies looking at the effectiveness of person-centred therapy in a variety of situations and conditions. They concluded that person-centred counselling is as effective as other approaches to therapy, and more successful than no treatment. There are published case studies that appear to show that, for some people, adopting a humanistic approach to therapy is the most effective intervention. Siebert (2000) describes the case of an 18-year-old girl diagnosed with severe paranoid schizophrenia and expected to remain institutionalised for life, whose symptoms all disappeared following person-centred counselling. Of course this is a one-off case and actually few psychologists would recommend a humanistic approach to schizophrenia. In general person-centred therapy is employed for working with less severe cases.

Rather less research has been published concerning the effectiveness of person-centred therapy with specific disorders than is the case for the other major psychological therapies. McLeod (1996) has suggested that this is why person-centred therapy currently has less of a foothold in the NHS than other therapies. The research that is available paints a fairly optimistic picture. Beutler (1991) assessed the effectiveness of person-centred therapy on 20 clients treated for depression and found moderate improvement, maintained at 10-month follow-up. More dramatic improvement was found in a study by Borkovec (1991), who found large improvements in 14 clients suffering from generalised anxiety.

## for and against

### person-centred therapy

**+** Research has supported the usefulness of person-centred therapy.

**–** The body of research supporting person-centred therapy is very small compared with that for other psychological therapies.

**+** Person-centred therapy may be particularly helpful to patients to whom spirituality is important.

## where to now?

**The following are good sources of further information on person-centred therapy:**

▶ **Mayhew, J. (1996)** *Psychological Change: A Practical Introduction.* **Basingstoke: Macmillan** – a very user-friendly book comparing the humanistic, learning and psychodynamic approaches to therapy.

▶ **Mearns, D. and Thorne, B. (1988)** *Person-centred Counselling in Action.* **London: Sage** – a detailed account of person-centred therapy, including some useful case material.

## Gestalt therapy

Although Rogerian or person-centred therapy has dominated the humanistic approach, there are other approaches worthy of discussion. Perhaps the most significant of these is the *gestalt* approach, developed by Fritz Perls (1965). Like Rogers, Perls believed in the human capacity for goodness and creativity; however, he also believed that people sometimes needed to be pushed to achieve their potential. Gestalt therapy thus involves a much wider range of techniques than does person-centred therapy, and in particular more challenge and confrontation.

### Awareness and bullshit

Like psychodynamic therapy, Gestalt therapy aims to give people insight into their interpersonal functioning, but rather than linking this past experience in the way a psychodynamic therapist would do, Gestalt therapists remain focused in the 'here and now', challenging clients to understand better how they are feeling and behaving at any given moment in therapy. The aim of this challenging is to give clients a better awareness of their real feelings. Perls believed that we lack awareness of our real feelings, and that our everyday understanding of our behaviour tends to be dishonest, 'bullshit' as he called it. However we have the capacity to choose to be honest with ourselves. Gestalt therapists can be quite ruthless in their refusal to accept bullshit and force clients to reveal their true feelings. Gaines (1974) gives an example of this. A young fan of Perls had got into a lift with him. At first he stammered what an honour it was to meet Perls. Perls ignored him totally until the lift door opened and the man said 'I'm really nervous.' Perls then smiled and said 'now let us talk.' Perls only acknowledged the man when he chose to reveal himself honestly. His initial approach was dismissed as bullshit.

## Unfinished business and closure

Whilst Gestalt therapists avoid focusing on past events during therapy sessions, they do recognise that people can be affected by their past. Perls called these unresolved past traumas 'unfinished business'. Gestalt techniques such as the empty chair (below) aim to resolve unfinished business and give clients a sense of *closure*. Only when we 'close' unfinished business in this way do we get the opportunity to move on from the effects of trauma.

## The empty chair

**Figure 6.3** The empty chair is a classic technique from Gestalt therapy

One of the most powerful techniques of Gestalt therapy involves asking clients to sit facing an empty chair, imaging a person or some aspect of himself or herself sitting there and talk honestly to them (Figure 6.3). This helps the client confront and resolve their feelings about unfinished business. Bereavement can be dealt with by talking to the chair as if the lost loved-one were sitting there, telling them all the things they would have liked to tell them before they died. Anger can be expressed by talking to the chair as if the person who had caused the anger were sitting there. By taking this opportunity to talk to the empty chair, the client is brought powerfully into contact with their real feelings about a situation, enabling them to be fully aware of their feelings and to express them. When a client expresses for the first time how they feel about a situation they can experience closure, and they can move on from the situation.

## Batting and catharsis

Gestalt therapy involves very powerful techniques for catharsis. As well as talking to the therapist, which achieves considerable catharsis in psychodynamic therapy, Gestalt therapists encourage patients to release anger by shouting and screaming, and in some cases *batting*. Batting commonly involves pounding pillows. Anger against another person can be expressed by screaming at an empty chair or, in the case of couples counselling, at the partner.

## Experimental techniques

Although Gestalt therapy is best known for batting and the empty chair technique, actually Gestalt therapists are not limited to a small range of orthodox techniques and instead take pride in finding novel ways of challenging their clients (Mackewn, 1994). Davison and Neale (1994) give the example of a therapist dealing with a married couple whose marriage was being dominated by the wife's mother. The therapist forced himself on to the settee, forcing the couple apart, and put his jacket over the wife's head. When the man asked him to move the therapist refused and the man pushed him to the floor. The therapist responded 'I wondered how long it would take you to do something!' He then challenged the wife for her passivity in not removing the jacket over her head. By doing this, the therapist demonstrated that the couple needed to be far more active in dealing with their situation.

## Discussion of Gestalt therapy

Gestalt techniques are controversial. There is little evidence that the extreme and rapid catharsis involved in Gestalt therapy benefits clients and it may in some cases be harmful. Mackewn (1994) suggests, however, that those not trained in Gestalt therapy have a stereotyped view that makes it appear ridiculous, and that in reality empty chair and batting may be only infrequently used. Davison and Neale (1994) suggest that Gestalt techniques are particularly open to abuse because of their power, but that responsibly used can be extremely helpful.

Despite the misgivings shared by many psychologists about the potential for harm in Gestalt techniques, research has provided strong support for the usefulness of such techniques when conducted appropriately. Paivio and Greenberg (1995) randomly assigned 34 clients with unresolved feelings towards a significant other to either an empty chair condition or a placebo condition consisting of education about unfinished business. On measures of unfinished business, symptoms and general well-being the empty chair group did significantly better, and their gains were maintained at one-year follow-up.

We might expect Gestalt therapy to lead to improvements in dealing with unfinished business, given that this is one of the major aims of the therapy, but how does Gestalt therapy compare with other models in tackling psychiatric disorders? Because of the wide range of techniques used, it is quite difficult to test the effectiveness of 'typical' Gestalt therapy. Research has therefore focused on the usefulness of particular techniques, for example the empty chair. A recent study from Johnson and Smith (1997) suggests that the empty chair technique compares well against a more standard treatment for phobias, systematic desensitisation (see p. 50).

# research now

## phobias and the empty chair

**Johnson, W.R. and Smith, E.W.L. (1997) Gestalt empty chair dialogue versus systematic desensitisation in the treatment of a phobia.** *Gestalt Review Special Issue, 1,* 150–162

**Aim:** It is well established that the empty chair technique is helpful for clients who wish to get in touch with their feelings towards other people or aspects of their own personality. However, very little research has been done to test the effectiveness of such techniques in tackling mental disorder. The aim of this study was to compare the effectiveness of the empty chair with that of systematic desensitisation, a more standard treatment for phobias.

**Method:** 23 undergraduate students were identified as suffering from ophidiophobia (fear of snakes) by means of interviews and by testing their responses to snake-related stimuli. They were randomly allocated to three conditions. In one condition they underwent systematic desensitisation, in another they were given the empty chair technique, in which they could talk to their phobia. The third group formed a control condition and underwent no therapy.

**Results:** Both the treatment conditions led to significant improvements in participants' fear of snakes. No difference in the effectiveness of these two treatments emerged. No improvements were noted in the control group.

**Conclusion:** Confronting a phobia using the empty chair technique is as effective as the standard treatment of systematic desensitisation. This suggests that Gestalt therapy may be a suitable treatment for simple phobias like ophidiophobia.

There are of course important limitations with this study. The number of participants was very small and, unlike most people treated for phobias, they had not sought therapy. This is important as it may indicate that the group had rather mild cases of ophidiophobia. We do not know how effective the empty chair might be with more severe cases. As a general validation of Gestalt therapy, this study and others like it have the further limitation that an isolated technique is being evaluated, rather than the full range of Gestalt techniques.

# for and against

## Gestalt therapy

+ Research has established that techniques like the empty chair can be helpful in tackling unresolved feelings and psychiatric disorders.

– There is only a relatively small body of research to support the effectiveness of Gestalt therapy.

– Gestalt techniques bring about very powerful catharsis and may therefore be dangerous if not carefully used.

## where to now?

**The following are good sources of further information about Gestalt therapy:**

▶ **Mackewn, J. (1994) Modern Gestalt – an integrative and ethical approach to counselling and psychotherapy.** *Counselling,* **5, 105–108** – a useful article defending Gestalt therapy against some of the common criticisms.

▶ **Wolfe, R. and Dryden, W. (1996)** *Handbook of Counselling Psychology.* **London: Sage** – contains a useful chapter on humanistic therapies with lots of information on Gestalt techniques.

## Conclusions

The humanistic approach is more of a philosophical position than a distinct theoretical approach to psychology. Humanistic psychologists see people as fundamentally good and emphasise their capacity to change and to choose their own destiny. Like psychodynamic psychologists, they see the roots of psychological problems in relationships. The most influential humanistic ideas of mental health come from Carl Rogers, who emphasised the human need to actualise and the requirement for unconditional positive regard to achieve this.

The two most important humanistic therapies are Rogers' person-centred approach and Perls' Gestalt approach. Despite sharing the basic humanistic assumptions, these models of therapy are very different. Person-centred therapy uses a minimum of intervention on the assumption that if a therapist can create the correct conditions then clients will work things out for themselves. By contrast, Gestalt therapy involves a range of powerful techniques designed to prod clients into greater awareness and honesty. There is a relatively small body of research into the humanistic therapies, but that research that does exist is supportive of their effectiveness.

1   Outline the ideas that distinguish the humanistic approach from other psychological models of mental health and therapy.

2   To what extent is humanistic theory and therapy supported by empirical evidence?

3   Compare and contrast person-centred and Gestalt therapies.

# 7

# The Social Approach

In this chapter we consider the alternatives to traditional psychological and biomedical models of abnormality. We begin by taking a look at three theoretical positions on abnormality that are critical of traditional approaches for ignoring social aspects of abnormality; social psychiatry, labelling theory and social constructionism. We then briefly examine the role of demographic variables – in particular socio-economic status and gender in mental disorder. The final part of this chapter discusses *Care in the Community*, a social programme of treatment used as an alternative to long-term hospitalisation for patients with chronic psychiatric conditions. There is a short discussion of two key professional roles involved in community care that are not often talked about in psychology: the psychiatric nurse and the mental health care worker.

## Assumptions of the social approach

The social approach has developed out of two main strands: first, theoretical approaches to the study of psychopathology and mental health; second, practical approaches based on therapies and interventions that are social in their outlook. Theoretical approaches include social constructionism and labelling theory, both of which are critical of mainstream psychological and biological approaches to mental health. Social therapies and interventions include psychiatric social work, community mental health support and drop-in centres provided by charities such as MIND. Therefore, the social approach should not be considered as a unified approach in the same way that learning theory unifies the behavioural approaches to explaining and treating mental disorder. Instead it can be seen as a collection of different theoretical and therapeutic approaches, which all have one thing in common: they all emphasise the existence of a social dimension in describing and explaining abnormality (Putwain *et al.*, 2000). Some of these assumptions include:

- The development of diagnostic categories (such as schizophrenia) and the actual process of diagnosis by a clinician (such as a psychiatrist or a clinical psychologist) are rooted in social processes, for example making judgements about what is and what is not abnormal.

- Social factors may partially cause, or trigger a predisposition to, a mental disorder. For example, depression is linked to poor relationships and social networks.

- Some disorders can be explained in social, rather than individual psychological or biological terms. For example, feminist approaches emphasise the role of the relative social power of men and women in the development of mental disorder in women.

- Patients suffering mental disorder can be aided by social as well as medical and psychological interventions. For example, those released from hospital into the community require social support such as social skills training and help with day-to-day living.

# Social perspectives on abnormality

## Social psychiatry

The social psychiatry movement in the UK (also referred to as the anti-psychiatry movement) tends to be associated with the radical psychiatrist R.D. Laing. Although trained as a psychiatrist, Laing rejected the medical model of mental disorders, which he saw as treating the symptoms first and the patient second. Laing advocated a more humane model of treatment, where first and foremost the patient was treated as a human being. He rejected the idea that psychotic disorders such as schizophrenia were 'illnesses', and that symptoms of such disorders were meaningless. In *Sanity, Madness and the Family*, Laing and Esterson (1964) presented a series of case studies, showing how the symptoms of patients diagnosed as schizophrenic could be seen to make sense in the context of their family relationships.

In *The Divided Self*, Laing (1965), inspired by the existential writings of the French philosopher Jean-Paul Sartre, argued that psychosis was an understandable reaction to living in an intolerable situation. Faced for a search for meaning, the person goes on a journey 'into themselves' where they experience a loss of identity, and become insightful into the contradictions and hypocrisies of a world gone mad. Laing's solution was to provide a space, a retreat, where people could complete their journey in a safe environment – notably *not* a psychiatric hospital. A community was set up in 1965 at Kingsley Hall in London with this aim. Several of the members became well known figures, including the nurse turned artist, Mary Barnes, whose 'journey' is recorded in the book *Two Accounts of a Journey Through Madness* (Barnes and Berke, 1973).

Laing's writings and practice came under sustained criticism from the medical profession, both personal and professional. From one side, it was argued that his methods of treatment (which they referred to as the 'Psychedelic' model) did not work and few if any of his patients emerged from their 'journey' as better people. As a result Laing was accused of lacking responsibility for the safety of his patients. From another angle, it was argued that Laing's writings only described a brief psychotic episode and thus did not apply to the more serious psychotic disorders. Laing's personal beliefs in mysticism, in particular his belief in the 're-birthing' technique (where a patient regresses to the womb and is metaphorically re-born) were heavily criticised as lacking any scientific credibility. Detractors pointed to his illicit lifestyle, and his abuse of alcohol and drugs, as evidence for his unsuitability as a practicing clinician.

**Figure 7.1** Laing's ideas helped to reduce the use of traditional psychiatric practices such as restraining patients

Despite these criticisms, Laing's work has been enormously influential (Figure 7.1). His books were popular with both mental health professionals (and radicals) and patients, who found in his writings an advocate who would not dismiss their experiences out of hand without a second thought. The radical element to Laing's work highlighted the power invested in the psychiatric profession, providing a voice to those who believed that the medical treatments (such as forcefully medicating a patient against their wishes) employed by psychiatrists were barbaric and abusive. Even if Laing's ideas about schizophrenia were rejected, there is no doubt that his campaign for the humane treatment of psychiatric patients was instrumental in raising awareness of the issues faced by users of mental health services. His legacy can still be seen today in, amongst others, *Psychology Politics Resistance* (who campaign against the oppressive and abusive uses of psychology), the magazine for democratic psychiatry *Asylum*, and the academic journal *Changes* (which places emphasis on humanitarian values than psychological therapy or professional boundaries).

## for and against

## social psychiatry

+ Laing's work drew attention to the power invested in psychiatry and the use of barbaric treatments, and led to psychiatric patients being treated in a humane manner.

− From a medical perspective, the psychedelic model was not effective (it did not reduce psychotic symptoms).

− Some of Laing's therapeutic techniques (e.g. the 're-birthing technique') were criticised for lacking scientific credibility.

## where to now?

The following is a good source of further information about social psychiatry:

▶ **Mullan, B. (1995) *Mad to be Normal: Conversations with R.D. Laing.* London: Free Association Books** – a biography of sorts, covering Laing's writings, Kingsley Hall and the social/anti-psychiatry movement.

## Labelling theory

A popular concept in social psychology in the 1960s was the idea that it is possible to explain people's behaviour in terms of social roles. Each of us has a number of roles (e.g. parent, teacher, student), which determine how we act in particular situations. According to Scheff (1966) mental disorders (in particular schizophrenia) can be seen as types of social roles. Essentially the diagnosis of a mental disorder is the application of a particular 'label' given to people who violate *social norms*; the implicit consensus about what is normal behaviour in any given society (e.g. what is the 'normal' way to approach a stranger).

Scheff believes that it is not uncommon for people to break these 'rules' occasionally, although consistent rule breakers are likely to attract attention from concerned people (family, GP, friends, police, etc.) and become referred to psychiatric services. These people are then labelled as having a mental disorder. This label functions as a social role, influencing how people behave and other people's reactions to them.

From a social perspective, labelling theory has a number of strengths. It highlights the power invested in the psychiatric profession and the ways in which the diagnostic process is open to abuse. This view is therefore popular with radicals who seek to challenge psychiatry as an oppressive and barbaric discipline. It also draws attention to how the definition of abnormality is rooted in social processes, how people decide what violates a social norm or not. Diagnostic procedures treat behaviours deemed as unusual or bizarre as characteristics of the person themselves and not as the product of a social decision, thereby diverting attention away from the social processes involved.

This position is not popular with mainstream psychologists and psychiatrists, who argue that some of the extremely bizarre behaviour they witness can't simply be the result of a label. For example, for such a serious and debilitating disorder as schizophrenia a 'label' trivialises both the extent of the problem and the suffering people experience. From a social perspective, the concept of 'role' has now gone out of fashion. It is seen as too inflexible and unable to account for the variability of behaviour when someone is supposed to be acting in a particular role. Social psychologists have now turned to language to examine the way in which particular discourses (e.g. the medical discourse) positions people in terms of what they can and can't do and what responsibilities they may or may not have.

## labelling theory

**+** Highlights how the concept of 'abnormality' rests upon social judgements.

**+** Has support from a classic study by Rosenhan (1973).

**−** Not all psychotic behaviours can be explained by people acting out a social role.

**−** The concept of 'social roles' is now out-of-date, replaced with the idea of social 'positions'.

**The following is a good source of further information on labelling theory:**

▶ **Heller, T.** *et al.* **(eds) (1996)** *Mental Health Matters.* **Basingstoke: Macmillan** – contains a chapter by Scheff outlining his ideas on labelling.

## Social constructionism

Social constructionism presents a serious challenge to the mainstream medical and psychological (learning, cognitive and psychodynamic) approaches to abnormality, by viewing the way in which knowledge is produced as a social process. Just as the cognitive approach does not refer to a single theory, but a group of approaches which are unified by several key assumptions (such as information processing), so the social construc-tionist approach does not refer to a single theory but is also unified by a set of common assumptions (Putwain *et al.*, 2000); see Box 7.1.

1 Doubt in the objective basis of knowledge: the claims made by scientific knowledge to provide an objective truth are rejected and instead the *production* of scientific knowledge becomes a topic of research.

2 Emphasis on historical and cultural context: psychological knowledge is specific to a particular time and a particular culture, so generalising findings beyond a particular time and culture is pointless.

3 An understanding of language is of central importance: our understanding of the world is constructed through language and so an analysis of language (e.g. discourse analysis) can reveal how certain versions of the world are constructed and function.

**Box 7.1** Assumptions of the social constructionist approach (adapted from Gergen, 1985)

Parker *et al.* (1995) examined how different accounts (medical, cognitive etc.) of psychopathology *position* those people who have been diagnosed with a mental disorder – e.g. what rights, responsibilities, attributes and so forth these people have. The traditional medical and psychological models of abnormality *individualise* mental disorders. That is, once a social judgement about whether someone is abnormal has been made, that abnormality is believed to exist inside somebody (e.g. biochemical imbalance, cognitive bias, etc.). Traditional models of abnormality also *pathologise* people with mental disorders – once somebody is deemed to have a mental illness, they are seen as different from other people, and are stigmatised (see p. 12 for a discussion of stigmatisation). Finally, traditional models of abnormality silence the 'voices' of people diagnosed with a mental disorder by treating their experiences as irrational or meaningless. The accounts of mental disorders given by psychologists and psychiatrists (e.g. in terms of learning or cognitive processes) become dominant over the accounts of the people who have to live with these disorders. This raises an ethical and moral dilemma in that the patient is encouraged to accept the knowledge and value system of the mental health professional as the correct or true version of events. Thus, people diagnosed with anorexia, for example, come to experience themselves as having 'faulty' or 'biased' thinking patterns.

## for and against

## the social constructionist approach

**+** The focus on language can highlight how traditional models of abnormality position people diagnosed with mental disorders in negative ways.

**−** The approach does not provide much of an alternative theory, although it comments on the traditional models of mental disorder (medical, cognitive, learning, etc.).

## where to now?

**The following are good sources of further information about social constructionism:**

▶ **Parker, I., Georgaca, E., Harper, D., McLaughlin, T. and Stowell-Smith, M. (1995)** *Deconstructing Psychopathology*. **London: Sage** – a super text, tracing the history and social practices that have led to psychology and psychiatry as it exists today. The hidden assumptions of mainstream models of abnormality are peeled away, revealing the contradictions and regulating practices that lie beneath. A thoroughly recommended read.

▶ **Putwain, D.W., Gray, M. and Emiljanowicz, C.M. (2000) Psychopathology: the social approach.** *Psychology Review,* **7(2), 8–11** – includes a short review of the social constructionist approach.

## Social explanations of mental disorders

A variety of social factors have been linked to mental disorders. Although there is considerable overlap between social and psychological factors it is possible to make a distinction between the two on the following basis. Psychological explanations of mental disorders such as cognitive, behavioural or psychodynamic factors provide *intra-psychic* (within the mind) explanations. That is, they all locate the cause of mental disorders within the individual. Social explanations on the other hand take a broader view, looking at how mental disorders are influenced by factors beyond the individual. These social factors tend to come in one of two types.

The first type of social explanation can be seen in feminist explanations of eating disorders (see Chapter 10). Feminist explanations of eating disorders are highly critical of mainstream psychological and biological models of mental disorder precisely because they are individual explanations. They argue that *individualising* a disorder such as anorexia ignores the political dimension associated with control of the female body and images of femininity. This approach deliberately sets out to look beyond individual explanations of eating disorders by looking at how such disorders are represented in discourse, and what positions these discourses offer for women. Such a move enables resistance by those who feel marginalized by mainstream psychology.

The second type of social explanation looks at how social factors may put an individual at risk from a particular disorder. For example, people who live in deprived inner-city areas are more at risk from schizophrenia (see Chapter 8) and people with weak social support are at risk from depression. These types of explanations are most likely to be incorporated into a stress-diathesis model, where no single factor is seen as entirely responsible for causing a disorder, but a combination of social, psychological and biological factors. For example, the cultural ideals about body size have been suggested as a possible cause of anorexia (see Chapter 10) and certain sections of the media have been heavily criticised for their role in presenting these images. However, not everyone who is subject to these images will develop anorexia. Therefore it has been suggested that cultural ideals about body size may be an additional factor for those already at risk from developing the disorder, perhaps through biological (e.g. a genetic predisposition) or psychological means (e.g. a cognitive vulnerability).

**Figure 7.2** Some psychologists believe that media images of thin glamorous women marginalise women of other body types and may even lead to eating problems

**for and against**

## social explanations

**+** Social explanations provide a contrast with the individual explanations offered by the other biological and psychological perspectives.

**–** Often social explanations are seen merely as adjuncts to individual explanations and are incorporated into a stress-diathesis framework.

## where to now?

**The following is a good source of further information about the social approach to mental disorder:**

▶ **Parker, I., Georgaca, E., Harper, D., McLaughlin, T. and Stowell-Smith, M. (1995)** *Deconstructing Psychopathology*. **London: Sage** – for a social account of psychopathology, look no further than this.

## Recent developments in the social approach: Care in the Community

In the 1950s and 1960s traditional care of chronic psychiatric patients in mental hospitals came under sustained criticism. It was claimed that in general conditions were poor, and that the emphasis was on containment, rather than rehabilitation of patients. As a result patients became *institutionalised*, unable to function outside of hospital, where their condition continued to deteriorate (see Figure 7.3). A graphic illustration of these conditions is shown in the novel and subsequent film *One Flew Over The Cuckoo's Nest*.

**Figure 7.3** A traditional psychiatric hospital or *asylum*

The 1970s and 1980s witnessed a move towards treating chronic mental disorders (such as schizophrenia) in the community. Old Victorian mental asylums were shut down and a variety of community-based care programmes established. The extent of this shift in health care policy can be seen in the number of in-patients receiving psychiatric care: in the 1950s there were approximately 150 000 patients on long-term psychiatric wards; in 1998 the figure had dropped below 30 000. The number of psychiatric patients is the same today as in the 1950s, but the type of care they receive has changed dramatically (Shepherd, 1998). The emphasis of these programmes is on rehabilitation of patients through providing a variety of social and health care services. The NHS aims to provide a 'Spectrum of Care' (Department of Health, 1997) involving the following elements:

1   Sheltered accommodation with 24-hour care.

2   Work and employment opportunities in sheltered social firms and co-operative businesses.

3   Specialist mental health outreach teams to provide long-term social support and care.

4   In-patient hospital care when required.

Patients living in the community may still require hospitalisation if their condition worsens. In a *revolving door policy*, patients requiring hospital treatment are admitted to a psychiatric ward on a short-term basis, until their condition stabilises. Sheltered accommodation is provided for patients who cannot live by themselves or with their family, when released from hospital, in *halfway houses*. These are communities of up to approximately 20 people with care staff who provide emotional support and help with day-to-day living. Residents are encouraged to be independent and responsible, setting their own rules and maintaining the community house themselves.

## Does Care in the Community work?

Outcome research has shown that Care in the Community has undoubted potential, but only when services are properly co-ordinated and funded. Leshner (1992) found that all too often communication between different agencies was poor with no overall strategy for co-ordinating patient care. For example, patients were given inconsistent advice by care staff and community care services would not be informed when a patient was released from hospital. In addition, patients on community programmes were not given the opportunity to develop the lasting trusting relationships with care workers essential to their progress.

Another problem is that community care is severely under funded. The government saved £2000 million by closing psychiatric hospitals between 1985 and 1991 alone, yet none of this money was reinvested in community care (Shepherd, 1998). The result is insufficient community-based programmes and halfway houses to provide adequate care and supervision. Patients are housed in low-cost private accommodation supported by welfare with no care staff to provide emotional support and help them rehabilitate. Essentially these patients are 'dumped' in the community rather than cared for, their condition worsens and they are re-admitted into hospital (Geller, 1992). Sadly, a large number of these patients end up homeless (Opler *et al.*, 1994).

## research now

## how successful is Care in the Community?

**Trauer, T., Farhall, J., Newton, R. and Cheung, P. (2001) From long-stay psychiatric hospital to Community Care Unit: Evaluation at 1 year.** *Social Psychiatry and Psychiatric Epidemiology*, 36, 416–419

**Aim:** To assess the effects of community care, one year after patients were released from hospital.

**Method:** Community care units (similar to halfway houses in the UK) were established to provide accommodation, clinical care and rehabilitation for patients discharged from long-term hospital care. Based in suburban settings, these units could house up to 20 patients each, providing 24-hour care from a multi-disciplinary clinical team. 125 patients were assessed one month before leaving hospital, 1 month after leaving hospital and 1 year after leaving hospital on measures of symptom severity, personal functioning, quality of life and residential preferences as well as the preferences and attitudes of care staff and relatives.

**Results:** After 1 year symptom levels and personal functioning had changed little, although the quality of life for patients had significantly improved. The community care units were much less regimented and restricted than hospital environments, giving the patients a greater sense of autonomy and responsibility. Care staff and relatives also preferred the community care units to hospitals.

**Conclusion:** A well-organised and resourced community care programme can improve the quality of life for patients released from long-term hospital care.

When community care services are properly funded and co-ordinated they show a range of potential benefits for patients. One study by Leff (1997) showed that patients suffering from schizophrenia cared for in the community, housed in long-term sheltered accommodation, showed much less severe symptoms (especially negative symptoms) than hospitalised patients. In a similar vein, Shepherd *et al.* (1996) showed a 40% improvement in social functioning for patients in sheltered accommodation compared with those receiving hospital care. The Shepherd study also highlighted how community care could improve patients' quality of life. The most important factor determining patient quality of life was choice, for example, choice over meals, mealtimes, access to bedroom, access to personal possessions. Although these factors may seem relatively insignificant, they are often difficult to provide in hospital.

Shepherd (1998) highlights a number of methodological problems in trying to assess the effectiveness of community care. The major problem is that there is not enough longitudinal research, especially in the UK. Living with a chronic psychiatric illness is a long-term problem and outcome research needs to reflect this by looking at long-term effects of community care. The other problem with research is poor definition of services and lack of consistency in the way that different types of community care is defined; simply referring to a service as 'community care' gives no information about hours of care available or how many patients a community team has to look after, for example. These are exactly the type of factors that may affect the success of community care and which need to be highlighted and researched.

## for and against

## Care in the Community

+ Patients on community care programmes are happier and make better progress than patients in long-term hospital care.

– Often community care is not well funded, patients receive inadequate care and end up back in hospital or homeless.

– Sometimes community care services are not well co-ordinated, and have no overall strategy for providing patient care.

## where to now?

The following book is a good source of further information about Care in the Community:

▶ **Comer, R.J. (1995)** *Abnormal Psychology*. **New York: Freeman** – contains an excellent section on the community care of schizophrenic patients in the United States.

▶ **Shepherd, G. (1998) Models of community care.** *Journal of Mental Health*, **7, 165–177** – a 'state of the art' overview of community care.

## media watch

### mentally ill face enforced treatment

Thousands of people with mental illness face compulsory treatment in the community under radical plans set out yesterday by the government. Alan Milburn, the health secretary, said the proposals would give 'proper protection to the public and to patients', but mental health groups warned they were too sweeping. As it became clear that the government had rejected advice on balancing new controls with strengthened patient rights, campaigners promised ministers a tough battle over the legislative blueprint. Judi Clements, chief executive of the mental health charity MIND, said: 'They are creating the illusion that this will make a huge difference to public safety, when it is more likely to backfire.'

Reform of the 1983 mental health act is widely advocated, as the focus of care for people with mental health problems has shifted from hospital to the community. Under the act, a patient can only be forced to have treatment in a hospital. Some inquiries into killings by people with severe mental illness have found that they had defaulted on prescribed medication and lost contact with mental health services. Mr Milburn said: 'For too many people, care in the community has become 'couldn't care less in the community, sometimes with the most tragic consequences'. The plans for a new act, outlined in a green paper, foreshadowed the biggest shake-up in mental health services for 40 years, he said, announcing an extra £53m for services next year.

The green paper, *Reform of the Mental Health Act 1983*, was published simultaneously with the recommendations of a government-appointed expert group led by Genevra Richardson, professor of law at Queen Mary and Westfield College, University of London. The group, which had been mandated to recommend compulsory treatment in the community, said that where patients were capable of giving consent, compulsion should be authorised only if they posed a 'substantial risk of serious harm' to themselves or others. But the green paper says the degree of risk must be paramount and proposes compulsion 'for the protection of others from serious harm' or 'for the protection of the patient from serious exploitation'.

The Richardson Group also said that until suitable alternative facilities were available, patients in the community should be taken to hospital for any compulsory treatment. The green paper does not specify where treatment should take place, although ministers have given assurances that it would not be 'on the kitchen table'. Cliff Prior, chief executive of the charity the National Schizophrenia Fellowship, said the green paper 'fails to take the chance to give people a right to decent care and treatment', a right demanded in a 20 000-signature petition delivered yesterday to Mr Milburn.

The Liberal Democrats branded the proposals 'illiberal and inadequate', and Julia Neuberger, chief executive of the King's Fund, an independent health policy think tank, said: 'Community care should help people with mental illnesses to live ordinary lives, not contain and control them.' But Michael Howlett, director of the Zito Trust, set up by Jayne Zito, whose husband was killed by a mental patient, welcomed the plans. Consultation on the green paper is open until March 31 next year. Mr Howlett said: 'We hope it goes ahead as stated and there isn't any kind of watering down over the next few months.'

*The Guardian*, 17 November 1999

## Questions

**1** What limitations of the current Care in the Community system are highlighted in the article?

**2** What issues are raised by attempts to 'tighten up' on Care in the Community?

## Community psychiatric nursing

The fundamental role of the psychiatric nurse is to enable people with mental health problems to meet their basic needs as far as possible (Putwain *et al.*, 2000). Clients' needs are assessed and appropriate interventions designed to meet these needs selected from a variety of models, particularly the medical, psychological and social models. The medical and psychological models of mental disorders have been dealt with in Chapters 2–6, so we will concentrate on social interventions here.

In the social model of mental health, relationships and the environment are seen as crucial to mental well-being. Disturbances to, or disruptions within, either of these can cause stress, resulting in an impaired ability to relate to others and function independently. The primary focus of this model therefore is on family and group relationships. The objective of social interventions is to facilitate the development of the individual's coping skills and social awareness to enable them to remain autonomous.

Social intervention is achieved in a number of ways through community care. In *social skills training*, clients are taught the necessary life skills and activities of daily living to help maintain their independence and ability to cope. Training is based on the principles of social learning theory (see Chapter 3) – guidance and instruction, demonstration and feedback, reinforcement and modelling – and is effective in helping individuals to improve and maintain their relationships with others. The promotion of a healthy lifestyle forms part of a health-education intervention. This would include reviewing the client's lifestyle and educating them in ways of identifying and coping with potential stress. Finally, group therapy, in which the objective is to increase the person's insight into their own behaviour and its effects on others, can be effective. In family therapy, the family is given space and support to work through and resolve conflicts, develop more effective ways of coping and relating, so as to provide support of other family members.

## where to now?

**The following is a good source of further information about mental health nursing:**

▶ **Ironbar, N.O. and Hooper, A. (1989)** *Self-instruction in Mental Health Nursing*. **London: Baillière-Tindall** – a good source of further information about mental health nursing.

## Mental health support work

The role of the mental health support worker is to empower clients and enable them to regain control over their mental health problems and day-to-day lives (Putwain *et al.*, 2000). In practice this involves providing the client with a wide range of social support. Depending on the degree of disability, the support needed may range from practical help with the basic activities of daily living to therapy and emotional support.

The type and level of support in each relationship must be tailored to the client, as each individual has different needs. For example, some clients may have experienced what they perceive to be a succession of failures within their families, careers and/or perhaps themselves; others may see themselves as naturally independent and for these people a high level of support may exacerbate feelings of uselessness and lack of adequate skills. For other individuals, however, a high level of support may emphasise their feelings of worthiness because they warrant a high level of attention. Providing the right level of support for each person in a manner acceptable to them is crucial in ensuring the success of that support in achieving the aims and wishes of the individual.

The success of the mental health worker is fundamentally based on building a good therapeutic relationship with the client based on Carl Rogers' care conditions of warmth, trust, empathy and a non-judgemental approach (see Chapter 6). It is important for the mental health worker to be perceived as a 'therapeutic ally' rather than a friend if the relationship is not to be damaging for the client, and therefore the needs of the client are paramount. An ongoing relationship founded on trust can be of enormous benefit to the client, in educating them about their condition and providing greater insight into their own behaviour. This education has an empowering effect, giving clients responsibility for dealing with their own problems, and allowing them to make informed choices with the support of mental health staff.

## where to now?

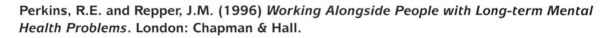

**The following is a good source of further information about mental health support:**

▶ Perkins, R.E. and Repper, J.M. (1996) *Working Alongside People with Long-term Mental Health Problems*. London: Chapman & Hall.

## Conclusions

Psychologists and psychiatrists working within the mainstream medical and psychological approaches have largely rejected the criticisms of theoretical social approaches. Some argue that these social approaches are simply trying to wish away the suffering experienced by people with mental disorders, who are 'ill' and require help. Such a humanitarian argument is commendable, but ignores the large number of psychiatric patients who feel that medical treatments are crude and abusive (e.g. a patient who refuses medication is pinned down by psychiatric nurses and forcibly injected). Perhaps these social approaches are too radical and people working within mainstream models feel threatened. Social interventions such as Care in the Community, with their emphasis on rehabilitation, have generally been welcomed by those working within mainstream psychology and psychiatry. However, community care has not always been a success story, with under-funded programmes leaving patients without the appropriate level of care.

what do you know?

1 What criticisms are made by social approaches of traditional psychological and medical models of abnormality?

2 What is the 'revolving door' policy?

3 Does Care in the Community work?

# 8

# Schizophrenia

what's
ahead?

This chapter begins with a description of the clinical characteristics of schizophrenia, including a case study and details of how it is diagnosed. The remainder of the chapter will deal with the causes of schizophrenia. There are important biomedical, psychological and social aspects to schizophrenia, and it therefore has a range of theoretical explanations, each focusing on one such aspect. Biomedical approaches emphasise the biological aspects of schizophrenia, including raised levels of a neurotransmitter called dopamine, and the role of genes in individual vulnerability to the condition. Psychological theories include the cognitive approach, which focuses on the abnormal ways in which patients with schizophrenia process information, and the psychodynamic approach, which looks instead at the possible role of family dynamics.

## Symptoms and phenomenology

This condition refers to a group of '*psychotic*' disorders characterised by major disturbances of thought, emotion and behaviour. The patient often withdraws from people and reality, often into a fantasy life of delusions and hallucinations (see Box 8.1). This debilitating disorder affects approximately one person in every hundred and is equally common in men and women. For men the disorder usually begins in their mid-20s and for women in their early 30s.

The condition was first termed 'dementia praecox' (youthful insanity) by Kraepelin (1896). Since then there has been some dispute over the diagnosis of schizophrenia, with different diagnostic systems (e.g. DSM-I, DSM-II) proposing different symptoms and different ways of diagnosing

Before her illness CR, aged 20, had left home and was contemplating marriage. The most striking feature at interview [clinical interview with a psychiatrist] was CR's disorganised behaviour. She would sit for only moments in a chair and then wander round the room, picking up articles and occasionally sitting on the floor. Her limited spontaneous speech consisted of abrupt commands to be given something. It was almost impossible to gain her attention. She repeatedly removed her dressing gown and made highly inappropriate sexual advances to the male staff, and then tore bits off a picture of a swan. She appeared neither depressed nor elated and moved slowly. She said that God talked to her, saying 'Shut up and get out of here'. When replying to an enquiry as to interference with her thinking the patient said: 'The thoughts go back to the swan. I want to keep the cross for ever and ever. It depends on the soldier Marcus the nurse.'

**Box 8.1** Schizophrenia: a case study (Macmillan, 1984)

the disorder. This had led to widespread criticism of the concept of the disorder called 'schizophrenia' and led some radical 1960s thinkers (known as social psychiatrists or anti-psychiatrists) to reject the medical approach, proposing that schizophrenia does not exist as a disease (*cf.* Laing, 1967). These historical changes in diagnostic criteria highlight how such diagnostic categories are not set in stone, but are socially constructed (Putwain *et al.*, 2000). The two diagnostic systems used in the UK today, DSM and ICD, are largely in agreement over the diagnosis (see Box 8.2).

A  Two characteristic symptoms for at least one month. Characteristic symptoms must include:
(1) delusions
(2) hallucinations
(3) disorganised speech
(4) grossly disorganised or catatonic behaviour
(5) negative symptoms (e.g. affective flattening)
*OR* one characteristic symptom if delusions are bizarre or hallucinations consist of a voice keeping up a running commentary on the person's behaviour or thoughts, or two or more voices conversing with each other.
B  Social/occupational functioning below levels prior to onset.
C  Continuous signs of the disturbance for at least six months.
D  No major changes in mood (depression or elation).
E  No evidence of organic factors (e.g. drugs) or medical conditions.
F  If there is history of a developmental disorder (e.g. autism) prominent delusions or hallucinations must be present for a month.

**Box 8.2** Characteristics of schizophrenia (American Psychiatric Association, 2000)

Although the cause of schizophrenia is not known, most psychologists and other mental health professionals believe that it has a biological basis, some kind of brain dysfunction that is triggered by psychosocial factors. Consequently, many psychiatrists and biologically oriented psychologists refer to schizophrenia as a disease. Strictly speaking, in medical terms, schizophrenia is not a disease: for a disorder to be called a disease it must have a set of core symptoms with an established cause, and schizophrenia has neither. A more accurate term for schizophrenia in medical termin-ology is a '*syndrome*', a set of signs and symptoms that appear to occur together and which probably have the same cause.

One of the key problems with establishing a diagnostic class called schiz-ophrenia and in diagnosing schizophrenia in practice, is that, compared with other disorders, schizophrenia has a very large number of signs and symptoms. A DSM-IV-TR diagnosis of schizophrenia requires only a very small number of these signs and symptoms to be present, and it is thus rare to find two schizophrenic individuals who present the same symptoms. This wide array of signs and symptoms has made the search for causes all the more difficult; however, a major breakthrough by Crowe (1980) was to distinguish between positive and negative symptoms. *Positive symptoms* refer to the bizarre experiences and beliefs that the patient tells the clinician about and are diagnosed by their presence. *Negative symptoms* (or more accurately signs) refer to abnormalities in behaviour, diagnosed by their absence. Box 8.3 gives some examples.

---

**Positive symptoms**

- **Hallucinations** – patients hear voices talking to them or commenting on what they are doing.

- **Delusions of control** – patients experience their actions as being con-trolled by outside forces.

- **Thought insertion** – patients experience thoughts coming into their minds from an external source.

**Negative symptoms**

- **Poverty of speech** – patients respond using the minimum number of words possible.

- **Social withdrawal** – patients withdraw from family and friends and refuse company.

- **Flattening of affect** – lack of expression in face and voice.

---

**Box 8.3** Positive and negative symptoms in schizophrenia

# Biomedical theories of schizophrenia

Biomedical theories of schizophrenia view schizophrenia as being caused by physiological processes. This is the kind of view taken up by many psychiatrists (who after all are medically trained doctors) and biologically orientated psychologists. The biological theories dealt with here offer *reductionist* explanations of schizophrenia. A complex psychological and experiential phenomenon, schizophrenia, is being *reduced* to a biological level of explanation. Reductionist explanations are traditionally thought of as more scientific by breaking down complex phenomena into their (more simple) parts. We can consider here three broad biological influences on schizophrenia. *Genetic factors* involve the link between schizophrenia and inherited genetic material. *Biochemical factors* involve the unusual brain chemistry associated with schizophrenia. *Neurological factors* involve the role of brain structure, which may be damaged in the womb or during birth.

## Genetic factors

### Adoption studies

Since the 1920s there have been many studies attempting to establish the role of genetics in schizophrenia using methods developed by behavioural geneticists (family, twin and adoptee studies – see p. 28 for a discussion). The first firm evidence for a role for genes in the development of schizophrenia came from an adoption study by Heston (1966).

## classic research

### the first evidence for a genetic component to schizophrenia

**Heston, L.L. (1966) Psychiatric disorders in foster home-reared children of schizophrenic mothers.** *British Journal of Psychiatry*, 112, 819–825

**Aim:** Before the 1960s, evidence from twin studies had suggested that schizophrenia was at least partly a result of genetic factors. However, no adoption studies had been carried out so there was a lack of direct evidence for a role for genes in schizophrenia. The aim of this study was to see how many adopted children of biological mothers with schizophrenia would go on to develop schizophrenia themselves. If a significant number did so, this would constitute powerful evidence for a role for genes in schizophrenia.

**Method:** 47 adults were identified who had been adopted at birth because their mothers were suffering from schizophrenia. A matched group of 47 adoptees whose mothers were believed to be mentally healthy were also identified. The 94 adults were interviewed in order to see whether any had gone on to develop schizophrenia themselves. It had been previously established that the risk of developing schizophrenia if one parent had it was about 10%. The incidence in the population at large is about 1%. The rationale of this study was that if there were no genetic influences on schizophrenia, we would expect none or perhaps one of the people with a biological mother with schizophrenia to go on to develop the condition. However, if it was passed on in genes, we would expect the same figure of 10% to develop the condition as would do so when living with a parent. A control group of adoptees without a parent suffering from schizophrenia was essential because, given the concern that early environment might cause schizophrenia, it was necessary to eliminate the possibility that the adoption itself was responsible for the high incidence of schizophrenia in the sample.

**Results:** The results were unequivocal. Of the 47 adults interviewed whose mother suffered schizophrenia, five had been hospitalised with the disorder. Three of these were chronically ill. Thus 10% of the adopted children of schizophrenic mothers developed schizophrenia – exactly the number that we would have expected had they not been adopted but brought up by the biological mother. None of the control group developed schizophrenia, indicating that the experience of adoption was not a factor in schizophrenia.

**Conclusions:** The results provided powerful evidence for the role of genes in schizophrenia. No evidence emerged from this study for any role at all for environmental factors in the development of schizophrenia.

Heston's results were dramatic, suggesting that schizophrenia may be entirely genetic in origin, and that environmental factors may play little or no role in its development. As we shall see, later research suggests a role for both genes and environment. On p. 147 we examine a much larger and more sophisticated adoption study that provides joint support for genetic and psychodynamic factors.

## Family studies

The simplest way of studying genetic factors in schizophrenia looks at the instances of schizophrenia in families. These studies, called *family studies*, ask the following question: If a person has been diagnosed with schizophrenia, how many members of their family have also been diagnosed with schizophrenia? If schizophrenia has a genetic component, then the chance of developing the disorder will increase the closer our genetic link to that individual. Twin studies compare the rates of diagnosis between identical (MZ) and non-identical (DZ) twins. MZ twins share 100% of their genetic material, whereas DZ twins share only 50%. If schizophrenia has a genetic component, MZ twins should show a higher rate of concordance than DZ twins. One very large-scale family study was carried out by Gottesman (1991), who pooled the data from 40 European studies published between 1920 and 1987 in a meta-analysis of the genetic influences on schizophrenia (see Table 8.1). Some of the older studies can be difficult to interpret as the diagnostic criteria for schizophrenia have changed over the years. However, in this analysis Gottesman used only data compatible with the diagnostic criteria used today.

| Relative | Percentage risk |
|---|---|
| General population | 1% |
| Uncles/aunts | 2% |
| Nephews/nieces | 4% |
| Grandchildren | 5% |
| Half-siblings | 6% |
| Siblings | 9% |
| Children | 13% |
| DZ twins | 17% |
| MZ twins | 48% |

**Table 8.1** The risk of developing schizophrenia (from Gottesman, 1991)

Superficially, Gottesman's results seem to support the genetic hypothesis. In general the data show that the more genetic material individuals share, the greater the chance of developing schizophrenia. For instance, the MZ twin of a schizophrenic has a much higher risk of developing schizophrenia than a DZ twin. However, before such an interpretation is uncritically accepted, several comments must be made and problems highlighted.

- These data show that schizophrenia can only be in part genetic. If the disorder were entirely genetic then MZ twins would show a 100% risk, as they are genetically identical. The 48% risk shows that other factors must be involved. Therefore genetic factors probably do not *cause* schizophrenia, but provide a *predisposition* to developing it.

- Family studies have been criticised, as they do not remove environmental influences. Members of the same family share a similar environment and so the higher risk for close family members could reflect elements of a common environment such as pychosocial stress or social learning rather than genetic factors.

## Molecular genetics

Recent research has focused on identifying the individual genes associated with developing schizophrenia. Several genes have been studied, and appear to be associated with schizophrenia. In the 1980s it appeared for a while that the *HLA* gene, a major gene important in the body's immune response, was associated with schizophrenia, although more recent and sophisticated studies have not confirmed this. However, there is currently a more promising line of research involving a variation in the *TPH* gene (so called because we know that it is involved with production of an enzyme called tryptophan hydroxylase). In one recent study, Hong *et al.* (2001) found that this variation in the *TPH* gene was significantly more common in Chinese patients with schizophrenia than in Chinese controls.

- Despite the strong support from family and adoption studies for the involvement of genes there are only very moderate associations between variations in particular genes and schizophrenia. This suggests that there are actually a number of genes involved. Kelly and Murray (2000) suggest that each of these genes is innocent in itself but that people who inherit a number of them are at high risk of developing schizophrenia.

### Discussion of genetic factors

Many textbooks on abnormal psychology take this and similar kinds of genetic data to indicate *strong* evidence for a heritable component in schizophrenia. Although there is no doubt these studies show that genetics does play *some* role in schizophrenia, it is possible that some biologically orientated authors are overstating the case for genetics. Genetics is only part of the picture and other factors must also be involved. One way of accounting for these findings is a *stress–diathesis* model of schizophrenia, where certain individuals may have a genetic predisposition to the disorder, but it is not certain that they will develop the disorder. Environmental factors are required to trigger off this predisposition and this is where social–psychological factors, such as urban living and expressed emotion, may come into play.

## for and against

### a genetic basis to schizophrenia

**+** There is support from family and adoption studies to suggest that genes play a significant role in individual vulnerability to schizophrenia.

**−** Evidence from family and adoption studies does not suggest that schizophrenia is entirely genetic in origin, but that environmental factors are at least as important.

**+** Molecular studies have found that variations in certain genes are more common in patients with schizophrenia than in controls.

**−** No single gene or cluster of genes has been found to be very strongly associated with schizophrenia.

## Biochemical factors: the dopamine hypothesis

A number of biochemical processes appear to work somewhat differently in the brains of people with schizophrenia. Research has focused in particular on the role of a neurotransmitter called *dopamine*. Our understanding of the link between dopamine and schizophrenia has been developed from several sources:

- *Amphetamine psychosis*, which closely resembles some forms of schizophrenia, is caused by an excess of dopamine, suggesting that perhaps schizophrenia might be caused by an excess of dopamine (Angrist *et al.*, 1974).

- When amphetamines are given to schizophrenics their symptoms worsen.

- Drugs used to treat schizophrenia such as chlorpromazine are *dopamine antagonists*. This means that they reduce activity in dopaminergic systems and are effective at treating some forms of schizophrenia (Johnstone *et al.*, 1978).

Evidence concerning the dopamine hypothesis is very mixed. For ethical reasons we cannot directly measure how much dopamine there is in the brains of live patients, but methods have been developed to suggest indirectly whether levels are higher than usual. Lindstroem *et al.* (1999) performed a PET scan study on 10 untreated patients with schizophrenia and 10 healthy controls. They injected a radioactively labelled chemical called L-DOPA, which is used in the production of dopamine, into subjects and used the PET scan to trace what happened to the radioactive L-DOPA. The L-DOPA was taken up more quickly in the patients with schizophrenia, suggesting that more dopamine was being produced.

Another way to test the hypothesis that schizophrenia is caused by excess levels of dopamine is to examine the dopamine metabolite *homovanillic acid*. Neurotransmitters are broken down into metabolites and passed out of the body like any other waste product. So if schizophrenia were linked to an excess of dopamine, then we would expect to find an excess of homovanillic acid in the urine or cerebrospinal fluid of schizophrenic patients. Studies (e.g. Donnelly *et al.*, 1996) consistently show that schizophrenic patients show levels of homovanillic acid that are significantly higher than those in control patients, suggesting that patients have higher levels of dopamine in their brain.

However, other lines of research have cast doubt on the dopamine hypothesis. A drug called *apomorphine*, which acts as a *dopamine agonist* (i.e. it increases the effects of dopamine) does not induce schizophrenic symptoms (Depatie and Lal, 2001). This finding is difficult to reconcile with the dopamine hypothesis. Another problem with the dopamine hypothesis relates to the effectiveness of anti-psychotic medication. Chlorpromazine only effectively treats about one-third of patients (those with positive symptoms), partially treats another third of patients (those with mixed positive and negative symptoms) and has no effect whatsoever on the remaining third of patients (those with negative symptoms). This finding suggests that there might be different forms of schizophrenia and it is only the form of schizophrenia with positive symptoms that is linked to overactive dopaminergic systems. See p. 36 for a review of studies into the effectiveness of antipsychotic drugs.

## for and against

### the dopamine hypothesis

**+** Much indirect evidence, for example reduced levels of the products of broken-down dopamine in patients' urine, supports the idea that schizophrenia is associated with very high levels of dopamine in the brain.

**−** There are ethical difficulties in directly testing the dopamine hypothesis, as this would involve extracting it from live brains.

**+** Anti-psychotic drugs appear to work by reducing the activity of dopamine.

**−** Some lines of research, for example use of dopamine agonists, have not found evidence for the dopamine hypothesis.

## Neurological factors

The idea that schizophrenia is linked to structural changes in the brain dates back to the early 1900s. It was not until new technology was developed in the 1970s, allowing for detailed brain scans, that researchers identified a consistent pattern.

Several studies using Computerised Axial Tomography (CAT) scans in the 1970s showed that approximately 25% of schizophrenic patients have enlarged ventricles in the brain (the ventricles in the brain are fluid-filled cavities that supply oxygen and blood to the densely packed neurons and remove waste product). Enlarged ventricles are usually caused by the death of brain tissue surrounding the ventricles and the fluid expanding to fill the space. More sophisticated studies have since shown more details about where there are deficits in brain tissue.

An MRI study by Crowe *et al.* (1989) has revealed that tissue is lost from an area of the temporal lobe, the hippocampus, particularly on the left-hand side of the brain. A more recent MRI study by Goldstein *et al.* (1999) demonstrated that the greatest reductions of brain matter are in an area called the paralimbic cortex. This region is shown in Figure 8.1.

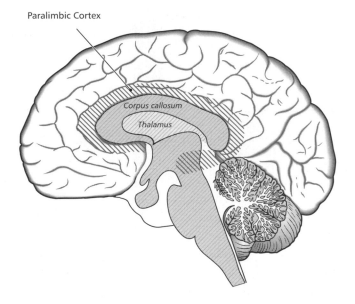

**Figure 8.1** The paralimbic cortex

# research
## now

### what parts of the brain are reduced in schizophrenia?

**Goldstein, J.M. *et al*. (1999) Cortical abnormalities in schizophrenia identified by structural magnetic resonance imaging.** *Archives of General Psychiatry*, 56, 537–547

**Aim:** It has been established by previous studies that schizophrenia is associated with reduced brain mass and larger ventricles. However, most published studies have focused on small regions. The aim of this study was to scan the whole of the brain cortex in a sample of patients with schizophrenia and compare the size of each region with that in a control group of healthy volunteers.

**Method:** Participants were 29 patients diagnosed with schizophrenia according to the DSM-III-R system and a control group of healthy adults. A matched pairs design was used in which the two groups were matched for sex, age, ethnicity, socio-economic status, handedness and catchment area. The brain of each participant was scanned using a MRI scanner, and the average sizes of 48 areas of brain were compared in the patients and the controls, controlling for head size.

**Results:** In the patients with schizophrenia, several areas of the cortex were significantly smaller than the control group. The greatest differences in size were in the paralimbic cortex and a related area called the middle frontal gyrus. Smaller differences were noted in a number of regions of the cortex that connected to the paralimbic cortex and fontal gyrus.

**Conclusions:** The finding that schizophrenia is associated with reduced brain mass is confirmed by this study. In addition, it demonstrates the particular importance of reduced mass in the paralimbic region and frontal gyrus.

Further research has confirmed the findings of Crowe *et al.* (1989) that the left side of the brain is more implicated in schizophrenia than the right. A simple neurological technique for testing general left and right brain function is to compare the motor skills of the left side of the body (controlled by the right brain) and the right side of the body (controlled by the left brain). Purdon *et al.* (2001) compared the persistent application of force using the right and left hand in 21 healthy controls matched for relevant variables. Ten of the treatment group were then given anti-psychotic medication and tested again. The untreated patient group was significantly weaker in the right hand, though not the left. This deficit disappeared after treatment. This suggests that schizophrenia involves a dysfunction of the left brain, and that anti-psychotic drugs rectify this dysfunction.

A general problem with identifying neurological differences in patients with schizophrenia is that these physical changes in the brain are not unique to schizophrenia. Patients with organic brain disease, such as Parkinson's disease, show similar kinds of structural changes in the brain. However, three factors suggest that this is not the same. First, in schizophrenia, there is no gliosis (a type of scar tissue) left in the brain from tissue death. Second, unlike organic brain disease, the ventricles do not continue to get larger, indicating that schizophrenia is not a progressive disease. Finally, a small number of cases have shown that schizophrenic patients had enlarged ventricles before the onset of the disorder (Weinberger, 1988).

### Possible causes of brain abnormality

In terms of explaining schizophrenia, identifying differences in the structure of the brain tells us only half the story. We also need to know what caused the structural abnormality. One possible answer is that one or more of the genes associated with schizophrenia leads to the development of a smaller brain. However, environmental factors may also damage the developing brain, leading to schizophrenia. One environmental variable that has been the subject of much research concerns exposure to the flu virus in the middle trimester of pregnancy.

O'Callaghan *et al.* (1991) looked at the influenza outbreak of 1957 and found that amongst those children who were in the fourth to sixth months of gestation during the outbreak there was a particularly high incidence of schizophrenia. Sham *et al.* (1992) examined the relationship between flu outbreaks and the reported incidence of schizophrenia across several decades. They concluded that schizophrenia was indeed more common amongst those who had been in the womb during such outbreaks. However, they also noted that most schizophrenics had not been exposed to 'flu in the womb and therefore prenatal 'flu alone is not a complete explanation of schizophrenia.

More recent research has suggested that, while people born in the late winter and early spring are more likely to develop schizophrenia, those whose mothers were directly exposed to flu are no more likely to develop schizophrenia than those who had no such contact. Battle *et al.* (1999) looked at the birth date of nearly 12 000 patients with schizophrenia and 735 000 controls and looked for correlations between the incidence of schizophrenia, measles and flu. Although a disproportionate number of people who later went on to develop schizophrenia were born in winter there was no correlation between incidence of schizophrenia and the prevalence of measles or flu during the gestation period.

Another cause of brain damage that has been linked to the later development of schizophrenia is having a difficult birth. Murray (1997) reviewed studies of birth difficulties and found that seven out of eight studies that used medical records to link difficult births to schizophrenia found an association. Low birth-weight, premature birth, prolonged labour and oxygen starvation have all been found to be associated with schizophrenia. Interestingly, Cantor-Graae *et al.* (1994) found that birth difficulties have been associated with schizophrenia more frequently in those who do not have a family history of the disease. This implies that some cases of schizophrenia are caused by genetic factors whilst others are due to brain damage.

## for and against

### a neurological basis to schizophrenia

+ A consistent finding has been that brains of patients with schizophrenia have lower mass than those of healthy controls.

+ There is evidence of neurological dysfunction in the left brain of people with schizophrenia.

+ There is evidence linking schizophrenia to prenatal exposure to flu and to difficult births.

− Findings are inconsistent and we do not have a good idea of what might lead to abnormal neurological functioning.

− There are also psychological and social factors not accounted for by a purely neurological model of schizophrenia.

## angles

The dominant biomedical model of schizophrenia views it as a physical illness with psychological symptoms. Having read the evidence for a biological basis to schizophrenia, what do you think? To what extent can the syndrome be accounted for by biological factors?

## where to now?

▶ **The following are good sources of further information on schizophrenia:**

**Gottesman, I.I. (1991)** *Schizophrenia Genesis: The Origins of Madness*. **New York: Freeman** – although best known for its analysis of family studies, this is an excellent general text on schizophrenia.

▶ **Lavender, T. (2000) Schizophrenia. In: Champion, L. and Power, M. (eds)** *Adult Psychological Problems*. **Hove, Psychology Press** – contains a good, critical account of the genetic, biochemical and neurological models of schizophrenia.

# Psychological theories of schizophrenia

Of the major psychological models of mental disorder, only two are of real importance when considering the causes of schizophrenia. The *cognitive* approach explains the symptoms of schizophrenia in terms of the ways in which people with schizophrenia process information. Of the psychological approaches to schizophrenia, the cognitive approach is currently the most popular in Britain and USA. The *psychodynamic* approach, based on the fundamental psychodynamic assumption that mental disorder has its roots in early relationships, is rather less popular in Britain and the USA, but is extensively used and researched in northern Europe.

## The cognitive approach

A comprehensive cognitive theory of schizophrenia was presented by Frith (1992). The aim of this cognitive approach is to explain the specific signs (behaviours) and symptoms (subjective experiences) of schizophrenia in terms of information-processing difficulties in a cognitive system referred to as the 'metarepresentation' system. *Metarepresentation* is a higher cognitive process referring to the ability to reflect upon thoughts, behaviour and experience. It is one of the most important features of conscious experience, affording us self-awareness of our own intentions and goals and allowing us to interpret the intentions of others. Information-processing difficulties in metarepresentation would seriously disrupt self-awareness, resulting in difficulties in self-initiated actions and the ability to recognise one's own actions and thoughts as being carried out by 'me' rather than someone else.

## Negative symptoms

According to Shallice (1988), we have two potential types of action. The first type are self-initiated or self-willed actions such as starting a conversation or planning a surprise party for a friend. The second type of actions is stimulus driven. These behaviours are responses to different types of environmental stimuli such as responding to someone else's questions. Shallice proposes that patients with negative symptoms have a deficit in the 'Supervisory Attention System'. The Supervisory Attention System is the cognitive process responsible for generating self-initiated actions. Such deficits can be seen as underlying negative symptoms such as lack of volition, poverty of speech and thought, social withdrawal and flattening of affect.

Evidence for this theory comes in the form of experimental fluency tasks, in which patients are asked to generate certain types of self-initiated actions and their responses are measured. In a verbal fluency task, participants were asked to generate as many responses as possible to a verbal prompt by the experimenter (e.g. 'Name as many types of fruit as you can'). Compared with control participants, schizophrenic patients with negative symptoms produced very few words (Frith and Done, 1986). Such patients either did nothing, repeated their previous response or responded to some irrelevant environmental stimulus.

In a design fluency task, participants were asked to generate as many designs as possible. Again, compared with a control group, schizophrenic patients with negative symptoms had great difficulty in producing spontaneous responses (Frith and Done, 1983). This evidence strongly supports the notion of a deficit in the ability to produce self-initiated actions underlying negative symptoms. This single cognitive deficit will produce different types of behaviour depending on what responses are acceptable: poverty of action (including speech and thought), stereotyped action (repeating the same response) or inappropriate stimulus-driven behaviour.

## Positive symptoms

Frith (1992) proposes that a deficit in the 'central monitoring system' underlies positive symptoms such as hallucinations and delusions. The central monitoring system is the cognitive process responsible for labelling actions and thoughts as 'being done by me' or as 'mine'. Hallucinations refer to unusual experiences such as hearing voices. Frith (1987) proposes that such experiences are caused when inner speech (the articulatory loop of working memory, see Jarvis et al., 2000) is not recognised as self-generated. Hallucinating patients misattribute self-generated inner speech to an external source and experience the speech as voices belonging to others. Even some pre-lingually deaf schizophrenic patients report they 'hear' voices (Critchley et al., 1981).

Such a theory would predict that people with hallucinations would be worse at remembering whether they had said something or not. This hypothesis was tested by Bentall *et al.* (1991), in a study where participants were to either generate category items themselves (e.g. animals beginning with the letter B) or read out category items. One week later, participants were given a list of words and were asked to decide whether they had generated the words themselves, read them or whether the words were new. Results showed that schizophrenic patients with hallucinations performed worse than schizophrenic patients without hallucinations. Both of these groups performed worse than a control group of non-schizophrenics. Although such results might indicate that hallucinating patients have a problem with memory, Frith (1992) suggests that at least provisionally there is some basis for the idea that hallucinations are a consequence of misattributing inner speech to external sources.

Delusions include *thought insertion* (experiencing thoughts being implanted into one's mind) and *delusions of control* (experiencing one's actions as being caused by others). Once again, such experiences suggest a deficit in self-monitoring. Thoughts and intentions are not labelled as 'mine', so are experienced as being controlled from external sources. Such a theory was tested by Frith and Done (1989). Participants were asked to follow a target on a videogame using a joystick. The task was deliberately designed to be difficult and induce errors. When participants could watch their responses on the screen, there were little differences between schizophrenic patients with delusions and control participants. However, when participants had no visual feedback for their errors, schizophrenic patients with delusions performed significantly worse than control group participants. Such patients had difficulty in monitoring their intended actions without visual feedback.

## for and against

### the cognitive approach

**+** The approach does not attempt to explain schizophrenia as a whole, but specific symptoms. Such a position avoids the problems of changing diagnostic criteria.

**+** Cognitive mechanisms not only give rise to cognitive deficits but also behaviours. Therefore hypotheses can be formed about patients' responses and measured using experimental tasks. This allows a degree of objectivity to be added to patients' subjective descriptions of their experiences (Frith, 1992).

**−** Schizophrenic patients have often been treated with anti-psychotic medication for a number of years. It is difficult (probably impossible) to find a comparable control group of patients to use in experiments who have also been treated with medication. This can make interpretation of results difficult and it may not always be possible to distinguish whether results are due to cognitive deficits or to the effects of anti-psychotic medication.

# Psychodynamic approaches

There are a number of theories from the psychoanalytic tradition that seek to explain the development of schizophrenia. They share the assumption that disruption to early family relationships can in some way drastically affect the way the developing child perceives reality and interacts with the world. Klein (1946) and Bion (1967) proposed that all children go through stages of development in which they are dominated by feelings of persecution and omnipotence. A poor relationship with the primary carer in infancy can prevent the child outgrowing these beliefs, rendering the individual very vulnerable to later developing schizophrenia. Bion (1967) suggested that when a child develops a 'schizophrenic core of personality' due to poor early social relations, they are likely as an adult to regress in response to stress to an early mental state characterised by feelings of persecution and omnipotence – classic symptoms of schizophrenia. Another psychodynamic approach came from Fromm-Reichmann (1948). Based on her patients' accounts of their childhoods, she proposed the existence of a *schizophrenogenic mother* (the term 'schizophrenogenic' refers to a factor that causes schizophrenia). Fromm-Reichmann proposed that where families were characterised by high emotional tension and secrecy, and where the mother was cold and domineering in her attitude, children were at high risk of developing schizophrenia.

## Evidence for the role of the family in developing schizophrenia

There is some evidence that certain types of family interactions are associated with schizophrenia. This idea was tested in a classic study by Schofield and Balian (1959).

# classic research

## a family basis to schizophrenia?

**Schofield, W. and Balian, L. (1959) A comparative study of the personal histories of schizophrenic and non-psychiatric patients.** *Journal of Abnormal and Social Psychology*, 59, 216–225

**Aim:** Psychodynamic writers had for some time suggested that schizophrenia was the result of poor or disrupted early family relationships. However, evidence for this was largely limited to case studies in which patients with schizophrenia reported unhappy childhoods. The aim of this study was to compare the childhood experiences of people with and without schizophrenia to see whether the patients really had more difficult childhood relationships.

**Method:** 178 patients with schizophrenia who were being treated at an American teaching hospital were given in-depth interviews regarding childhood traumas, maternal characteristics and the quality of relationships between parents. A control group of 150 non-psychiatric participants matched for education, socio-economic status and marital status received the same interviews. The two groups were compared.

**Results:** With regard to the quality of relationships between parents, no differences emerged between the two groups. Patients with schizophrenia were significantly less likely to report childhood trauma, poverty or an invalid parent. There was no difference in the frequency of parental divorce, death or alcohol abuse. There were, however, significant differences in the reported quality of mothering. Mothers of patients were less likely to have been affectionate and more likely to be domineering and overprotective.

**Conclusions:** Results were consistent with Fromm-Reichmann's theory of the schizophrenogenic mother. The only childhood circumstances that appeared to increase the risk of schizophrenia in adulthood were related to the quality of the maternal relationship.

In another early study, Lidz *et al.* (1965) investigated the family backgrounds of 50 schizophrenic patients. Forty-five of these (90%) were found to have seriously disturbed families and 60% of the patients had one or both parents with serious personality disorders. Parental marriages were typically characterised by either constant discord or one dominant and one submissive parent. Parents frequently made considerable emotional demands on children. Fathers of male schizophrenics were typically very passive, whilst mothers of female schizophrenics were typically cold and dominant.

The studies carried out by Lidz *et al.* and Schofield and Balian both have the serious limitation that they were carried out *retrospectively* (i.e. the researchers gathered data about families after the patient had developed schizophrenia). It is quite possible that the pre-schizophrenic child *caused* the unusual patterns of family interaction. For example, parents might wish to be unusually protective of a child who appeared to be very vulnerable because of the early symptoms of schizophrenia.

Traditionally it has been widely believed that adopting a psychodynamic approach to treating schizophrenia is at best ineffective and potentially harmful. This belief has in turn damaged the credibility of the approach as an explanation. However, recent studies are more supportive of the usefulness to sufferers of schizophrenia of exploring their early family dynamics.

# Alanen's integrated psychodynamic–genetic theory

Until the work of Heston (1966), psychologists tended to believe that schizophrenia was entirely psychodynamic in origin. Many psychologists now believe that schizophrenia is principally biological in origin. However, given the accumulated evidence for both biomedical and family factors it is difficult to take an entirely biomedical or psychodynamic stance. Alanen (1994) has attempted to resolve this by producing an integrative model that explains the role of both genes and family dynamics.

Unlike early psychodynamic theories, Alanen's theory is based on large-scale studies of families of people with schizophrenia, as well as clinical case studies. He proposed a five-point theory of how the family social environment can lead to schizophrenia:

- Vulnerability to schizophrenia is largely determined by the quality of relationships within the family. The whole family is important, not just the primary carer.

- Parental personalities and their impact on their relationship with the child are critically important in the development of schizophrenia.

- Families in which feelings of persecution or omnipotence are fostered encourage the development of schizophrenia.

- Family relationships that encourage dependence rather than independence are associated with the development of schizophrenia.

- Genes play an important role because they determine the *temperament* of the child (its in-born personality characteristics), which is important in determining the role the child plays in family interactions.

To summarise these five points, Alanen is proposing that genes determine the ability of a child to cope with difficult family dynamics. A child who is genetically vulnerable but who has a happy childhood with a supportive family will thus not go on to develop schizophrenia, nor will a child who has a difficult family life but is resilient to its effects because of their genes. However, a genetically vulnerable child who experiences poor family relationships is vulnerable to developing schizophrenia.

Alanen's theory differs from the early psychodynamic viewpoint by taking into account research into the behaviour of the whole family as well as the relationship with parents. Alanen has also updated psychodynamic thinking by acknowledging the importance of genes and the active role the child takes in family dynamics.

Perhaps the best evidence for Alanen's theory of schizophrenia comes from the Finnish adoption study, a longitudinal study that has been running since the 1960s of children born to

Finnish mothers with schizophrenia and adopted at or shortly after birth. Tienari (1992) followed up 200 children in this position. It was found that around 10% went on to develop schizophrenia – the same percentage as we would expect to find were schizophrenia entirely genetic in origin. However, the most significant finding of this study was *which* children made up the 10%: children that developed schizophrenia were almost all from families that had been previously assessed by the researchers as in some way dysfunctional.

A more recent analysis of results of the Finnish adoption study comes from Wahlberg *et al.* (1997). They compared 56 adoptees from mothers with schizophrenia with a control group of 96 children adopted from parents without mental health problems, looking at communication patterns in the adoptive families. In direct support of Alanen's theory it emerged that neither a parent with schizophrenia nor deviant communication in the adoptive family alone was associated with schizophrenia. However, there was a massive interaction between genes and environment, i.e. a child with *both* a mother suffering from schizophrenia *and* an adoptive family with deviant communication was at greatly increased risk of schizophrenia.

## for and against

## psychodynamic explanations

**+** There is considerable evidence to suggest that poor family dynamics increase the risk of schizophrenia in individuals already vulnerable because of their genes.

**−** However, there is little or no sound evidence to suggest that family dynamics alone can lead to the development of schizophrenia. Early studies that implicated family dynamics were methodologically flawed.

**+** In contrast, there is a large body of sound evidence to support the biological aspects of schizophrenia.

**−** By attributing responsibility for schizophrenia to families, when some individuals are highly genetically vulnerable or have suffered biological insults like maternal flu or birth complications, psychodynamic psychologists risk adding to the misery of families with a schizophrenic member by blaming them.

**+** Alanen has successfully integrated psychodynamic and genetic explanations and shown how psychodynamics is an important, though incomplete model of schizophrenia.

## Communication patterns and relapse from schizophrenia

While the possible role of the family in *causing* schizophrenia remains a very contentious issue, family intervention studies have highlighted that the family does play some role in *relapse*. In particular, structural family therapy has drawn attention to faulty communication patterns. A study by Brown (1972) investigated these factors more directly by studying family communication patterns in schizophrenics returning home following a period of hospitalisation. Results showed that communication patterns were a critical variable in whether patients would relapse into a psychotic state. The key factor was the level of expressed emotion; patients returning to homes with a high level of expressed emotion were much more likely to relapse than those returning to homes with a low level of expressed emotion. *Expressed emotion* (EE) refers to the attitudes expressed by family members when talking about the schizophrenic family member along five separate scales (Leff and Vaughn, 1985):

1  **Critical comments about family members.** Criticisms are rated on the basis of content and/or tone. Remarks are considered to be critical if there is a clear and ambiguous statement that the relative dislikes, disapproves of, or resents a behaviour or characteristic. The dissatisfaction is expressed intensely and emphatically; the relative must use phrases such as 'It annoys me' or 'I don't like it'. Vocal aspects of speech such as pitch, speed, inflection, and loudness are used to identify critical tone.

2  **Hostility.** Hostility is rated as present when the patient is attacked for what he or she *is* rather than for what he or she *does*. Negative feeling is generalised in such a way that it is expressed about the person himself or herself rather than about particular behaviours or attributes.

3  **Emotional overinvolvement.** Emotional overinvolvement is rated when there is an exaggerated emotional response to the patient's illness, marked concern reflected in unusually self-sacrificing and devoted behaviours, or extremely overprotective behaviours.

4  **Warmth.** Ratings of warmth are based on the sympathy, concern, and empathy relatives show when talking about the patient, the enthusiasm for and interest in the patient's activities, the number of spontaneous expressions of affection, and the tone of voice used when talking about the patient.

5  **Positive remarks.** Positive remarks are statements that express praise, approval, or appreciation of the behaviour or personality of the patient.

This theme was taken up by Vaughn and Leff (1976), who followed up 128 patients who had been hospitalised for schizophrenic episodes and subsequently discharged to their families. Communication patterns between family members were rated for expressed emotion. The crucial finding was that patients' families who were rated high in negative EE (scales 1–3 above) were more likely to relapse and be re-hospitalised than patients whose families were rated low in negative EE (see Table 8.2 for a more detailed breakdown of the results).

| Expressed emotion (EE) | Relapse rates |
|---|---|
| Low in negative EE | On medication 12% <br> Not on medication 15% |
| High in negative EE (<35 h exposure) | On medication 15% <br> Not on medication 42% |
| High in negative EE (>35 h exposure) | On medication 53% <br> Not on medication 92% |
| Note: Relapse rates after 9 months for 128 patients diagnosed with schizophrenia and the amount of contact time with family members for patients whose families rated high in negative expressed emotion (in hours). | |

**Table 8.2** Relapse rates after 9 months associated with expressed emotion (Vaughn and Leff, 1976)

Relatives rated high in negative EE were likely to be hostile and critical in their communications about the patient. Their response to the patient is one of fear and is characterised by lacking insight into and understanding of the patient's condition. In contrast, relatives rated low in negative EE displayed an insight and understanding into the schizophrenic condition and consequently made less demands and had lower expectations of their relatives. Leff and Vaughn (1985) found that a high level of positive EE with communication patterns displaying warmth and positive comments is associated with prevention of relapse.

# for and against

## the role of EE in relapse

**+** A large number of studies have replicated the original findings of Vaughn and Leff; one study even found a 0% relapse rate for patients from families rated low in negative EE.

**+** The role of EE is not limited to families. The association between high rates of negative EE and higher rates of relapse has been demonstrated with patients living in community care. This suggests that the significant factor could be communication patterns between patients and those they live with rather than specifically with the family.

**—** There is evidence that during periods where the patient is displaying fewer symptoms, rates of negative EE drop and vice versa. Therefore, high rates of negative EE may only reflect the strained communications that occur when the schizophrenic family member is undergoing a severe phase.

**—** The term 'expressed emotion' has become associated with high levels of negative emotion and in some cases this has been misinterpreted such that families should not express emotions at all. Expression of positive feelings can help to create a healthy emotional atmosphere, which is less likely to result in relapse.

EE research raises the psychodynamic spectre of blaming families. Some families may feel guilty that they are responsible for their relative developing schizophrenia. Remember that EE is not considered a cause of schizophrenia, but a factor that may influence the incidence of relapse. Coupled with appropriate psycho-educational intervention, family therapy can have a positive influence to reduce suffering.

Based on Sarason and Sarason (1998)

## where to now?

The following are good sources of further information on psychodynamic theories of schizophrenia:

▶ **Putwain, D.W. (2000) Living with schizophrenia: Family, communication and expressed emotions.** *Psychology Review* **6(4), 15–18** – this article charts the progression from psychodynamic theories of schizophrenia, through family therapy to the present-day research into expressed emotion.

▶ **Warner, R. (2000)** *The Environment of Schizophrenia*. **Hove: Taylor and Francis** – intended as a practical clinical guide to managing schizophrenia, this also includes good general information of psychological factors in schizophrenia.

## Social theories of schizophrenia

Biological and psychological theories of schizophrenia both provide individual explanations of schizophrenia. Social theories provide a contrast, in that they look beyond the individual. One line of social research examines the relationship between urban living and schizophrenia. In the clinical psychology literature, these factors are not presented as direct causes of the disorder. Rather, they are thought of as factors that may trigger schizophrenia (see the stress-diathesis model). Some writers (e.g. Parker *et al.*, 1995) are sceptical of such a position, believing that it diverts attention away from the social nature of schizophrenia and back to the individual.

### Schizophrenia and urban living: social drift and social causation

A consistent finding in Western industrialised nations for the past 40 years has been that the incidence of schizophrenia is much higher in urban than rural areas. For example, studies in Stockholm, Manheim, Chicago, London, Nottingham and Salford have all shown an above average incidence of schizophrenia compared with the incidence in the normal population (Freeman, 1994). Some psychologists have framed this relationship in terms of social class, as in most cases the individuals who live in deprived inner city areas tend to belong to the lowest social classes. There are two traditional explanations for the relationship between schizophrenia and urban living.

1  According to the 'social causation' hypothesis, living in an urban area may be a cause of schizophrenia in itself. Several characteristics associated with urban living (social deprivation, unemployment, high population density, poor housing and low social status) may provide a high level of psychological stress, leading to a schizophrenic breakdown in people who are vulnerable.

2  The alternative explanation, referred to as the 'social selection' hypothesis, is that higher rates of schizophrenia in cities are a result of migration (Freeman, 1984). Individuals who develop schizophrenia may drift into inner-city areas where they can obtain cheap single-person accommodation, do casual/low paid work and have few social and emotional demands. The other side of the coin is that mentally healthy people migrate away from undesirable inner-city areas, leaving such areas with a high rate of schizophrenia. According to this hypothesis, living in an urban area is not a cause of schizophrenia, but a consequence.

**Figure 8.2** Schizophrenia is more common in urban areas

## Comparing the two explanations

A number of studies have attempted to establish which explanation can provide the best account of the relationship between schizophrenia and social class. One such study by Castle *et al.* (1993) tested the social selection hypothesis by comparing the birthplace of schizophrenic individuals in Camberwell (an area of south London) with a control group of non-schizophrenic patients. The results did not support the social selection hypothesis. They showed that most schizophrenic individuals were born into deprived, urban areas and had not 'drifted' into such areas following the onset of the disorder. The results of this and a range of other studies suggest that, although migration (usually of mentally healthy people out of inner city areas) does occur, it is only in small numbers and is not enough to account for the high incidence of schizophrenia in inner-city areas (Freeman, 1994).

It would therefore seem plausible to suggest that, as the social causation hypothesis suggests, some aspect of urban life is responsible for causing schizophrenia. However, the development of schizophrenia does not tend to reflect the characteristics of a stress-related breakdown, making it unlikely that the *social* aspect of urban life is responsible for causing schizophrenia (Jablansky, 1988). The alternative is that some *non-social* aspect of urban life could be the cause. One clue provided by the Castle *et al.* study, is that schizophrenic individuals tend to be born in deprived inner-city areas. Such areas are well known for high rates of birth complications and infectious diseases (Jablansky, 1988). When combined with the finding that maternal influenza and maternal dietary deficiency are risk factors for schizophrenia (O'Callaghan *et al.*, 1991), it is possible to see how a link could be established between environmental factors and the development of schizophrenia.

Although the social causation hypothesis in its pure form is not supported, social factors such as overcrowded housing and unemployment may contribute to poor health leading to maternal influenza infection. Maternal influenza in turn may provide the neurodevelopmental basis for schizophrenia, as seen in the neurological changes in the brains of schizophrenic individuals.

## Conclusions

The evidence from the different theories considered here suggests that schizophrenia should be seen as a developmental disorder, i.e. it develops through childhood due to a combination of biological and psychological factors. On a biological level the disorder is linked to the neurotransmitter dopamine and to abnormalities in brain structure. On a cognitive level changes in brain function may appear as certain deficits in information processing. Genetic factors, family dynamics, urban living and maternal influenza all constitute risk factors. Remember, however, that the whole idea of schizophrenia as a single condition is controversial. There is, for example, a definite possibility that two distinct forms of schizophrenia exist, based on positive and negative symptoms, each of which has different causes, courses and outcomes.

1    Describe the clinical characteristics of schizophrenia (e.g. diagnostic criteria, different types of symptoms).

2    Describe one biological factor (genetics, biochemistry or neurology) that may be linked to the development of schizophrenia. What is the evidence for that biological factor?

3    Describe one psychological factor (e.g. cognitive processing) that may be linked to the development of schizophrenia. How strong is the evidence for that factor? What is the evidence for that psychological factor?

4    Discuss one social factor (e.g. urban living) that may be linked to the development of schizophrenia.

# 9

# Depression

what's ahead?

This chapter opens with a description of the clinical characteristics of depressive, seasonal and bipolar disorders, including details of diagnosis using the DSM system. The bulk of the chapter is devoted to theories of the origins of depression. Like schizophrenia, depression has important biological, psychological and social aspects, and there have been various theoretical attempts to explain it from the biomedical, cognitive and psychodynamic psychological perspectives. Social factors also appear to be important in depression, and we shall examine in particular social explanations of why depression affects women more commonly than men, and lower rather than higher socio-economic groups.

## Symptoms and phenomenology

We have almost certainly all described ourselves at some point as depressed. We might. for example feel sad, dejected or lonely. These feelings are a perfectly normal part of human existence, often in a response to losses and disappointments that we all encounter. Depression as a mental disorder is defined by a particular set of symptoms. Most professionals, particularly those writing from a medical perspective, tend to see *clinical depression* – depression that meets the criteria for psychiatric diagnosis – as a distinct condition, quite different from our everyday life experience of sadness.

### Categories of clinical depression

To receive a diagnosis of clinical depression, one must have a certain number of symptoms for a certain period of time. Both the ICD-10 and the DSM-IV make a distinction between *major depressive episode* or *major depressive disorder* and *dysthymia* or *dysthymic disorder*. Both also recognise an additional condition, bipolar depression, which is commonly called 'manic depression'.

## Major depressive disorder

The symptoms of major depression come and go in cycles. During a depressive episode, symptoms can be extremely severe. Most people who experience a major depressive episode go on to experience further episodes. Usually depressive episodes last from four to six months, but there are exceptions and some episodes last over a year. Thornicroft and Sartorius (1993) calculated that the average patient with major depression is depressed 27.5% of the time. The criteria for diagnosis of a major depressive episode according to the DSM-IV-TR are shown in Box 9.1.

---

**A**  Five (or more) of the following symptoms have been present during the same two-week period and represent a change from previous functioning; at least one of the symptoms is either (1) depressed mood or (2) loss of interest or pleasure.

**Note**: Do not include symptoms that are clearly due to a general medical condition, or mood-incongruent delusions or hallucinations.

(1) Depressed mood most of the day, nearly every day, as indicated by either subjective report (e.g. feels sad or empty) or observation made by others (e.g. appears tearful). **Note**: In children and adolescents, can be irritable mood.

(2) Markedly diminished interest or pleasure in all, or almost all, activities most of the day, nearly every day (as indicated by either subjective account or observation made by others).

(3) Significant weight loss when not dieting or weight gain (e.g. a change of more than 5% of body weight in a month), or decrease or increase in appetite nearly every day. **Note**: In children, consider failure to make expected weight gains.

(4) Insomnia or hypersomnia nearly every day.

(5) Psychomotor agitation or retardation nearly every day (observable by others, not merely subjective feelings of restlessness or being slowed down).

(6) Fatigue or loss of energy nearly every day.

(7) Feelings of worthlessness or excessive or inappropriate guilt (which may be delusional) nearly every day (not merely self-reproach or guilt about being sick).

(8) Diminished ability to think or concentrate, or indecisiveness, nearly every day (either by subjective account or as observed by others).

(9) Recurrent thoughts of death (not just fear of dying), recurrent suicidal ideation without a specific plan, or a suicide attempt or a specific plan for committing suicide.

**B**  The symptoms do not meet criteria for a mixed episode.

**C**  The symptoms cause clinically significant distress or impairment in social, occupational, or other important areas of functioning.

**D**  The symptoms are not due to the direct physiological effects of a substance (e.g. a drug of abuse, a medication), or a general medical condition (e.g. hypothyroidism).

**E**  The symptoms are not better accounted for by bereavement, i.e. after the loss of a loved one, the symptoms persist for longer than 2 months or are characterised by marked functional impairment, morbid preoccupation with worthlessness, suicidal ideation, psychotic symptoms, or psychomotor retardation.

---

**Box 9.1** DS MR-IV-TR criteria for a major depressive episode

## Dysthymia

In contrast to major depression, which is characterised by periods with no symptoms, followed by episodes of often severe depression, dysthymia involves constant but generally less severe symptoms. Depression must last for longer than two years for dysthymia to be diagnosed. Of course treatment of the symptoms can begin earlier. Dysthymia tends to be most severe in those in which it begins before age 21. Diagnostic criteria for dysthymia according to the DSM-IV-TR are shown in Box 9.2.

---

A   Depressed mood for most of the day, for more days than not, as indicated either by subjective account or observation by others, for at least 2 years.

**Note:** In children and adolescents, mood can be irritable and duration must be at least 1 year.

B   Presence, while depressed, of two (or more) of the following:

(1) Poor appetite or overeating
(2) Insomnia or hypersomnia
(3) Low energy or fatigue
(4) Low self-esteem
(5) Poor concentration or difficulty making decisions
(6) Feelings of hopelessness.

C   During the 2-year period of the disturbance (1 year for children or adolescents), the person has never been without the symptoms in Criteria A and B for more than 2 months at a time.

D   No major depressive episode has been present during the first 2 years of the disturbance (1 year for children and adolescents), i.e. the disturbance is not better accounted for by chronic major depressive disorder, or major depressive disorder, in partial remission.

**Note:** There may have been a previous major depressive episode provided there was a full remission (no significant signs or symptoms for 2 months) before development of the dysthymic disorder. In addition, after the initial 2 years (1 year in children or adolescents) of dysthymic disorder, there may be superimposed episodes of major depressive disorder, in which case both diagnoses may be given when the criteria are met for a major depressive episode.

E   There has never been a manic episode, a mixed episode, or a hypomanic episode and criteria have never been met for cyclothymic disorder.

F   The disturbance does not occur exclusively during the course of a chronic psychotic disorder, such as schizophrenia or delusional disorder.

G   The symptoms are not due to the direct physiological effects of a substance (e.g. a drug of abuse, a medication) or a general medical condition (e.g. hypothyroidism).

**Box 9.2** DS MR-IV-TR diagnostic criteria for dysthymic disorder

## Bipolar disorder

Bipolar disorder, more commonly known as manic depression, is diagnosed when patients suffer from episodes of *mania* (i.e. states of high arousal and irritability or excitement; the opposite of depressive symptoms). Goodwin and Jamison (1990) calculated that 72% of those diagnosed as having a manic episode also suffered depression. Periods of depression are not, however, necessary for a person to receive a diagnosis of bipolar disorder. Patients typically feel full of energy and they may feel elated or irritable. There is a reduced need for sleep and there may be an increased sexual appetite. Manic patients are often extremely impulsive and their judgement is impaired, for example leading to spending sprees and bizarre business schemes. Bipolar disorder is much less common than unipolar depression, occurring in 0.7–1.6% of the population. Box 9.3 shows the criteria according to DSM-IV-TR for a manic episode.

---

**A**  Presence of only one manic episode and no past major depressive episodes.

**Note**: Recurrence is defined as either a change in polarity from depression or an interval of at least 2 months without manic symptoms.

**B**  The manic episode is not better accounted for by schizoaffective disorder and is not superimposed on schizophrenia, schizophreniform disorder, delusional disorder, or psychotic disorder not otherwise specified.

Specify if:
**Mixed**: if symptoms meet criteria for a mixed episode.

If the full criteria are currently met for a manic, mixed, or major depressive episode, *specify* its current clinical status and/or features:

- **Mild, moderate, severe without psychotic features/severe with psychotic features.**

- **With catatonic features.**

- **With postpartum onset.**

If the full criteria are not currently met for a manic, mixed, or major depressive episode, *specify* the current clinical status of the bipolar I disorder or features of the most recent episode.

---

**Box 9.3** DSMR-IV-TR diagnostic criteria for a manic episode

## Seasonal Affective Disorder

*Seasonal Affective Disorder* (SAD) is a mood disorder experienced in the short days of winter by as many as 10% of the population (Ferenczi, 1997). As well as depression the symptoms of SAD include craving for high-carbohydrate foods and sleepiness. The frequency of SAD among people in latitudes where winter nights are very long suggests that it may be related to day length. In the lighter, longer days of spring and early summer the symptoms of SAD disappear.

During long winter nights secretion of a chemical called melatonin peaks then lowers as summer approaches. This pattern has tempted psychologists to search for a relationship between low exposure to light, high melatonin and SAD. This relationship is supported by the effectiveness of light therapy (see Figure 9.1). SAD sufferers exposed to intense artificial lighting (1000 lux or more) during the winter generally find relief from their depression. Even as little as half an hour a day is effective, lifting depression within a week. How this exposure to light affects mood is, however, unclear. Ferenczi (1997) has suggested that it may either reset the circadian cycle or increase the secretion of serotonin, which is also implicated in mood disorders. Light therapy is not effective in all cases, although failure may be attributable to misdiagnosis rather than ineffectual treatment. The timing of light sessions has been the subject of much research, and certainly simulated 'early dawn' is effective but brightness and total exposure, rather than timing, appear to be the key factors.

**Figure 9.1** A phototherapy box

# Biomedical theories of depression

In medical circles depression is widely regarded as a physical illness. Hammen (1997) suggests four types of circumstantial evidence why we might believe that depression is a biological condition:

- Some symptoms of depression are physical, for example disruption to sleep and appetite.

- Depression runs in families.

- Antidepressant medication reduces the symptoms of depression.

- We know that certain medical conditions and certain drugs induce depression.

At first glance these might seem pretty convincing. However, as Hammen points out, none of these facts is in itself particularly strong evidence for the biological nature of depression. It is well known than psychological factors can lead to physical symptoms; patterns of family interaction and the modelling of depressed behaviour can cause patterns of behaviour, thinking and feelings to be passed on through families. Just because depression can be induced and treated biologically, this does not mean that that is how depression naturally occurs.

## Evidence for a genetic element to depression

We have long known that the children of depressed parents are more vulnerable to depression than comparable children without depressed parents. The strongest evidence for a genetic element to depression comes from twin studies. McGuffin *et al.* (1996) obtained a sample of 214 pairs of twins, at least one of whom was being treated for major depression. They found that 46% of monozygotic (identical) twins and 20% of dizygotic (fraternal) twins of the patients had also suffered major depression, suggesting moderate genetic influence. Of course, identical twins may be reared more similarly than fraternal twins; therefore once again genes may not be the only factor affecting this finding. Silberg *et al.* (1999) examined both the role of genes and life events in a twin study.

# research
## now

## depression: genes, environment or both?

**Silberg, J. *et al.* (1999) The influence of genetic factors and life stress on depression among adolescent girls.** *Archives of General Psychiatry*, 56, 225–232

**Aim:** Previous twin studies have suggested a moderate role for genetic factors in the development of depression, but most have revealed little about the environmental factors that appear to be rather more important. Other lines of research have suggested that depression is a response to life events. The aim of this study was to assess both the role of genes and recent life events.

**Method:** 902 pairs of twins took part in the study: 182 girls and 237 boys of pre-pubertal age, 314 girls and 171 boys at puberty. The participants were taken from an ongoing project called the *Virginia Twin Study of Adolescent Behavioural Development*. Each adolescent completed a standard psychiatric interview to assess depression. Life events were measured both by a questionnaire given to the young people and an interview with their parents. Using this data it was possible to examine the importance of genes and recent life events, to see whether their importance differed between boys and girls, and to see how genes and life events worked together to cause depression.

**Results:** Overall, girls suffered more depression than boys. On average they were more susceptible to depression in response to recent life events. Interestingly, however, there were wider individual differences among girls in their response to life events, and girls who suffered depression after a negative life event were often those whose twin also suffered depression. This suggested an important role for genes in determining individual differences in vulnerability to depression in response to life events.

**Conclusions:** The study supported a role for both genes and environment (in the form of life events) in the development of depression. Importantly, it also tells us something about the way genes operate. It seems that rather than causing depression directly, genetic factors make us particularly susceptible to the depressing effects of life events.

The findings of Silberg *et al.* are particularly interesting because they suggest that there is not a gene for depression as such, but rather that some people are predisposed to be particularly vulnerable to depression when unpleasant things happen to them. Because there appear to be a number of neurochemical and neurological factors associated with depression, it seems likely that more than one gene may be involved. It also appears that the more severe the depression the greater the extent to which genes are involved. Kendler *et al.* (1992) carried out a twin study on sufferers of relatively mild major depressive disorder, and found little difference between the probability of identical and fraternal twins sharing depression (49% and 42% respectively). Compared with the wider disparity between identical and fraternal twins in the more severe cases looked at in the McGuffin *et al.* (1996) study, this suggests that milder depression may have little genetic influence whereas severe cases have a substantial genetic component.

Interestingly, although major depressive disorder and dysthymia are distinct disorders, the genetic influences on them may be the same. Klein *et al.* (1995) examined depression in the families of 100 patients suffering from dysthymia or major depression. They found that both dysthymia and major depression were more common in the families of *both* groups of patients than in the general population. Slightly different results are found in the case of bipolar disorder; the families of patients with unipolar disorder are at no increased risk from bipolar disorder than the rest of the population, although relatives of patients with bipolar disorder are at greater risk from unipolar disorder (Weissman, 1984). This suggests that bipolar disorder may be a particularly severe form of major depression rather than a distinct disorder. 80% of identical twins and only 16% of fraternal twins share bipolar disorder. Bipolar disorder thus appears to be rather more influenced by genes than unipolar depression.

## for and
## against

## a genetic basis to depression

**+** Twin studies have shown that depression is more likely to be shared by identical twins than fraternal twins.

**−** Twin studies suggest only a moderate genetic component to unipolar depression, especially in milder cases.

**−** Studies of gene–environment interaction suggest that rather than causing depression, genes influence how susceptible we are to the effects of life events.

**+** It appears that bipolar disorder has a larger genetic component than unipolar depression.

## Biochemical and neurological factors

The *monoamine* neurotransmitters noradrenaline, dopamine and serotonin appear to be present in lower levels in depressed patients than in the rest of the population. The main evidence for this comes from the action of antidepressant drugs, which are known to increase monoamine levels and to relieve the symptoms of depression. Monoamine oxidase inhibitors prevent the de-activation of the monoamines in the synapse, thus increasing their effectiveness. Serotonin re-uptake inhibitors (such as Prozac) prevent the synaptic reuptake of serotonin, thus increasing the effectiveness of serotonin alone. Furthermore, reserpine, a drug which is used for the treatment of hypertension, but which also lowers levels of serotonin and noradrenaline, induces the symptoms of depression (Lemieux *et al.*, 1965).

The role of the chemical 5-HT in depression has been strongly supported by metabolite studies. Depressed patients show lower levels of the serotonin metabolite, 5-H1AA, in cerebrospinal fluid than in controls, strongly suggesting that they have lowered levels of serotonin (McNeal and Cimbolic, 1986). It appears that the association of serotonin with mood is not a direct effect, but rather occurs because of the role of serotonin in regulating the other monoamines (Barlow and Durand, 1999).

Recent research has focused on the role of noradrenaline, which may directly affect mood. Some new antidepressant drugs (e.g. reboxetine) work by increasing the action of noradrenaline, thus supporting the importance of noradrenaline (Moffaert and Dierick, 1999). Further evidence for the importance of noradrenaline in depression comes from a post-mortem study by Klimek *et al.* (1997). They compared an area of the brain called the locus coeruleus, which produces noradrenaline, in 15 sufferers of major depression with that in 15 control participants, and found significant differences in structure. This suggests that production of noradrenaline may be impaired in depression.

Although research has firmly established that depression is associated with biochemical abnormalities, and although our understanding of the role of particular chemicals is growing, this does *not* necessarily mean that depression is a direct result of biochemical abnormality. A strict biomedical explanation for depression might be that genetic factors directly lead to abnormal production of monoamines. However, we know from twin studies that genes are less important than environmental factors in depression. It is thus safer to think of biochemical factors as being involved in depression and contributing to its symptoms rather than being its general cause.

Neurological factors have also been identified in depression. We have already noted the possible role of the locus coeruleus in noradrenaline production. Other studies have suggested a role for the frontal lobes, the region at the front of the brain cortex particularly involved in thinking. Coffey (1993) compared the size of the frontal lobes in depressed patients and non-depressed controls using MRI scanning technology, and found that the mean frontal lobe volume in the depressed patients was significantly smaller. A recent PET scan study by Milo *et al.* (2001) has also shown that the frontal lobes in depressed patients do not draw on blood flow in the brain as they do normally (this is called *hypoperfusion*). Interestingly, Milo *et al.* found that blood flow to the frontal lobes improved immediately following ECT (see p. 38 for a discussion of ECT), suggesting that this might be the mechanism by which ECT works.

## for and against

## biochemical and neurological models of depression

**+** There is substantial evidence from drug trials and from post-mortem studies that depression is associated with biochemical abnormalities.

**+** There is also substantial evidence from brain scanning studies that the frontal lobes of the brain are less active in depression.

**—** There is little evidence to suggest that biochemical and neurological abnormalities are causes rather than features of depression.

## where to now?

**The following are good sources of further information on the biochemical and neurological models of depression:**

▷ **Plomin, R. *et al.* (1997) *Behavioural Genetics*. New York: Freeman** – contains an excellent discussion of the role of genes in depression.

▷ **Hammen, C. (1997) *Depression*. Hove: Psychology Press** – a very clearly written book containing good sections on the genetic, biochemical and neurological aspects of depression.

▷ **Barlow, D.H. and Durand, V.M. (1999) *Abnormal Psychology*. Pacific Grove: Brooks/Cole** – a very good general text on atypical psychology with a useful chapter on depression, discussing genetic, biochemical and neurological models.

# Psychological theories of depression

As for schizophrenia, the cognitive and psychodynamic models are probably the most helpful psychological approaches to understanding depression. Interestingly, although there are differences in emphasis, the cognitive and psychodynamic models of depression are similar in that they both see depression as a result of early experience. Cognitive theories are concerned with the way depressed patients think, which is characterised by a highly negative outlook and a sense of hopelessness. Psychodynamic theories are more concerned with the emotional impact of early relationship-based experiences, for example significant losses and insecure attachment.

## The psychodynamic approach

### Freudian theory

From the psychodynamic perspective, the most important determinants of later mental health are the quality of parent–child relationships and the patterns of family interaction. Freud (1917) proposed that many cases of depression were due to biological factors. However, Freud also believed that some cases of depression could be linked to experiences of loss of, or rejection by, a parent. Freud drew a parallel between the feelings we have as adults when in mourning for a lost loved one and the experience of depression years after a childhood loss experience. An important part of adult mourning is anger, and Freud proposed that the same anger is important in children's responses to loss. The child's anger at being 'abandoned' through separation or rejection cannot be expressed because of love for the object of the anger, and instead is repressed, turning inwards and causing guilt and low self-esteem as the ego 'rages against itself' (Freud, 1917, p. 257).

Freud's theory of depression provides an alternative to the biomedical model in explaining depressive symptoms. Whereas the biomedical model might explain disruption to appetite in terms of the effects of monoamine disruption, Freud suggested that it is the result of regression to early childhood where nurturance is associated with the primary carer and, following their loss, is not present. The lack of energy associated with depression can be explained according to Freud's *hydraulic model* of the mind (see p. 83 for a discussion), as energy is expended in maintaining the repression of the rage against the abandoning loved one.

Although in some ways Freud's account appears dated, for example in his use of the hydraulic model, Champion and Power (2000) suggest that Freudian theory is still helpful in contemporary psychology in two ways: it draws our attention to the links between loss and depression and it links depression and anger. We can examine research into both these ideas. There is a substantial body of research into the relationship between early loss experiences and later depression, and in general results have supported Freud's view that early loss predicts later depression. In one recent study, Maier and Lachman (2000) surveyed 2998 adults aged 30–60 by questionnaire and telephone interview. They found that symptoms of depression were more common in those who had lost a parent in childhood by divorce or death. Particularly interesting in view of Freudian theory was the finding that self-acceptance was sharply lower in those who reported an early loss experience.

Research into the link between anger and depression has produced partial support for Freud. Swaffer and Hollin (2001) gave 100 young offenders questionnaires to assess anger and health. Depression, along with general health, was associated with levels of anger, those who suppressed their anger having a greater tendency for depression. This association between depression and anger has also been found in different types of study. In a study of the psychological factors underlying headaches Venable *et al.* (2001) found that headaches were associated with both suppressed anger and depression. Both these studies suggest that Freud was correct to propose a link between depression and anger, however they do not provide *direct* support for the idea that loss causes anger, which is turned inwards leading to depression.

### Attachment theory

A number of studies have found that type C attachment, which is characterised by anxiety and aggression in children and preoccupation with and difficulty in discussing attachment relationships in adulthood, is associated with depression (e.g. Rosenstein and Horowitz, 1996). Other studies have found that depression is more associated with type A attachment, being characterised by avoidant behaviour in childhood and dismissal of the importance of attachment in adulthood (e.g. Patrick *et al.*, 1994). Type D attachment, which is associated with an unresolved attachment-related trauma such as abuse or neglect by the primary carer, also increases the risk of suffering depression. Bowlby (1980) suggested that insecure attachment predisposes people to depression for a number of reasons. Children who fail to form secure attachments never internalise a working model of themselves as lovable, hence suffer low self-esteem. They also develop working models of others as rejecting and hostile, meaning that they come to expect this in future relationships. A child who develops internal working models of themselves as unlovable and of others as unloving exists in an essentially loveless world, a situation we are not psychologically equipped to deal with.

Attachment theory represents a compromise between traditional Freudian theory and more mainstream non-psychodynamic perspectives on depression. It explains the emotional impact of early experiences without reliance on the outdated hydraulic model. A limitation of the attachment approach to depression is that most studies have been retrospective, assessing attachment type in adulthood, once symptoms are established. Unfortunately, one of the symptoms of depression is a negative outlook on life, and it seems possible that this general negativity may at least partially explain why sufferers of depression report insecure attachments.

## for and against

## the psychodynamic model of depression

+ Depression is associated with early trauma and disruption to early relationships.

+ In keeping with Freudian theory, early experiences of loss predict depression in adulthood.

– Although depression is associated with suppressed anger, it is difficult to directly test Freud's idea that anger at early loss becomes turned inward against the self.

– It is unclear to what extent the effects of early loss are emotional in nature as opposed to cognitive and behavioural.

## The cognitive approach

Psychologists adopting a cognitive approach to depression would generally not quibble with Freud's idea that early loss predisposes us to later depression. However, cognitive theory differs in rejecting the Freudian emphasis on emotion and focusing instead on the effects on the developing child's thinking. Cognitive–behavioural therapy differs as well from psychodynamic therapy in ignoring the developmental history of the individual and focusing on altering the types of cognition that characterise depression. The rationale is that by making people think in more positive ways we can make them feel better.

### Beck's theory

Aaron Beck (1976) described in detail the irrational thinking that characterises depression in his cognitive theory. Beck proposed three factors that contribute to a person's *cognitive vulnerability* to depression. Cognitive vulnerability refers to the ways in which our individual style of thinking and responding to information makes us more or less vulnerable to depression. These three factors are the cognitive triad of negative automatic thinking, faulty information processing and negative self-schemas.

### The cognitive triad

Beck identified three types of very negative thoughts that appeared to be automatic in depressed patients. These are a negative view of self, negative view of the world and negative view of the future. The cognitive triad is shown in Figure 9.2.

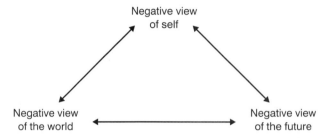

**Figure 9.2** Beck's cognitive triad of automatic thoughts

Beck called these *automatic* thoughts because they occur spontaneously. You can imagine that it would be at best discouraging, at worst disabling, to be plagued with hopeless and self-critical thoughts.

### Faulty information processing

Beck proposed that depressed people tend to selectively attend to the negative aspects of a situation and ignore the positive aspects. This leads to a tendency to overestimate the 'downside' of any situation. We are all illogical in that we attend to some stimuli and not others, and in that we jump to conclusions. The illogic of depression is of a particularly unfortunate kind – the depressive attends to the negative and jumps to the most negative possible conclusions.

### Negative self-schemas

Schemas are packets of information in which our knowledge of each aspect of the world is contained. The self-schema contains all our information, beliefs, etc. concerning ourselves. Beck suggested that in childhood we acquire a negative set of beliefs about ourselves through experiences of negative or critical parents. We interpret new information relevant to our beliefs about ourselves in the light of our existing self-beliefs. Any situation that requires us to examine information relevant to ourselves will activate the self-schema, and bring to mind those negative beliefs. Once we have a negative self-schema, it becomes difficult for us to interpret any new information about ourselves positively.

### Research into Beck's theory

It is a simple matter to demonstrate that depressed people display faulty information processing and negative thinking. However, this is only of limited use to us as these may be symptoms of depression rather than causes. One way of testing Beck's theory is to examine the incidence of depression in people with different levels of cognitive vulnerability. In one recent study Grazioli and Terry (2000) assessed cognitive vulnerability in 65 women in the third trimester of their pregnancy and found that those with high levels of cognitive vulnerability were more likely to suffer post-natal depression.

Research has also supported Beck's notion of faulty information processing in depression, at least in major depression. Perez *et al.* (1999) compared sufferers of major depression with non-depressed participants in whom a sad mood had been induced by playing sad music and recalling unhappy memories on a Stroop task involving unhappy stimuli. The major depressive group, but not the sad-mood participants, paid significantly more attention to unhappy words in the Stroop task. This phenomenon, where depressed people pay more attention to unhappy stimuli, is called *negative attentional bias*.

Beck's idea that early experience leads to the formation of negative schemas is further supported. In a recent study by Parker *et al.* (2000) 96 depressed patients whose self-reports of their symptoms included the idea of a negative schema being activated under certain circumstances were interviewed about their early experiences. There were significant associations between reports of early experiences and the existence of maladaptive schemas that were in turn associated with the experience of depression. This suggests that early experiences do induce cognitive vulnerability; however, remember that psychodynamic theories can explain the link between early experience and later depression in other ways, and certainly account more easily for the link between early experience, depression and anger. Beck's theory may therefore not be a complete explanation of the experience–depression link.

what's
new ?

## the hopelessness model of depression

There have been newer cognitive models of depression since the pioneering work of Beck. Abramson *et al.* (1989) put forward the *hopelessness model*, in which hopelessness is seen as the main negative cognition underlying depression.

Hopelessness consists of two elements: negative expectations of the likelihood of positive events and negative beliefs about the ability of the individual to influence events (helplessness). When the vulnerable individual experiences a negative life event they feel helpless to respond to it, and this helplessness leads to the sense of hopelessness that directly causes depression. Once they are in the pattern of experiencing negative events and not being able to respond positively to them, a general sense of hopelessness results. Note that Abramson *et al.* were not aiming to explain all depression by this model, but rather to identify a particular group of people who are particularly vulnerable.

Following up the idea that there is a subset of people who suffer from a lack of hope, Rose *et al.* investigated the characteristics of people who displayed hopelessness. They found that hopeless people were particularly likely to have a diagnosis of personality disorder, have suffered sexual abuse and a highly controlling family. These last two are critical as they are both circumstances in which the person will have experienced profound helplessness in childhood. It thus appears that childhood experiences in which the child experiences long-term helplessness in the face of negative events leads to their learning a helpless and hopeless cognitive style.

In general, research has supported the role of hopelessness in depression. Kapci (1998) tested the idea that depressive symptoms follow a helpless response to life events. 34 depressed and 36 non-depressed participants completed the Beck Depression Inventory, a standard test for depression, and a 'hopelessness scale' on two occasions, three months apart. On the second occasion they also completed a questionnaire to assess their recent life events. It was found that worsened depression was associated with negative life events, in particular in those who scored high on helplessness and hopelessness, suggesting that the helpless response to the life events led to an increase in depression. Joiner (2000) tested the same idea in 9–17-year-old children in psychiatric care. Once again, both negative life events and a sense of hopelessness preceded worsening in symptoms.

## for and against

# the cognitive approach

**+** There is strong support for the idea that depression is associated with negative thinking.

**+** There is also strong support for the idea that early experience can lead to the negative cognitive style that predisposes people to depression.

**–** Cognitive theories fail to neatly explain the link between depression and anger. They thus probably give an incomplete understanding of depression.

## where to now?

**The following are good sources of further information on psychological approaches to depression:**

▶ **Champion, L. and Power, M. (2000)** *Adult Psychological Problems*. **Hove: Taylor and Francis** – an excellent general text on psychopathology, particularly strong on psychological models.

▶ **Comer, R.J. (1995)** *Abnormal Psychology*. **Freeman: New York** – again, a good general text on atypical psychology, with some useful material on psychological models of depression.

## interactive angles

The cognitive and psychodynamic models of depression are similar in that they both explain depression as a response to early experiences of loss.

### Questions

**1** How do the two approaches differ?

**2** Do you think either model has a distinct advantage over the other?

## Social factors in depression

The distinction between social and psychological factors in depression is a tricky one. In this chapter we have classified social factors as those that involve social interaction, whether this takes place on an individual or societal level. A classic study by Brown and Harris (1978) demonstrates the impact of social factors on the individual. We can look at this study in *classic research*.

Brown, Harris and colleagues continued to research social factors in depression, and Brown (1996) has summarised their overall conclusions. Depression is strongly associated with negative life events. Some individuals are particularly vulnerable to depression following life events as a result of both psychological factors such as cognitive vulnerability, low self-esteem and a history of loss experiences (discussed earlier in the chapter). *Social factors* such as lack of social support, low socio-economic status, unemployment and family discord also lead some people to be especially vulnerable.

# classic
## research

# life experiences, social support and depression

**Brown, G.W. and Harris, T.O. (1978)** *The Social Origins of Depression: A Study of Psychiatric Disorder in Women*. London: Tavistock

**Aim:** Brown and Harris (1978) aimed to investigate the link between depression and both current and past life events in the lives of sufferers. They focused on working-class women, as women tend to experience more depression than men, and because working-class people tend to experience more stress than middle class.

**Method:** A complex structured interview called the Life Events and Difficulties Scale (LEDS) was developed and interviewers were trained in its use. 539 women in Camberwell, London were interviewed using the LEDS. Interviewers obtained details of what stressful events had occurred in the previous year, along with the background circumstances in which they occurred. The LEDS also aimed to uncover stressful childhood events. Interviewers had to prepare a written account of each event of source of stress, which could be rated by a panel of researchers as how stressful it would be for a typical person. To avoid bias, these raters had no knowledge of whether the person they were looking at had suffered depression. It was later ascertained which interviewees suffered from depression. Researchers then looked for associations between who suffered depression, who had recently had a stressful life or who had had stressful events in their childhood.

**Results:** It emerged that both recent high levels of stress and having suffered a stressful childhood event left people particularly vulnerable to depression. 80% of the women who suffered depression had had a major stressful life event in the previous year, as opposed to 40% of those who did not suffer depression. Three of the four factors that had the strongest associations with depression involved recent levels of stress. These were the lack of an intimate relationship, lack of paid employment and the presence of three or more children in the home. However, childhood events were also important, especially the death of the woman's mother before she reached the age of 11.

**Conclusions:** It was concluded that there was a link between recent negative life events and the onset of depression. It was also concluded that loss in childhood, especially of the mother, also made women more vulnerable to depression. Lack of social support and family discord made women more vulnerable to depression.

## Socio-economic status and depression

Most mental disorders are found more frequently in lower socio-economic groups, and this is certainly true of depression. In Chapter 7, which deals with social models of psychopathology, we talked about social drift and social causation as explanations for this relationship. To briefly recap, social causation is the idea that low socio-economic status (SES) causes psychopathology, whereas social drift is the idea that individuals and families with mental disorders tend to drift into lower socio-economic groups. Ritsher *et al.* (2001) tested for social causation and drift effects in a study of 756 participants across two generations. It was found that low parental educational level was associated with increased rates of depression in the following generation even when there was previously no depression in the family history. Parental depression did not predict lower SES in offspring. The study thus supports the role of causation and fails to support a role for social drift in depression.

A number of explanations have been proposed for why depression should be associated with low SES. A study by Lupien *et al.* (2000) suggests that high levels of stress in parents affect children's development by affecting their own levels of stress. A total of 139 mothers were regularly assessed for stress and depression by telephone interview. Their children (217 in total) were assessed for salivary cortisol levels (a measure of stress) and for cognitive functioning. Low SES mothers reported more stress, which in turn was reflected in the cortisol levels and cognitive functioning of their children. It seems that the stressed low SES mothers in some way transmitted this stress to their children, and it seems likely that this early stress contributes to later depression. So how might this transmission of stress from one generation to the next take place? One explanation might lie in parenting styles. Radziszewska *et al.* (1996) compared rates of depression in 15 year olds whose parents had adopted different parenting styles. The lowest rates of depression were found in *authoritative* parents (who adopted firm but kind strategies with a degree of democracy) and the highest rates in *unengaged* parents who took little interest in their children's behaviour (Figure 9.3). Authoritarian (strict and harsh) and permissive (few rules or boundaries) parents had children with intermediate levels of depression. Authoritative parenting was most frequent in the higher socio-economic groups, perhaps because this is the most time-consuming and demanding style of parenting and is very difficult to maintain in the face of the high levels of stress experienced by low SES parents.

**Figure 9.3** Unengaged parenting is associated with depression

## Gender and depression: feminist perspectives

A consistent finding is that depression is more common in women than in men (Weissman and Olfson, 1995; Culbertson, 1997). Precise figures are difficult to come by but it seems that depression is two to three times more common in women. This *could* be explained from a biological perspective, in which depression rates are attributed to genetic and hormonal sex differences. However, feminist psychologists have generally adopted a more social approach, emphasising a number of ways in which women are socially disadvantaged compared with men.

We have already looked at the work of Brown, Harris and colleagues, who have extensively researched depression in women, and found links with early loss, recent life events and current social support. From a feminist perspective, Stoppard (2000) has attacked the Brown and Harris approach for tackling depression only at the level of the individual and for neglecting the reasons why women experience so many negative life events and have inadequate social support. These factors are undoubtedly linked, at least in part, to discrimination against women.

Discrimination against women begins early in their lives. Women are about twice as likely as men to suffer sexual abuse in childhood and this pattern of victimisation is maintained in adulthood, where women make up the overwhelming majority of victims of physical assault (Koss *et al.*, 1994). Recall from Chapter 5, which deals with psychodynamic approaches to mental disorder, that sexual abuse is associated with a range of psychological problems including depression. The lower average earnings of women further contribute to a sense of helplessness and practical difficulties in leaving violent relationships (Stoppard, 2000).

A further factor that appears to be implicated in the higher rates of depression in women is the manner in which men and women respond to the experience of psychological distress. In European and American societies, where women suffer more depression than men, it is also the case that it is the social norm for women to respond passively to distress. By contrast, it is more socially acceptable for men to respond actively to distress, for example by alcohol abuse and physical aggression. It seems likely that the passive responses that our culture encourages in women increase the likelihood of depression. Support for this explanation of depression comes from statistics showing that the lower rates of depression in men are matched by higher rates of drug abuse and violent crime in men (Rogers and Pilgrim, 1996).

## where to now?

The following are good sources of further information about social factors and depression:

▶ Brown, R. (1996) Life events, loss and depressive disorders. In: Heller T *et al*. (eds) *Mental Health Matters*. Basingstoke: Macmillan – a review of the Brown and Harris tradition of research.

▶ Stoppard, J.M. (2000) *Understanding Depression: Feminist Social Constructionist Approaches*. London: Routledge – an advanced and detailed account of the possible factors influencing the higher incidence of depression in women.

## Conclusions

There are a number of categories of mood disorder. Whilst these are probably influenced by both genes and environment it appears that genes are more important in the origins of bipolar disorder and more severe cases of major depression. Both brain chemistry and structure appear to be involved in depression, and depression can be treated with drugs, which compensate for the biochemical abnormalities. However, it is not clear to what extent these biological factors are underlying causes of depression and to what extent they are symptoms.

It seems that in most cases of depression the environment is more critical than genes. Experiences of early loss are particularly associated with later depression – a finding compatible with both the major psychological models of depression, the psychodynamic and cognitive approaches. These models differ however in their interpretation of how early experience leads to depression. Social factors are also important in depression. At the individual level, lack of social support and negative life events influence depression. At the societal level low socio-economic status is associated with depression, perhaps because it generates stress in parents, which in turn affects parenting style and so children's development. Women suffer depression more frequently than men. From a feminist perspective this is at least partially a result of social inequalities, which lead women to have more stressful lives, less opportunity to change them and fewer opportunities to respond actively to distress.

1   Discuss the importance of biological factors (e.g. genes, biochemistry and neurology) in the origins of depression.

2   Compare the evidence to support cognitive and psychodynamic models of depression.

3   How important are social factors in the origin of depression?

# 10

# Eating Disorders

what's
ahead?

This chapter will explore two of the more common eating disorders, anorexia and bulimia. The chapter begins with a description of the symptoms and clinical characteristics of anorexia and bulimia before moving on to consider a diverse range of factors which may cause these disorders. Our section on social perspectives deals with the influence of body image in Western culture with a particular emphasis on the feminist position. The section on psychological perspectives looks at two mainstream approaches, psychodynamic and cognitive. Finally we examine the role of genetic, biochemical and neurological factors in the development of eating disorders.

## Symptoms and phenomenology

*Anorexia nervosa* is a condition in which individuals have an intense preoccupation with body size and a distorted body image. Even those individuals who are emaciated feel fat. The incidence of anorexia rose markedly in late twentieth-century Western society, leading some researchers to believe that the disorder is a cultural product of this historical period, but not everyone agrees with this view. Colman (1993) argues that, contrary to popular belief, anorexia is not a new disorder. He points to historical medical records showing disorders characterised by extreme weight loss and a refusal to eat were diagnosed as long ago as the eleventh century. However, such a view ignores the possibility that people's experiences and actions had different meanings in different historical periods (Putwain *et al.*, 2000). In the late twentieth century, anorexia is bound up with cultural standards of beauty, but this does not mean that similar disorders in the eleventh century were too.

The term anorexia nervosa was first used in the medical literature in 1874 by Sir William Gull of Guy's Hospital, London. *Anorexia* comes from a

**Figure 10.1** In the Middle Ages anorexia was associated with religious piety rather than a belief in being overweight

Greek term meaning severe loss of weight, and *nervosa* meaning for emotional reasons. There are no universally accepted diagnostic criteria for anorexia and, according to Colman (1993), most doctors diagnose on the basis of intuition rather than by applying rigorous diagnostic criteria. According to DSM-IV-TR, anorexia is diagnosed when an individual has lost 15% of their body weight and refuses to eat (see Box 10.1). These individuals are obsessed with food and some will engage in frantic exercise to shed imaginary fat. They fear a loss of control, show a lack of inner resources and self-esteem, a fear of sexuality and of being controlled by others. In addition to abnormal eating attitudes and behaviour, there are other outward signs of anorexia, many of which are the physical consequences of starvation. These include a loss of menstruation, low blood pressure and insomnia.

---

A   Refusal to maintain body weight at or above a minimal normal weight for age and height (e.g. weight loss leading to maintenance of body weight less than 85% of that expected or failure to make expected weight gain during period of growth, leading to body weight less than 85% of that expected).

B   Intense fear of gaining weight, or becoming fat, even though underweight.

C   Disturbance in the way in which one's body weight or shape is experienced, undue influence of body weight or shape on self-evaluation, or denial of the seriousness of the current low body weight.

D   Amenhorroea, the absence of at least three consecutive menstrual cycles.

---

**Box 10.1** DSM-IV-TR criteria for anorexia (American Psychiatric Association, 2000)

According to Colman (1993) two factors make it difficult to establish the prevalence of anorexia. First, it is difficult to draw a line between excessive dieting (which is very popular) and mild cases of anorexia. Second, most anorexic individuals deny their symptoms and claim there is nothing wrong with them other than being too fat. Between 90 and 95% of cases are female, the disorder is more common in adolescents than other age groups and two thirds of reported cases belong to the top two social classes (professional and managerial) even though they only make up one-fifth of the population. Anorexia seems to take a prolonged course, although the outcome is mixed (see Table 10.1).

| | |
|---|---|
| Fully recovered | 69% |
| Met full criteria for anorexia | 3% |
| Met full criteria for bulimia | 5% |
| Died | 0% |

**Table 10.1** Results of a 10-year follow-up of individuals diagnosed with anorexia (Herpertz-Dahlmann *et al.*, 2001)

During the 1970s reports began to appear of an eating disorder related to anorexia that had not been previously described. This was termed *bulimia nervosa*. Individuals with bulimia are also concerned with body image, with an intense fear of becoming fat although, unlike anorexics, the bulimic individual does not necessarily have a low weight. Originally bulimia nervosa was considered as an attachment to anorexia, but under DSM-IV-TR the disorder is considered as separate (see Box 10.2). Affected individuals feel intense anxiety after eating and induce vomiting or use laxatives to avoid weight gain, which is followed by feelings of shame, guilt, depression and a lack of control.

---

1   Recurrent episodes of binge eating (rapid consumption of a large amount of food in a discrete period of time, usually less than two hours).
2   At least three of the following:
    i.   consumption of high-calorie, easily ingested food during a binge
    ii.  inconspicuous eating during a binge
    iii. termination of such eating by abdominal pain, sleep or self-induced vomiting
    iv.  repeated attempts to lose weight by severely restricting diets, self-induced vomiting, or the use of cathartics or diuretics
    v.   frequent weight fluctuations greater than 10 pounds due to alternating binges and fasts.
3   Awareness that the eating pattern is abnormal and fear of not being able to stop eating voluntarily.
4   Depressed mood and self-depreciating thoughts following eating binges.
5   The bulimic episodes are not due to anorexia nervosa or any known physical disorder.

**Box 10.2** DSM-IV-TR criteria for bulimia (American Psychiatric Association, 2000)

---

Estimating the prevalence of bulimia is even more difficult than for anorexia as bulimic individuals may have normal body weight and size and because the bulimic individual may be very secretive about their bizarre eating habits. A 1980 survey by *Cosmopolitan* magazine invited letters from readers who used vomiting as a means of weight control. An analysis revealed that 83% of respondents met diagnostic criteria for bulimia (Fairburn, 1982). Another study of visitors to a family planning clinic revealed a 1.9% incidence of bulimia, a figure which tallies with American studies of college students. This evidence suggests that bulimia is more common than anorexia. The vast majority (99%) of reported cases are female, most sufferers belong to social classes one and two (managerial and professional) and the condition tends to develop in the early twenties.

Frequent vomiting or laxative abuse can also lead to physical problems including severe tooth decay, and stomach rupture. The loss of body fluids can cause cardiac problems, epileptic seizures and kidney damage. Half of the individuals with anorexia also show the features of bulimia and are referred to as bulimarexics.

Initially it was believed that eating disorders had a purely psychological cause, but since the 1950s it has been generally accepted that the disorder stems from an interaction of psychological, physical and social roots.

what's new?

## binge eating disorder

As we have already said, anorexia appears to have been around for many years, but bulimia has only been recognised as a separate disorder since the 1970s. Over the past decade, much of the attention of eating disorders researchers has shifted to the phenomenon of binge eating in the absence of bulimia. Currently binge eating without other bulimic symptoms is not classified as an eating disorder in ICD-10, although it does appear in the DSM-IV-TR.

According to a large community survey by Spitzer et al. (1993), up to 30% of overweight Americans and 2% of the whole population indulge in binge eating behaviour. In a minority of cases, binge eating disorder (or BED) also occurs in normal-weight individuals. If we were to accept binge eating as an eating disorder, it would be more common than anorexia and bulimia put together.

Proper procedures for recognising and treating BED have the potential to save a large number of lives. Currently in Britain BED is not widely recognised by doctors or dieticians. This is a serious problem because conventional treatments for obesity, such as dieting, appear to make BED worse. This means that sufferers, being overweight, frequently receive the worst possible medical advice (Romano and Quinn, 1995). Binge eating can be distinguished from over-eating by the consumption of large volumes of food in short periods, accompanied by a sense of being out of control and feelings of shame or guilt.

Binge eating presents psychologists with something of a problem. Behavioural therapies have been found to be ineffective and in fact may worsen the problem. It seems likely that psychodynamic and cognitive–behavioural therapies may be more successful, although there is currently a lack of evidence for this.

## Theories of eating disorders

Although anorexia and bulimia are considered as separate disorders under DSM-IV-TR, and have separate diagnostic criteria, this distinction has not really been matched in the academic literature. Anorexia and bulimia are almost treated as if they were different manifestations of the same disorder. Therefore the theories outlined below can be considered as explanations of both anorexia and bulimia, unless specified otherwise. The section on social perspectives will consider the role of contemporary culture in providing idealised images of beauty and a radical perspective offered by feminist psychotherapist Colleen Heenan. The section on psychological perspectives will consider the more individualistic explanations offered by the more mainstream cognitive and psychodynamic approaches. Finally, the section on physiological perspectives will consider the role of genetic and neurological factors in the development of eating disorders.

## Social perspectives

The two social perspectives explored here are closely linked by the assumption that eating disorders originate not in the mind or body of the individual but in social processes. The *socio-cultural approach* focuses on the impact of changing cultural ideas of beauty and the role of the media in bringing these ideas to the individual. *Feminist theory* takes this a logical stage further and shows how cultural ideas of beauty have been used to oppress women.

### The socio-cultural approach

According to socio-cultural theory, anorexia and bulimia are caused by pressure in Western society to conform to an idealised notion of beauty. For women, there is an ideal shape presented by models and film stars, which has become more and more thin over the past 30 years. For example, Owen and Laurel-Seller (2000) examined the vital statistics of Playboy Centrefolds from 1985 to 1997 and found that 53.2% of the models were underweight, 46% severely underweight and 30.5% reached the weight criteria for anorexia. The average bust and hip measurement did not change much over this period; however, as the models were becoming taller, they were becoming more underweight.

In 1959 the average model weighed 9% less than the average weight for their height (Garner *et al.*, 1980) and by 1997 they weighed 17% less than the average for their height. In conclusion, the centrefolds of today are thinner and weigh less than the centrefolds of the 1960s and 1970s (Figure 10.2). This is in contrast to the average weight of the female population, which has increased in the same period. The social pressure to become and stay slim has increased as the average woman has drifted further away from the cultural ideal.

The theory is supported by research showing that anorexia and bulimia are more common in Western industrialised countries than in non-industrialised countries, where a more rounded body shape is preferred (Hsu, 1990). Furthermore, Arab and Asian women are more likely to develop eating disorders if they move to the West (Mumford *et al.*, 1991). Similarly, the rate of anorexia is increasing for Chinese residents in Hong Kong, coinciding with a culture slowly becoming more westernised (Lai, 2000).

**Figure 10.2** Models have become much thinner over the last few decades

Within Western society, socio-cultural theory predicts a higher incidence of eating disorders for groups where a premium is placed on thinness, and evidence tends to support this prediction. Crisp *et al.* (1976) surveyed 16–18-year-old London schoolgirls and found that dancers and fashion models were more likely to develop the disorder. This theory can also potentially explain the gradual increase in the incidence of anorexia and bulimia in men as idealised notions of male beauty become more commonplace in the media.

Although the evidence seems to suggest that exposure to an idealised body image is linked to an increase in eating disorders, only a fraction of the people in Western culture exposed to these idealised media images go on to develop eating disorders. These images might prompt some excessive dieting but, as mentioned earlier, this is not necessarily the same as an eating disorder. As a result most researchers conclude that this theory can be only a contributory factor in the development of anorexia and bulimia.

# for and against

## socio-cultural theory

**+** In the West, idealised notions of body shape presented in the media have become more and more thin over the past 30 years.

**+** Anorexia and bulimia are more common in Western countries and individuals who live in the East are more likely to develop an eating disorder if they move to the West.

**–** Only a fraction of the people exposed to these images develop eating disorders, so idealised notions of body image can only be a contributory factor to eating disorders.

# media watch

## Are eating disorders a female disorder?

In 1991, 5% of sufferers with eating disorders were men, by 1999 that figure had doubled to 10%, which has prompted the question over why more men are developing the disorder. One suggestion is that in the past decade there has been a decline in societal double standards over body size; now men are under pressure to have an ideal body image. However, there are differences in how the disorder manifests itself. Girls tend to develop the disorder at a younger age than boys and although like girls, boys are more likely to develop bulimia rather than anorexia, they are more likely to exercise obsessively whereas girls are more likely to use laxatives. One alternative explanation is that men have always suffered from eating disorders but that in the past ten years they have become more likely to report it.

*Psychology Today* (July/August, 1999)

## Questions

**1** What theories of eating disorders might best explain the greater incidence of eating problems in girls?

**2** What reasons can you think of to explain the increasing incidence of eating problems in boys?

### The feminist approach

Most people with eating disorders are female, yet traditional social, psychological and physiological models fail to contextualise eating disorders in terms of gender, or how culture or history may contribute to the gendered nature of eating disorders (Heenan, 1996a). What makes the feminist approach different from other models is that it attends to the dynamics of gender and power in culture and society. From a feminist position, there must be more to anorexia and bulimia than simply conforming to social pressure to be thin.

Heenan (1996a) argues that the size and shape of a woman's body reflects changing historical and economic trends. Eating disorders are a physical expression of the contradictions facing women in attempting to meet their emotional needs, symbolised through food and body image. Orbach (1986) argues that cultural representations of femininity involve instances of self-denial. In order to be feminine, a woman must ignore her own emotional needs and attend to the needs of others. Women therefore become 'starved' of affection.

The cultural representations of thinness replicates self-denial as seen in phrases such as 'naughty but nice', 'tempting but I shouldn't' and so forth. Our culture markets food for consumption, but simultaneously denies its consumption. Eating disorders arise out of this social context and removing eating disorders from this context functions to 'problematise' women. From a feminist perspective, the symptoms of eating disorders are interpreted as expressions of living in a society that promotes this self-denial.

> Women who starve themselves, binge and vomit or eat compulsively can be understood not simply as 'victims' of media hype but as challenging social norms by being very, very good at dieting to extremes; by defying the sanction against women having an appetite, or by being more than 'little women'. (Heenan, 1996b, p. 60).

Through being disordered women are expressing problems of a societal nature by saying 'no' to what is expected of them. Rather than positioning some women as 'normal' and others as 'abnormal' it makes more sense to have a continuum (Burstow, 1996). At one end are women who occasionally worry about food and at the other, those with troubled eating (Burstow's term for eating disorders).

## for and against

## the feminist approach

**+** Provides a contrast with mainstream psychological and biological approaches by looking at how eating disorders are bound up with the way that femininity is constructed in society.

**–** Focusing on the social and cultural context of the disorder could be seen as ignoring the severity of individual distress experienced by women with eating disorders.

> ✚ Women with eating disorders are not seen as 'abnormal'. Instead, eating disorders are seen as a physical manifestation of the contradictions and self-denial facing women living in Western culture.
>
> ▬ The feminist approach cannot account for different manifestations of eating disorders, i.e. why some women develop anorexia and others bulimia.

## where to now?

The following are good sources of further information about social approaches to eating disorders:

▶ **Hepworth, J. (1999)** *The Social Construction of Anorexia Nervosa*. **London: Sage** – advanced and complex, but very well written. Addresses socio-cultural and feminist perspectives.

▶ **Petkova, B. (1997) Understanding eating disorders: a perspective from feminist psychology.** *Psychology Review*, **4(1), 2–7** – a more straightforward and simple introduction to what can be a complex theoretical position.

## Psychological perspectives

There are two major psychological models of eating disorders: the psychodynamic approach and the cognitive approach. The psychodynamic approach focuses on the role of patterns of interaction in the family, whilst the cognitive approach focuses on the atypical ways in which sufferers of eating disorders think about food.

### The psychodynamic approach

One psychodynamic theory put forward by Hilde Bruch (1982) claims that the origins of anorexia can be found in childhood. She distinguishes between different types of parenting based on how parents respond to the needs of their children.

● The *effective parent* is able to correctly distinguish between a child's biological and emotional needs, for example, giving food when the child is crying from hunger and comfort when it is crying from fear.

● The *ineffective parent* does not respond to the child's needs, but imposes their own definitions of needs on their children. These types of parents arbitrarily decide whether children are tired, hungry or cold without correctly interpreting the child's actual condition. They may feed a child when it is anxious and comfort a hungry one.

According to Bruch, the children of these different types of parent will follow different developmental patterns. Children of effective parents are able to distinguish between their own internal emotional and physiological states (this is called *introceptive awareness*). They follow a 'normal' developmental pattern, acquiring control and autonomy as they move into adolescence. In contrast, children of ineffective parents cannot differentiate between their own internal needs. As a result they do not experience themselves as being in control of their own behaviour, needs and impulses. They feel like they do not own their bodies and do not develop a coherent sense of self. The child does not develop as an autonomous individual, but according to the wishes and expectations of their parents. During adolescence, the child becomes desperate to overcome their sense of helplessness and exert control over some aspect of their lives. In an attempt to defy the demands of others, the child attempts a form of extreme control over their body and eating habits. Those that are successful at redirecting their need for control go on to develop anorexia and those that are less successful end up in a binge–purge cycle (bulimia).

Although the theory was developed out of Bruch's clinical observations during therapy, subsequent research has begun to systematically test different aspects of the theory. Several studies have analysed interactions between individuals diagnosed with anorexia and bulimia with other family members. Results of such studies have shown that the families of anorexic and bulimic individuals communicate in complicated ways, providing support for various aspects of Bruch's theory.

Within the families of anorexics, parental messages often contain a 'double bind' showing both affection and a disregard for any attempted autonomy (Humphrey, 1989). Anorexic patients have described their own mothers as being excessively dominant, intrusive and overbearing (Dare and Eisher, 1997). Parents of anorexics tend to define the needs of their child themselves, rather than allowing the child to develop their own needs. Individuals with eating disorders tend to be conformist, approval seeking and tend to perceive themselves as having little control over their lives (Vitousek and Manke, 1994).

One problem with these kinds of studies is that, while they show that families of individuals with eating disorders show certain types of communication patterns, it is unclear whether these are causing the disorder or simply a response to living with an anorexic or bulimic individual. In a different kind of study, Leon *et al.* (1993) found that anorexic individuals showed a lack of introceptive awareness (awareness of internal cues such as hunger and emotional states) compared with individuals without an eating disorder and that a low level of introceptive awareness could predict the onset on anorexia 2 years in the future. These results therefore suggest that such factors do play a causal role.

# for and against

## Bruch's theory

**+** A range of studies have found support for different parts of the theory by examining communication patterns in the families of patients with eating disorders.

**−** It is not clear whether these factors are a cause of the disorder or represent a response to living with a family member with an eating disorder.

### The cognitive approach

One of the defining features of eating disorders is a distorted body image, where individuals perceive themselves as being overweight when they are not. This suggests some kind of bias in the way that visual information about the body is processed. Early research supported this view, finding that anorexic patients tended to overestimate their body size by 25–55%, compared with a control group of non-anorexic participants who made roughly accurate estimates (Slade and Russell, 1973). At the time this discovery was held as a breakthrough because it seemed to show that body image disturbance lies at the heart of anorexia, and this view has persisted to the present day.

However, this view has been seriously challenged by research showing that body image disturbance may not be unique to anorexia. Crisp and Kalucy (1974), using the same body size estimation technique as Slade and Russell, found that, while anorexic patients overestimated their body size after eating a fattening meal, so did a group of normal patients. Shortly after these results were published it was found that ordinary people tend to estimate their body sizes more accurately as they grow older. As it happened, the control group patients in Slade and Russell's study were significantly older than the anorexic patients, which may help to explain why the group of patients overestimated their body size more than the control group.

Another problem for the body disturbance hypothesis is that recovery from eating disorders is unrelated to patients' estimation of their body size. Fernandez *et al.* (1999) compared estimated body image in groups of anorexic and bulimic patients before and after a course of cognitive–behavioural therapy. Results showed that estimation of body size did not change during the course of therapy and, crucially, patients who recovered from their eating disorder still overestimated their body size.

The evidence from these two studies suggests that, contrary to popular belief, distorted body size is not a causal factor in eating disorders. Fernandez *et al.* suggest that eating disorders are not caused by a cognitive bias in the way that patients with eating disorders see their body, but are about the way they feel about their body – a disturbance in the emotional aspects of body image, not the visual aspects. These emotional aspects of distorted body image will be expressed in negative attitudes and beliefs about one's body.

Cooper and Turner (2000) examined these emotional aspects of body perception in anorexic patients using the *Eating Disorder Belief Questionnaire*. Compared with a group of dieters and a control group, the anorexic patients held more negative beliefs about themselves, believed that acceptance from others depended on body shape and size, perceived themselves as having little control over their eating and judged self-esteem on body shape and size.

These negative beliefs may play an important role in the development of eating disorders, although at this early stage it is not clear whether these negative beliefs are a cause of eating disorders or whether they simply reflect the cognitive biases of patients with eating disorders. Negative beliefs have been shown to play a causal role in other emotional disorders such as depression and anxiety disorders and so it is possible that this is also the case with eating disorders. Some evidence has come from outcome studies of cognitive–behavioural therapy. One such study (Newman *et al.*, 2000) showed that cognitive–behavioural therapy which aimed to reduce negative beliefs relating to eating, size and shape was an effective treatment for bulimia. These results suggest that negative beliefs do indeed play a causal role in the development of eating disorders, but further research is required before such a conclusion can be uncritically accepted.

# for and against

## the cognitive model

+ The symptoms of eating disorders suggest an obvious source of cognitive bias; that individuals with anorexia and bulimia have a distorted body image. They overestimate their body shape and size.

− Research does not support this view. Anorexic patients do not overestimate their body shape and size any more than non-anorexic people.

+ Another line of research has shown that anorexic patients hold negative beliefs about themselves, food and eating, leading to a distorted emotional component of body image.

− It is not clear at this stage whether these negative beliefs are a cause of eating disorders, or whether they reflect the type of thinking shown by patients with eating disorders.

# where to now?

The following are good sources of further information about psychological theories of eating disorders:

▶ **Champion, L. and Power, M. (2000)** *Adult Psychological Problems*. **Hove: Psychology Press** – contains a good chapter on eating problems, focusing on psychological models.

▶ **Szmukler, G., Dare, C. and Treasure, J. (1995)** *Handbook of Eating Disorders*. **Chichester: Wiley** – contains chapters on psychodynamic and cognitive perspectives by leading experts in those approaches.

## Biological perspectives

Biological approaches to understanding eating disorders have included examinations of the role of genetic factors, biochemistry and neurology. Regardless of our theoretical views on the origins of eating problems, a sound medical understanding of eating disorders is essential for anyone working with patients, as sufferers of eating problems experience serious physical symptoms, sometimes to a life-threatening degree.

### Genetic factors

Biological theories of anorexia have suggested that eating disorders may be in part genetic as there is an increased risk of developing an eating disorder for first-degree relatives (parents, siblings, etc.). Twin studies have provided more direct evidence for a role of genes.

# research now

## twins and eating problems

**Kortegaard, L.S., Hoerder, K., Joergensen, J., Gillberg, C. and Kyvik, K.O. (2001)**
**A preliminary population-based twin study of self-reported eating disorder.**
*Psychological Medicine*, 31, 361–365

**Aim:** To establish whether anorexia and bulimia have a genetic component by comparing the rates of co-occurrence of eating disorders in identical and fraternal twins. If the identical twins are more likely to share an eating problem than the fraternal twins, then this suggests that it has a genetic component.

**Method:** A questionnaire was sent to all 34 076 members of the Danish Twin Register asking three simple questions:

Q1   Have you ever experienced anorexia?
Q2   Has anyone else ever described you as anorexic?
Q3   Have you ever experienced bulimia?

Questionnaires would only be included for analysis if both twins had responded. A narrow definition of anorexia was used if respondents answered yes to question 1 and a broad definition of anorexia was used if respondents answered yes to questions 1 and 2.

**Results:** 29 424 questionnaires were returned (86.2% of register), revealing a group of 1270 individuals who replied yes to one of the above questions. Concordance rates are as in Table 10.2:

| | MZ (identical) | DZ (non-identical) |
|---|---|---|
| Anorexia (narrow definition) | 0.18 | 0.07 |
| Anorexia (broad definition) | 0.25 | 0.13 |
| Bulimia | 0.26 | 0.11 |

**Table 10.2** Concordance rates for study group

**Conclusions:** The results show that MZ (identical) twins have a higher chance of developing both anorexia and bulimia than DZ (non-identical twins), suggesting that genes might play some role in the development of eating disorders.

Superficially, the evidence from this study suggests that genetic factors contribute to the development of eating disorders (see Chapter 8 for a more thorough discussion of the different types of studies used in behavioural genetics). If eating disorders were 100% genetic, then the concordance rate would be 1.00 for MZ twins. As the concordance rates for MZ twins were so low in this study (0.18 for anorexia (narrow definition) and 0.26 for bulimia), genetic factors can play only a small role at best in eating disorders. Using the stress–diathesis model, genetic factors could be seen as providing a slight predisposition to eating disorders, which could be triggered by other psychological variables (such as family background) or socio-cultural variables (such as pressure to be thin). The self-report method used in this study has the advantage of using many more participants than could be included in a clinical trial. However, as participants had not received a formal diagnosis, there is no consistent standard against which participants are judged as having an eating disorder other than their own subjective views.

## for and against

### a genetic element

**+** Evidence from twin studies such as that of Kortegaard *et al.* suggests that genetic factors may play a small role in the development of eating disorders.

**+** Genetic factors could provide a predisposition to the development of eating disorders, which is triggered by psychological or socio-cultural variables.

**–** Twin studies may not remove the influence of environmental factors and so it is possible that they overestimate the influence of genetic factors.

### *Biochemical factors*

One biochemical theory of bulimia comes from the basic premise that the disorder is linked to a lack of the monoamine neurotransmitters, and in particular serotonin. This theory has been developed from two main sources: the drugs used to treat eating disorders, such as Prozac, and diet – see Box 10.3.

---

1  Eating disorders tend to co-occur with other disorders linked to low levels of serotonin (e.g. depression and obsessive–compulsive disorder), suggesting that eating disorders might also be linked to low levels of serotonin.

2  Prozac (a selective serotonin reuptake inhibitor) is effective at treating bulimia; the symptoms of bulimia reduce in severity with increased dosage. Prozac works by preventing the synaptic reuptake of serotonin (therefore increasing serotonin activity), suggesting that eating disorders might result from a lack of serotonin.

3  Patients with eating disorders who have a low tryptophan diet (an essential component of serotonin), and therefore lower levels of serotonin, experience more severe symptoms than patients with a high tryptophan diet. This finding suggests that severity of symptoms is linked to levels of serotonin.

---

**Box 10.3** Origins of the serotonin hypothesis

A neurotransmitter is broken down into a metabolite to pass out of the body like any other waste product. One way to test the serotonin hypothesis would be to test levels of the serotonin metabolite, 5-H1AA in cerebrospinal fluid (CSF) and urine to give an indication of levels of neurotransmitter in the brain. If eating disorders are linked to low levels of serotonin, low levels of 5-H1AA should be found in CSF and urine. Jimerson *et al.*. (1992) measured levels of CSF 5-H1AA in bulimic patients classified into high bingers (average 23 binges/week), medium bingers (average 10 binges/week) and a control group of individuals with no history of eating disorders. Results supported the serotonin hypothesis; both groups of bulimic patients showed lower levels of 5-H1AA over a one week period than the control group. Furthermore, high-frequency bingers showed lower levels of 5-H1AA than the medium-frequency bingers, supporting the finding that symptom severity is linked to levels of serotonin.

Measuring neurotransmitter metabolites in urine and CSF is not always an accurate index of neurotransmitter levels in the brain. However, the metabolite studies and Prozac treatment studies lead to the same conclusion, that eating disorders are linked to low levels of serotonin. One problem is in establishing the direction of causality; do low levels of serotonin cause eating disorders or vice versa? Psychiatrists and biologically oriented psychologists tend to assume that low levels of serotonin *cause* the eating disorder because of their reductionist belief that psychological phenomena are caused by biological phenomena. It would be a mistake to uncritically accept such an interpretation without further evidence.

## for and against

### the serotonin hypothesis

+ A range of factors suggest that low levels of serotonin are linked to bulimia.

+ Drugs used to treat bulimia (e.g. Prozac) work by raising levels of serotonin.

+ High levels of the serotonin metabolite (5-H1AA) are found in the cerebrospinal fluid of bulimic patients.

− It is unclear whether low levels of serotonin are a cause or an effect of bulimia.

Serotonin is not the only biochemical associated with eating disorders. A number of hormone levels are disrupted in eating disorders, and it has long been a subject of debate whether these may be implicated in the origins of eating pathology. A classic study by Fichter and Pirke (1986) suggests that, on the contrary, hormone levels are disrupted by not eating and thus they are probably not a causal factor in eating disorders.

# classic
## research

## starvation vs anorexia

**Fichter, M.M. and Pirke, K.M. (1986) Effects of experimental and pathological weight loss on the hypothalamo-pituritary-adrenal axis.** *Psychoneuroendocrinology*, 11, 295–305

**Aim:** The aim of the study was to induce starvation in participants and measure the resulting changes in hormone levels. The idea was to see whether the hormonal changes resulting from starvation were the same as those in anorexia. If they were the same then we could take it that the hormone disruption seen in eating disorders, particularly anorexia, is the result of not eating rather than a cause of the condition.

**Method:** Five healthy male volunteers were selected and studied over four phases. In the first phase, body weight was maintained and the concentrations of several hormones in the blood were measured every 30 minutes over a 24-hour period in order to establish the normal hormone levels for the five individuals. The hormones measured included growth hormone, cortisol and thyroid-stimulating hormone. In the second phase participants were deprived completely of food for 3 weeks, and the concentrations of hormone levels measured, again over a 24-hour period. In a third phase, the weight of the volunteers was restored to normal and hormone levels measured. In the final phase, participants were monitored for a time as normal body weight was maintained.

**Results:** In the starvation phase there were significant changes in hormone levels. For example, growth hormone levels increased, cortisol levels increased and thyroid-stimulating hormone levels decreased. When weight was restored to normal, the hormone levels returned to normal. The changes in hormone levels were compared with those recorded in eating disorders during previous studies. The hormonal changes in starvation and eating disorders were found to be the same.

**Conclusions:** The hormonal changes induced by starvation were the same as those measured in patients with eating disorders. This implies strongly that the abnormal hormone levels in patients with eating disorders are symptoms of the disruption to eating patterns rather than the underlying cause of eating disorders.

*Neurological factors*

Simmonds (1914) reported the case of a patient who died from emaciation whose pituitary gland was atrophied. For the next 25 years, cases of anorexia were assumed to be caused by the same problems and were unsuccessfully treated with pituitary extracts. Eventually it became clear that anorexia produces different symptoms to this case, which subsequently became known as Simmonds' disease, and pituitary malfunction rejected as the cause of anorexia.

In the past 20 years, more sophisticated techniques have been used to examine the neurological factors in eating disorders. Computed Tomography (CT) and Magnetic Resonance Imaging (MRI) scans have identified structural changes in the brains of patients with eating disorders compared with the brains of control group patients who have no eating disorders. Krieg *et al.* (1989) found that patients with anorexia had enlarged ventricles in the brain (the fluid-filled cavities that supply nutrients to the brain and remove waste products). This might indicate that some of the brain tissue around the ventricles had been destroyed, however ventricles return to their normal size following weight gain, suggesting that ventricular enlargement is not a cause of anorexia. Husain *et al.* (1992) found that the thalamus and midbrain were smaller in anorexic patients. Both of these brain regions have been linked to emotion and, since it is not known whether these changes are reversible or not, they could be casual factors in anorexia.

Positron Emission Tomography (PET) and functional Magnetic Resonance Imaging (*f*MRI) scans have been used to identify changes in brain function. One such study (Ellison *et al.*, 1998) showed a 5-minute film containing pictures of labelled high- and low-calorie drinks to a group of patients with anorexia and another group of healthy volunteers without eating disorders. Results found that anorexic patients showed much higher levels of brain activity in the amygdala and hippocampus (both areas of the limbic system). Both of these regions have been implicated in controlling emotion, especially anxiety, and so it is possible that these patients have an uncontrollable fear reaction to certain stimuli (e.g. high-calorie foods). At present it is unclear whether such changes in brain function are causes of anorexia or whether they are simply a result of the disorder, and if they are causal how they might be implicated in the development of eating disorders.

## for and against

## the neurological model

+ Several areas of the brain have been implicated in eating disorders using structural scanning techniques (CT and MRI scans) and functional scanning techniques (PET and *f*MRI scans).

– Some of these changes are reversible (e.g. enlarged ventricles) and so are not likely to be causal factors in the development of anorexia.

+ Other changes (e.g. increased activity in the amygdala and hippocampus) may be linked to fear responses to certain foods.

– Many patients with eating disorders also suffer from depression and obsessive–compulsive disorder and so it is possible that neurological changes reflect these disorders and not eating disorders.

**where to now?**

**The following are good sources of further information about the neurological model:**

▶ **Chowdhury, U. and Lask, B. (2001) Clinical implications of brain imaging in eating disorders.** *Psychiatric Clinics of North America*, **24, 227–234** – a highly accessible review of the literature on neurological correlates of eating disorders.

▶ **Fichter, M.M. and Pirke, K.M. (1995) Starvation models and eating disorders. In: Szmukler, G., Dare, C. and Treasure, J. (eds)** *Handbook of Eating Disorders*. **Chichester: Wiley** – a good chapter on the relationship between the symptoms of eating problems and the effects of not eating.

## Conclusions

A familiar theme begins to emerge when viewing the literature on the causes of eating disorders. There seems to be evidence that each factor seems to play *some* role in the development of eating disorders, but it is often difficult to establish whether it is a *casual* factor. The common-sense interpretation of these findings would be to suggest that eating disorders are multi-causal; an interaction of social, psychological and physiological factors, but feminists warn us against such a straightforward explanation. An alternative interpretation would be to view each factor as providing an explanation of the disorder at a different level of analysis. For example, rather than the biochemical explanation competing against the psychodynamic explanation for the 'true' cause of eating disorders, the disorder can be seen as simultaneously psychodynamic and biochemical, with one explanation operating at the biological level and another operating at the psychological level. No one particular explanation can be seen as superior to any other. There is no straightforward resolution to this debate, but one can rest assured that over the coming decades the debate will continue.

what
do you
know?

1   Describe the clinical characteristics of anorexia (e.g. diagnostic criteria).

2   Describe one biological factor (e.g. genetic factors) that may be linked to the development of anorexia. What is the evidence for that biological factor?

3   Describe one psychological factor (e.g. psychodynamics) that may be linked to the development of anorexia. How strong is the evidence for that factor?

4   Discuss one social factor (e.g. media images of the body) that may be linked to the development of anorexia. How strong is the evidence for that factor?

# 11

# Anxiety Disorders

what's
ahead?

Like depression (see Chapter 8), we have all experienced the sensation of anxiety at some point our lives. Anxiety can take the form of recognisable mental disorder. In this chapter we focus on five anxiety disorders recognised by DSM-IV and ICD-10: generalised anxiety disorder, panic disorder, phobias, obsessive–compulsive disorder and post-traumatic stress disorder. Anxiety disorders can be explained in biological or psychological terms, and we look here at some depth at biomedical, learning and psychodynamic explanations. We also examine briefly the newer cognitive perspective on anxiety in the form of *attentional bias*.

## Symptoms and phenomenology of anxiety disorders

### Generalised anxiety disorder

This is characterised by unusually high levels of anxiety and worry related to normal everyday events such as performance at work. Diagnosis requires that the person is anxious on most days for a period of 6 months, and that this is accompanied by restlessness, irritability, fatigue, concentration problems, muscle tension or sleep disturbance.

### Panic disorder

This is characterised by recurrent panic attacks (a single panic attack does not warrant a diagnosis). The DSM criteria for a panic attack are shown in Box 11.1.

**Note**: A panic attack is not a codable disorder. Code the specific diagnosis in which the panic attack occurs (e.g. 300.21 Panic disorder with agoraphobia).

A discrete period of intense fear or discomfort, in which four (or more) of the following symptoms developed abruptly and reached a peak within 10 minutes:

1   palpitations, pounding heart, or accelerated heart rate
2   sweating
3   trembling or shaking
4   sensations of shortness of breath or smothering
5   feeling of choking
6   chest pain or discomfort
7   nausea or abdominal distress
8   feeling dizzy, unsteady, light headed, or faint
9   derealisation (feelings of unreality) or depersonalisation (being detached from oneself)
10  fear of losing control or going crazy
11  fear of dying
12  paraesthesias (numbness or tingling sensations)
13  chills or hot flushes.

**Box 11.1** DSM-IV-TR diagnostic criteria for a panic attack

Diagnosis under DSM-IV-TR also requires that at least one attack has been accompanied by a month of worry about having further attacks, concern over the significance of panic attacks (e.g. are they heart attacks?) or major changes in behaviour as a result of the attack.

## Phobic disorders

### Specific phobias

Specific phobias involve fear of a single, simple stimulus, such as spiders, snakes or heights. About 13% of people experience a specific phobia at some time in their lives, more than half of sufferers being women. The mean age for the appearance of specific phobias is 4 years. The intensity of most specific phobias declines throughout the lifespan. Interestingly, fear of snakes differs from other specific phobias in that it does not appear to decline with age. Some of the common specific phobias are shown in Table 11.1, and the criteria for diagnosis under DSM-IV-TR are shown in Box 11.2.

| Name | Feared stimulus |
|------|-----------------|
| Arachnophobia | Spiders |
| Ophidiophobia | Snakes |
| Ornithophobia | Birds |
| Hydrophobia | Water |
| Brontophobia | Thunder |
| Taphenophobia | Being buried alive |

**Table 11.1** Examples of simple phobias

---

**300.29 Specific phobia (formerly Simple phobia)**

A  Marked and persistent fear that is excessive or unreasonable, cued by the presence or anticipation of a specific object or situation (e.g. flying, heights, animals, receiving an injection, seeing blood).

B  Exposure to the phobic stimulus almost invariably provokes an immediate anxiety response, which may take the form of a situationally bound or situationally predisposed panic attack. **Note:** In children, the anxiety may be expressed by crying, tantrums, freezing, or clinging.

C  The person recognises that the fear is excessive or unreasonable. **Note:** In children, this feature may be absent.

D  The phobic situation(s) is avoided or else is endured with intense anxiety or distress.

E  The avoidance, anxious anticipation, or distress in the feared situation(s) interferes significantly with the person's normal routine, occupational (or academic) functioning, or social activities or relationships, or there is marked distress about having the phobia.

F  In individuals under age 18 years, the duration is at least 6 months.

G  The anxiety, panic attacks or phobic avoidance associated with the specific object or situation are not better accounted for by another mental disorder, such as obsessive–compulsive disorder (e.g. fear of dirt in someone with an obsession about contamination), post-traumatic stress disorder (e.g. avoidance of stimuli associated with a severe stressor), separation anxiety disorder (e.g. avoidance of school), social phobia (e.g. avoidance of social situations because of fear of embarrassment), panic disorder with agoraphobia, or agoraphobia without history of panic disorder.

**Box 11.2** DSM-IV-TR diagnostic criteria for specific phobias

## Social phobias

Social phobias are those that relate to other people. Common examples of situations that social phobics find difficult can include public speaking, eating and drinking in front of others and using public toilets. A degree of anxiety before social situations is quite normal and reported by about 40% of the population, but it becomes a clinical condition when it interferes with work and social life. About 2% of the population suffer from social phobias, which affect men and women equally. Social phobias most commonly appear between 15 and 20 years of age.

*Agoraphobia*

Agoraphobia is often described as fear of open spaces but this is rather misleading. Agoraphobics actually fear *public* places, sometimes particularly crowded and difficult to escape situations. The dominant anxiety experienced in agoraphobia is of being unable to escape. Public transport is thus particularly difficult for agoraphobics. Agoraphobia occurs in 2-3 % of the population. Two-thirds of sufferers are women. The mean age for onset is 24 years, older than the other phobic disorders.

media watch

## What are you afraid of?

These extracts are taken from an article by health journalist Helen Saul, published in the magazine *Hotline*.

So what links Dennis Bergkamp with Hans Christian Andersen? Or Kim Basinger with Sir Isaac Newton? Success in very different careers, obviously, but also some extreme, irrational fears. Fears of travelling for the first pair, and for the second agoraphobia, which is a fear of public places.

Footballer Bergkamp is so afraid of flying that he has a clause written into his contract ensuring that his club cannot insist on it. If he can't get to a match by car, coach or train he can't play. Storyteller Andersen would not leave home without a rope, so that he could escape through a window in the case of fire. The rope is now in a museum in Denmark, proof that the fires were only in Andersen's mind.

Newton was housebound with agoraphobia for years after a period of severe stress. Basinger had a similar experience after the birth of her daughter. It's much harder to imagine an agoraphobic actress: academics can succeed with limited socialising, whereas actresses are subject to intense public scrutiny. But in both cases phobia severely impinged on their lives.

*Hotline*, Summer 2001

## Questions

**1** Why are phobias so disabling? Give examples.

**2** Suggest how people may cope with severe phobias. How effective are these strategies?

## Post-traumatic stress

Post-traumatic stress disorder (PTSD) follows psychological trauma, defined as an extreme stressor that is beyond the range of ordinary human experience. Hunt (1997) suggests five categories of trauma:

1   Subjecting or being subjected to attack or torture in war.

2   Acts of terrorism.

3   Personal attacks, such as rape, sexual abuse and physical assault, within families or on the street.

4   Natural disasters, such as earthquakes (see Figure 11.1).

5   Man-made catastrophes.

Symptoms include dreams and waking *flashbacks* (in which the experience is relived), avoidance of circumstances that remind the patient of the traumatic event, increased arousal and partial amnesia for the traumatic event. Other problems often occur alongside the clinical symptoms of PTSD. Sufferers may be prone to guilt or anger, and there is a tendency for serious relationship problems and substance abuse, as patients *self-medicate* with alcohol or illegal drugs in order to ease their distress.

**Figure 11.1** People exposed to natural disasters such as earthquakes frequently suffer PTSD

The prevalence of PTSD in the population is thought to be 1–2%: most people who experience a traumatic event do not go on to suffer PTSD. In one survey in Detroit, USA, Breslau *et al.* (1991) found that 39% of people reported having suffered a psychological trauma. Of these, about a quarter went on to develop PTSD. Pynoos *et al.* (1993) found higher incidence in high-risk groups. 60% of children who had been exposed to sniper attack and the majority of children surviving the Armenian earthquake suffered PTSD.

## Obsessive–compulsive disorder

Obsessive–compulsive disorder (or OCD) is characterised by persistent and intrusive thoughts that can take one or both of two forms:

1 **Obsessions**: thoughts that can take the form of doubts, fears, images or chains of future events. These 'invade' the consciousness of the sufferer and dominate their waking life.

2 **Compulsions**: desires to carry out a repetitive task, most commonly washing or cleaning.

We are virtually all prone to minor obsessions and compulsions. You will all have had the experience of not being able to get a song out of your head, even though it may be one you hate! Only the bravest of us walk on cracks in the pavement or under ladders, even though we are aware of how irrational these superstitions are. Some of our rituals are helpful, even therapeutic. Comer (1995) suggests that religious rituals, such as fingering rosary beads, are beneficial in helping us deal with stress (Figure 11.2). However, when obsessions or compulsions either cause distress or significantly interfere with someone's everyday life, we classify them as a mental disorder. About 1.5% of the population suffer from OCD. The mean age of onset is 20–25 years. Most cases are preceded by stressful life events. Diagnosis of OCD under the DSM-IV-TR system requires that either obsessions or compulsions (or both) are present for more than one hour per day or that they interfere with the routine of the sufferer.

**Figure 11.2** The tradition of fingering rosary beads can be a helpful ritual to deal with stress

# Biomedical explanations of anxiety disorders

There is no doubt that some of the symptoms of anxiety reactions, such as increased heart rate and blood pressure, are biological. What is more controversial is whether biological factors are part of the underlying *cause* of anxiety. We can look here at an early theory of biological susceptibility to anxiety, contemporary studies of genetic influence and studies of brain functioning in patients with anxiety.

## Emotional lability theory

Eysenck (1967) suggested that the biological basis of individual differences in anxiety lies in the reactivity of the autonomic nervous system. The autonomic nervous system controls the body's arousal. Eysenck described individuals with high autonomic reactivity as *emotionally labile*. Such people are very easily aroused by fear-provoking stimuli. As you can imagine, people who are more easily frightened are more likely to acquire phobias. Eysenck (1967) proposed that emotional lability, which underlies the development of phobias, is determined by genetic factors. Although current research supports the link between anxiety and the autonomic nervous system we know that different anxiety disorders are associated with distinctive patterns of autonomic activity. In one recent study, Friedman and Thayer (1998) compared the responses of 16 patients suffering from panic attacks, 15 blood phobics and 15 control patients without an anxiety condition to laboratory stressors such as electric shocks. The panic group displayed the fastest heart rate but the least variation between stressed and non-stressed states. The blood phobic group displayed the largest variation between physiological states when relaxed and when stressed. This suggests that the autonomic nervous systems of patients with different anxiety disorders function differently, thus Eysenck's idea of emotional lability is over simple.

## Evidence for a genetic predisposition to anxiety

It seems likely that some people are more vulnerable to acquiring phobias than others because of the inherited characteristics of their nervous system. Skre *et al.* (2000) looked at the contributions of genes and environment in phobias by comparing the concordance rates in 23 pairs of identical twins and 38 pairs of same-sex fraternal twins. Identical twins were significantly more likely to share phobic conditions than fraternal twins and this effect was greater for specific phobias than for agoraphobia. This suggests that some people are more likely to acquire phobias (particularly specific phobias) than others as a result of their genetic make-up.

There is also some evidence for a genetic factor in other anxiety disorders. True *et al.* (1993) studied the twins of patients who had developed PTSD following the Vietnam War. Identical twins were more likely than fraternal twins of the soldiers to share PTSD, suggesting that their genetic make-up influenced their susceptibility. Studies of genetic susceptibility to OCD have produced conflicting results. McKeon and Murray (1987) found that relatives of OCD sufferers were more likely than the rest of the population to suffer from anxiety disorders in general, but no more likely to suffer specifically from OCD. In a large family study, Black *et al.* (1992) found that relatives of OCD sufferers were likely to suffer a variety of mental disorders, but no more likely than the general population to suffer OCD.

In a recent attempt to isolate the size of genetic influences on different anxiety disorders Hetterna *et al.* (2001) reviewed the results of many twin and family studies concerned with generalised anxiety, panic disorder, phobias and OCD. Results of studies of panic disorder and generalised anxiety disorder were meta-analysed and revealed inheritabilities of 0.43 for panic disorder and 0.32 for generalised anxiety disorder. Overall, family members of a patient with an anxiety disorder were four to six times as likely as others to develop an anxiety condition themselves. For all anxiety disorders it was concluded that there is an element of genetic susceptibility but in all cases this was less important than environmental factors.

## for and against

### a genetic basis to anxiety

**+** Twin studies have shown that identical twins are more likely to share anxiety disorders than fraternal twins.

**+** Family studies have shown that family members of a patient with an anxiety disorder are several times more likely than non-family members to suffer an anxiety disorder themselves.

**—** In all anxiety disorders the environment has emerged as more important than genetic make-up.

## Biochemical and neurological factors

We have already looked at Eysenck's lability theory and concluded that anxiety disorders are associated with distinctive patterns of functioning in the autonomic nervous system. In a recent study of autonomic function in Vietnam veterans Muraoka *et al.* (1998) monitored the blood pressure and heart rate of 11 patients with PTSD and a control group of seven veterans without a diagnosis. The PTSD patients had significantly higher heart rate and blood pressure throughout the 24-hour cycle, including when asleep. Findings like this have been explained by Krystal *et al.* (1989) in terms of the trauma physically damaging the brain, leading to higher output of the neurotransmitter noradrenaline (norepinephrine). However, although we know that trauma is associated with physiological changes, there is no direct evidence to suggest that the trauma directly *causes* the physiological change. It may well be that the psychological symptoms of PTSD – flashbacks, amnesia, etc. – are sufficiently stressful to result in high arousal.

Neurochemical abnormalities have been found in patients with OCD, particularly associated with the neurotransmitter serotonin. Hollander *et al.* (1992) found that the drug M-CCP, which reduces levels of serotonin, made OCD symptoms worse. Pigott *et al.* (1990) found that antidepressant drugs, which increase serotonin levels, can reduce symptoms. Generally, however, it is not believed that low serotonin levels alone can explain OCD. Some studies have pointed to malfunction of an area of the brain called the *caudate nucleus*. Baxter *et al.* (1992) used PET scanning to observe the differences in brain function in patients before and after successful treatment. They found that the main difference following treatment was that the right caudate nucleus became more active. Johanson *et al.* (1998) carried out a study on 16 women suffering from arachnophobia. By radioactive labelling of oxygen and PET scanning they were able to track the areas of the brain that were active when responding to images of spiders. All the participants displayed changes in blood flow to the right frontal lobe. Eight participants who responded with severe panic to the sight of spiders showed *reduced* blood flow to the right frontal lobe, whereas the other eight, who showed some fear but controlled it successfully, showed an *increase* in blood flow to the same area. This suggests that the right frontal lobe plays a role in the regulation of fear responses and that severe phobias are linked to lack of activity in that region.

## for and against

## biochemical and neurological factors

**+** There is evidence from drug studies that serotonin is implicated in anxiety.

**+** There is evidence that anxiety disorders are associated with particular patterns of autonomic function.

**−** There is an important question of cause and effect. We do not know whether the biological differences found in people with anxiety disorders are causes or results of their condition.

## where to now?

The following is a good source of further information about biomedical theories of anxiety:

**Comer, R.J. (1995)** *Abnormal Psychology*. **New York: Freeman** – the chapter on anxiety disorders explores some different biological approaches to those we have covered here.

# Learning theory and anxiety disorders

Learning theory can be used to explain all the anxiety disorders. Actually, learning theory remains more important in explaining anxiety disorders than it does in most other conditions. Classical conditioning, operant conditioning and social learning are all implicated in the development of anxiety disorders.

## Avoidance conditioning

The simplest account of how people acquire anxiety disorders is the *avoidance–conditioning model*, based on classical conditioning. This involves the pairing of the phobic-stimulus-to-be with another object or event that already provokes fear. The sufferer comes to associate the new stimulus with the fear caused by the already-feared stimulus. This approach explains well how some specific phobias are acquired. For example, if you have been involved in a serious car crash, you might become afraid of driving. In an early and now classic study of avoidance learning, Watson and Rayner (1920) used classical conditioning to create a phobia in a baby.

# classic research

# the case of Little Albert

**Watson, J.B. and Rayner, R. (1920) Conditioned emotional responses.** *Journal of Experimental Psychology*, 3, 1–14

**Aim:** In the 1920s, the early learning theorists like J.B. Watson were emphasising the importance of classical conditioning in learning human behaviour. The aim of this study was to demonstrate that a fear response to a non-threatening stimulus could be created by classical conditioning.

**Method:** The design was an *n* = 1 experiment, i.e. an experimental procedure carried out on a single participant. The participant was an emotionally stable male infant called Albert, aged 9 months at the start of the study. Albert was assessed on his responses to a number of objects, including a white rat, and he displayed no fear. Two months later Little Albert was again shown the white rat. This time, when he reached for it, the researchers struck a four-foot metal bar behind his ear, making a loud noise and frightening the baby. This procedure was repeated five times a week later and twice more 17 days later. Albert's responses to the rat and to other white, fluffy objects were recorded.

**Results:** In the first trial when the metal bar was struck, Albert displayed some distress, sticking his face into a mattress. The second time he was a little suspicious of the rat, and by the third session he leaned away from the rat as soon as it was shown to him. When a rabbit was placed next to Albert, he cried. Seven weeks later Albert cried in response to the rat and a variety of other white, furry objects.

**Conclusions:** The researchers had succeeded in creating a phobic response to a previously non-threatening stimulus. This demonstrates that phobias can be learnt by classical conditioning.

The avoidance–conditioning model can also be applied to social phobias. The former Prime Minister Harold Macmillan suffered severe social phobia before Prime Minister's Question Time. Now that this event is televised, you can see that it is characterised by highly aggressive confrontation, which would naturally cause anxiety. It would be impossible now to find out whether Macmillan had a social phobia before becoming Prime Minister, or whether he acquired it when he began the job. However, it does seem likely that it was the anxiety regarding confrontation in public that triggered the bouts of anxiety before Question Time (Figure 11.3).

**Figure 11.3** Public speaking can be an extremely anxiety-provoking experience

It seems likely that avoidance conditioning plays a part in the development of agoraphobia. After the first attack of anxiety in a public place, agoraphobics typically display a *fear of fear*. This means that one of the reasons why they avoid going out is the fear of *becoming afraid* once they are out. It seems that going out becomes associated with becoming afraid, causing further fear. Of course, this model of agoraphobia does not explain how the first bout of anxiety occurred, but it might explain the ongoing development of agoraphobia.

Avoidance learning is also the simplest explanation of PTSD. For example, the victim of a mugging may come to associate going out with being attacked. Going out then causes a fear reaction, which in turn reinforces the avoidance of going out. Ferguson and Cassaday (1999) have suggested that a similar process can explain *Gulf War Syndrome*, a set of symptoms including memory, sexual and sleep problems, nausea, headaches, depression, rashes and increased sensitivity to pain. Typically, each individual suffers only some of these symptoms. Ferguson and Cassaday have proposed a classical conditioning model that suggests that a sickness response has been acquired by association with a range of stimuli including oil fire fumes (present throughout the fighting) and stressful events such as witnessing injuries during the war. The symptoms of Gulf War Syndrome can be explained as the body's conditioned responses to these stimuli. Following the war exposure to any of these conditioned stimuli would produce the conditioned sickness response.

Classical conditioning can be used to treat anxiety conditions through the processes of behaviour therapy. This might involve systematic desensitisation, implosion or flooding (see Chapter 3 for a discussion). The fact that we can treat specific phobias so easily by classical conditioning techniques suggests that this is how they were acquired in the first place. However, whilst there is nothing controversial about the existence of avoidance learning, we are unsure about just how many cases it can account for. When Menzies (1996) surveyed phobic patients on the origins of their fears most reported either that they had 'always' had the phobia or that other types of experience accounted for it. We can acquire phobias of things we have never encountered (perhaps most commonly snakes), and with which we could have no conditioning experiences. Moreover, as Lovibond (2001) points out, when we have a 'near-miss' experience (e.g. being in a car that nearly crashes) that does not have a negative outcome we can still acquire a phobia. According to simple classical conditioning this should not be possible, and it suggests that at least some of the time we use more advanced cognitive processes to acquire phobias.

## Other learning mechanisms

Although classical conditioning remains the most common learning explanation for acquiring anxiety, operant conditioning and social learning have also been implicated in some cases. For example OCD can be explained in terms of operant conditioning, symptoms being seen as learned rituals for reducing anxiety. Thus compulsive hand washing has been explained by Meyer and Chesser (1970) as being learnt as a way of reducing the anxiety from an obsessional fear of dirt or germs. The obsession thus comes *before* the compulsion. There is empirical support for this view of how compulsions develop. Hodgson and Rachman (1972) placed OCD sufferers with washing compulsions in the presence of 'contaminated' objects. Researchers found that anxiety levels increased. They were then allowed to wash, whereupon anxiety levels decreased again. This demonstrated that compulsive rituals reduce anxiety. However, although learning explanations like this explain well how obsession leads to compulsion, they find it much harder to explain where the obsession came from in the first place.

Social learning theory can also explain the development of phobias. Mineka *et al.* (1984) performed a classic study on the social learning of fear of snakes in rhesus monkeys. Monkeys were reared with parents who had an intense fear of snakes. During sessions of observational learning, adolescent monkeys saw their parents react fearfully to snakes. After only six sessions of observation, the adolescent monkeys exhibited the same reactions as their parents. In humans, this process can account for cases where children develop the same phobias as their parents.

## for and against

## learning theory as an explanation of anxiety disorders

+ There is clear evidence that classical conditioning can account for some cases of specific phobias and for some symptoms of PTSD.

+ Other phobias are probably acquired by social learning.

− There are some aspects of anxiety disorders that cannot be explained by learning theory, for example individual differences in susceptibility to acquiring disorders.

− Learning theory cannot explain how we can acquire anxiety disorders following near-miss experiences.

## what's new?

## cognitive bias and anxiety disorders

One of the limitations of learning theory in explaining the development of anxiety disorders is that it fails to explain why some people are more vulnerable to acquiring conditions than others. A further problem is in understanding instances where it appears that simple conditioning does not account for the condition, for example in the cases of near misses. These problems have been addressed by recent research from the cognitive perspective. Various cognitive processes seem to operate somewhat differently in phobic patients, in particular attention. Eysenck (1992) has suggested that anxiety disorders are caused or at least maintained by *attentional bias* (the tendency to attend more than most people to threatening stimuli). Bradley *et al.* (1999) tested this idea on 14 patients suffering generalised anxiety disorder and 33 control participants, who were exposed to slides of happy or threatening faces. The anxious group responded with greater vigilance to all the faces than did the control group, providing partial support for Eysenck's theory. In another recent study, Friedman *et al.* (2000) asked generalised anxiety patients and non-anxious control participants to silently read words, some of which were intended as neutral and some as threatening. They were then asked to recall as many words as possible. The anxiety patients recalled a disproportionate number of threatening words.

A different approach to investigating cognitive bias has been employed in the Netherlands. In a series of studies Kindt and Brosschot (1997) have used the Stroop task to test processing of spider-relevant information in arachnophobics. In the Stroop task participants are asked to name the ink colour of each word in a multicoloured word list. There are a number of variations in the task, including substituting pictures for words. The task is difficult because participants find themselves attending to the meaning of the words or pictures rather than to the ink colour. Kindt and Brosschot compared arachnophobic and non-phobic participants on Stroop tasks involving spider words or images. The arachnophobics took significantly longer to name the ink colours for spider-related items whether presented as words or pictures, suggesting that phobias involve an automatic process of selectively attending to the phobic stimulus.

Cognitive bias may be important in explaining individual differences in susceptibility to anxiety disorders. It is adaptive to attend to threatening stimuli in our environment, but if some people are born with or develop a particularly strong attentional bias towards threatening stimuli then those individuals may be particularly likely to become conditioned to respond to threatening stimuli and so acquire anxiety disorders.

## where to now?

**The following is a good source of further information about learning theory and anxiety disorders:**

**Champion, L. and Power, M. (2000)** *Adult Psychological Problems*. **Hove: Psychology Press** – contains separate chapters on anxiety and obsessive–compulsive disorders, the latter in particular giving good coverage of learning approaches.

## Psychodynamic approaches

### Freudian theory

Psychodynamic approaches emphasise the unconscious influence of early events and the family context in which these events take place. In his early work, Freud (1909) emphasised the role of Oedipal conflict (see p. 82–85 for a discussion), exemplified by his classic case of Little Hans who, Freud suggested, displaced anxiety from his father onto horses, leading to a phobia of horses.

# classic
## research

# a case of the Oedipus complex?

**Freud, S. (1909) Analysis of a phobia in a five-year-old boy.** *Collected papers, Vol. III,* *149–295*

**Aim:** Little Hans, a 5-year-old boy, was taken to Freud suffering from a phobia of horses. As in all clinical case studies, Freud's most important aim was to treat the phobia. However, Freud's therapeutic input in this case was extremely minimal, and a secondary aim of the study was to explore what factors might have led to the phobia in the first place, and what factors led to its remission. By 1909 Freud's ideas about the Oedipus complex were well established and Freud interpreted this case in line with his theory.

**Case history:** Freud's information about the course of Hans' condition was derived partially from observation of Hans himself, but mostly from Hans' father, who was familiar with Freud's work, and who gave him weekly reports. Hans' father reported that from the age of 3 Hans had developed considerable interest in his own penis or 'widdler' and that at age 5 his mother had threatened to cut it off if he didn't stop playing with it. At about the same time Hans developed a morbid fear that a white horse would bite him. Hans' father reported that his fear seemed to be related to the horse's large penis. At the time Hans' phobia developed his father began to object to Hans' habit of getting into bed with his parents in the morning. Over a period of weeks Hans' phobia got worse and he feared going out of the house in case he encountered a horse. He also suffered attacks of more generalised anxiety.

Over the next few weeks Hans' phobia gradually began to improve. His fear became limited to horses with black harnesses over their noses. Hans' father interpreted this as related to his own black moustache. The end of Hans' phobia of horses was accompanied by two significant fantasies, which he told to his father. In the first, Hans had several imaginary children. When asked who their mother was, Hans replied 'Why, mummy, and you're their Grandaddy' (p. 238). In the second fantasy, which occurred the next day, Hans imagined that a plumber had come and fitted him with a bigger widdler. These fantasies marked the end of Hans' phobia.

**Interpretation:** Freud saw Hans' phobia as an expression of the Oedipus complex. Horses, particularly horses with black harnesses, symbolised his father. Horses were particularly appropriate father symbols because of their large penises. The fear began as an Oedipal conflict was developing around Hans being allowed in his parents' bed. Freud saw the Oedipus complex happily resolved as Hans fantasised himself with a big penis like his father's and married to his mother with his father present in the role of grandfather.

**Discussion:** The case of Little Hans does appear to provide support for Freud's theory of the Oedipus complex. However, there are difficulties with this type of evidence. Hans' father, who provided Freud with most of his evidence, was already familiar with the Oedipus complex and interpreted the case in the light of this. It is also possible therefore that he supplied Hans with clues that led to his fantasies of marriage to his mother and his new large widdler. There are also other explanations for Hans' fear of horses. For example, it has been reported that he saw a horse die in pain and was frightened by it. This might have been sufficient to trigger a fear of horses. Of course, even if Hans did have a fully fledged Oedipus complex, this shows that the Oedipus complex *exists* but not how *common* it is. Freud believed it to be universal.

Neglect, abuse or other trauma, and the conflict between the child's desires to act as it wishes and fear of parental disapproval, leads to *free floating anxiety*, which can then be projected onto specific stimuli, leading to a phobia. This is what Freud was getting at in the case of Little Hans, and this idea of displacement of anxiety remains interesting to contemporary psychologists even if we reject the importance of the Oedipus complex.

In his later work, Freud (1926) suggested that a degree of anxiety is a positive thing as it activates psychological defence mechanisms (see Jarvis *et al.*, 2000, for a discussion of defence mechanisms), which protect the individual from the distress of a situation. However, when a current event triggers the memory of a childhood trauma the resulting anxiety can be too powerful to be contained by psychological defences, and the resulting internal conflict becomes expressed in symptoms. Thus, someone who experienced a traumatic separation from parents in early childhood and then faces a situation in adulthood that re-enacts this trauma (such as being left by a partner) is particularly vulnerable to being overcome by a flood of anxiety. The psychological defences that would normally help with this anxiety are overwhelmed because the anxiety released is the sum of that produced by both the current and early experiences.

## Contemporary research

In a study of attachment and psychopathology Fonagy *et al.* (1996) found that in anxiety, as in other mental disorders, most patients were classified as having type D attachments. This suggests that anxiety conditions in general have some association with early family experiences. This is not to say that simpler processes such as conditioning are not important: contemporary psychodynamic writers Brown and Pedder (1991), whilst maintaining the emphasis on the family environment in which phobias develop, have conceded that in the case of specific phobias, learning theories such as avoidance conditioning can provide a simpler and neater explanation. However, Brown and Pedder point out that social phobias and agoraphobia are more complex and cannot be explained by simple learning approaches. Research suggests that early family relationships have an impact on vulnerability to all types of phobia. Magee (1999) looked at the history of patients developing specific phobias, agoraphobia and social phobia and concluded that long-term childhood trauma in the form of physical aggression, sexual abuse (women only) and verbal aggression between parents were all risk factors for developing phobias. Looking at social phobia in particular, Chartier *et al.* (2001) searched for risk factors in the history of 8116 Canadians taken from the National Risk Survey. A number of psychodynamic risk factors for social phobia emerged, including the lack of a close relationship in childhood, parental discord and sexual abuse. The psychodynamic emphasis on family environment thus remains an important part of understanding vulnerability to phobias.

Psychodynamic approaches have proved useful both in explaining the symptoms of PTSD and in offering an explanation for why some people are more susceptible than others to PTSD. Horowitz (1990) suggested that the flashbacks and dreams associated with PTSD resulted from the attempts of the unconscious mind to integrate the traumatic event into the person's beliefs about themselves and the world. Avoidance behaviour could be seen as an unconscious attempt to suppress memory of the trauma by avoiding memory cues. Repression may also be associated with more serious symptoms. Joseph *et al.* (1997) assessed the expression of emotion in survivors of the *Herald of Free Enterprise* disaster and found that those who did not freely express emotions had worse symptoms. Breslau *et al.* (1991) found that individuals whose parents had divorced when they were children were more vulnerable to PTSD than those from intact families. Davidson *et al.* (1991) also demonstrated a link between physical abuse in childhood and vulnerability to PTSD as an adult. Studies like this are important because they demonstrate that the quality of early relationships is one factor in the development of anxiety conditions, and hence that PTSD has a psychodynamic component (Callanan, 2000).

The contemporary psychodynamic model sees obsessive and compulsive behaviour as the result of an extreme emotional response to trauma. This trauma can take place in childhood or adulthood. Salzman (1995) suggests that obsessional thoughts represent the memories of trauma breaking through to the conscious mind, while compulsive behaviour represents the mind's attempts to reduce the anxiety that results from this. There is some case-study evidence for links in some people between childhood trauma and later OCD but there is little empirical support for the importance of childhood trauma in cases of OCD, other than clinical case studies, which are not representative of OCD patients as a whole. However, as Lemma-Wright (1996) reports, about 66% of cases of OCD follow shortly after a significant stressful event in adulthood or adolescence. This does suggest that OCD is at least in part an emotional response to trauma.

## for and against

# psychodynamic explanations for anxiety disorders

**+** Research clearly shows that psychodynamic factors including sexual abuse and poor family relationships increase vulnerability to anxiety disorders.

**+** Insecure attachment, in particular type D, predisposes people to anxiety disorders.

**–** Some ideas, such as explaining avoidance behaviour as a strategy to suppress anxiety into the unconscious mind, are speculative and untestable.

## Conclusions

There are a number of anxiety disorders recognised by DSM-IV and ICD-10. On a biological level these have been explained by emotional lability, the genetic tendency for a highly autonomic nervous system. Research has partially supported the notion of lability, and there appear to be some genetic influences on susceptibility to anxiety. Learning theory provides a simple explanation of and highly effective therapies to tackle anxiety conditions, in particular specific phobias. There are however limitations to learning theory in its classic form, and these have been addressed by the newer cognitive perspective. The psychodynamic perspective takes a different and complementary approach, emphasising unconscious influences on anxiety, and seeing susceptibility as the result of factors like poor childhood relationships, insecure attachment and sexual abuse.

1  Compare and contrast the cases of Little Hans and Little Albert.

2  What does learning theory explain and fail to explain about anxiety disorders?

3  To what extent are biological factors involved in anxiety disorders?

4  Do we still need a psychodynamic perspective on anxiety disorders?

# glossary

*Actualisation* An important concept in humanistic psychology, meaning the achievement of one's potential.

*Antisocial personality disorder* Commonly called 'psychopathy', this condition is characterised by lack of conscience and empathy, and is associated with violent criminality.

*Anxiety* A negative emotional state, characterised by high physiological arousal and nervousness or fear.

*Biomedical* A way of looking at mental disorder, characterised by an emphasis on biological aspects of a condition (bio) and the processes of diagnosis and treatment (medical).

*Bullshit* A term used in Gestalt therapy to mean the self-defensive distortions to our perception of our own behaviour.

*Catharsis* A term used in psychodynamic psychology to mean the release of emotion. An example would be crying to release sadness.

*Closure* A term used in Gestalt therapy to mean the emotional experience of moving on from a past trauma.

*Cultural relativism* In the context of atypical psychology, the acknowledgement that symptoms may differ across cultures.

*Culture* A system of values, beliefs and practices that characterise a particular group, for example a national or ethnic group.

*Culture-bound syndrome* A mental disorder that appears to be confined to the members of a particular cultural group.

*Delusion* Characteristic of certain mental disorders. For example, schizophrenia (a delusion) is an irrational belief that one is someone else.

*Diathesis-stress model* An approach that explains mental disorder in terms of a combination of genetic vulnerability (diathesis) and environmental stress.

*Discourse analysis* A research method associated with the social constructionist approach to psychology, discourse analysis involves 'unpacking' hidden meanings in discourse – what people say or write.

*Feminism* A social movement united by the belief that women are socially disadvantaged as compared to men. In atypical psychology, feminists have pointed to the role of social disadvantage in the origins of disorders such as depression.

*Free association* A psychodynamic technique in which a patient is encouraged to talk at will, allowing them to make their own connections between events and allowing preconscious material to come to consciousness.

*Iatrogenesis* The process whereby techniques can inadvertently create a mental disorder in the diagnosed individual.

*Individualism* In the context of mental disorder, the tendency to treat mental disorder as occurring within the mind of the individual, thus disregarding the role of social processes (for example, social construction, labelling).

*Insight* An important concept in psychodynamic psychology; an awareness of one's own thoughts and emotions, and their origins.

*Institutionalisation* In the context of atypical psychology, the tendency of patients kept in institutions for long periods to become adapted to institutional life to the extent that it becomes difficult to adjust to life outside the institution.

*Maladaptive behaviour* Behaviour that is harmful to the individual, as opposed to adaptive behaviour, which benefits the individual in some way.

*Mental illness* A term meaning mental disorder, 'mental illness' is now rarely used because it is so theoretically biased towards the biomedical model of mental disorder.

*Metarepresentation* The cognitive ability to be aware of one's own mental processes.

*Mood disorders* A category of mental disorders, characterised by their dramatic effect on the mood of sufferers. Mood may be characterised by depression or its opposite, mania.

*Multiaxial diagnosis* The process now employed in the DSM system whereby patients are assessed on a number of medical and social criteria, as well as their clinical condition.

*Neuroanatomy* The structure of the nervous system.

*Observational learning* Important in social learning theory, the term given to the acquisition of new behaviours by imitation of another individual.

*Psychiatry* The branch of medicine devoted to the diagnosis, explanation and treatment of mental disorder. Note that unlike psychologists, psychiatrists are medical doctors.

*Psychoanalysis* 1. A body of classical psychodynamic theory, including the work of Sigmund Freud. 2. A long-term and intensive psychodynamic therapy.

*Psychotherapy* A term meaning mental disorder or the study of mental disorder.

*Psychosis* Mental disorder, characterised by distortions of subjective reality, including delusions and hallucinations.

*Reductionism* The tendency to focus on one aspect of a psychological phenomenon (e.g. observable behaviour or physiology), neglecting other aspects.

*Reinforcement* In learning theory, any consequence of a behaviour that increases the probability of it being repeated.

*Scriptotherapy* The therapeutic technique of writing about one's situation and feelings towards it.

*Schizophrenogenic* Contributing towards the development of schizophrenia.

*Seduction theory* Freud's term for the explanation of mental disorder in terms of child sexual abuse.

*Self-esteem* The emotional experience of how much an individual likes themselves.

*Self-medication* Using non-medicinal drugs to alter one's psychological state in response to distress, for example, using alcohol to relax in the face of stress.

*Social constructivism* A collection of approaches to psychology linked by the belief that there is no single universal truth, and that we construct meaning through our use of language.

*Social norms* Conventional standards of behaviour for a particular society.

*Spirituality* Important in humanistic psychology, the subjective experience of one's relationship with the universe.

*Stigmatisation* The consequence of having a socially unacceptable characteristic such as mental disorder, characterised by isolation and discrimination.

*Syndrome* A collection of symptoms that tend to be found together. Unlike the terms 'condition' or 'disorder', 'syndrome' does not imply a single cause or set of causes for those symptoms.

*Unconscious* Mental processes of which we are not aware. In psychodynamic theory, the unconscious mind has a powerful effect on our behaviour, thinking and emotional states.

# references

Abrams, M. and Ellis. A. (1996) Rational emotive behaviour therapy in the treatment of stress. In: Palmer, S. and Dryden, W. (eds) *Stress Management and Counselling*. London: Cassell.

Abramson, L.Y., Alloy, L.B. and Metalsky, G.I. (1989) Hopelessness depression: a theory-based subtype of depression. *Psychological Review*, 96, 358–372.

Ainsworth, M.D.S. and Wittig, B.A. (1969) Attachment theory and the exploratory behaviour of one-year-olds in a strange situation. In: Foss, B.M. (ed.) *Determinants of Infant Behaviour, Vol. 4*. London: Methuen.

Alanen, Y. (1994) An attempt to integrate the individual-psychological and interactive concepts of the origin of schizophrenia. *British Journal of Psychiatry*, 164, 56–61.

American Psychiatric Association (2000) *Diagnostic and Statistical Manual of Mental Disorder*. Washington DC: American Psychiatric Association.

Andrews, G., Slade, T. and Peters, L. (1999) Classification in psychiatry: ICD-10 versus DSM-IV. *British Journal of Psychiatry*, 174, 3–5.

Angrist, B., Sathananthan, G., Wilk, S., and Gershon, S. (1974) Amphetamine psychosis: behavioural and biochemical aspects. *Journal of Psychiatric Research*, 11, 13–23.

Ayllon, T. and Azrin, N.H. (1968) *The Token Economy: A Motivational System for Therapy and Rehabilitation*. New York: Appleton-Century-Crofts.

Bandura, A. (1965) Influence of models' reinforcement contingencies on the acquisition of imitative responses. *Journal of Personality and Social Psychology*, 1, 589–595.

Bandura, A. (1973) *Aggression: A Social Learning Analysis*. Oxford: Prentice Hall.

Bandura, A. (1974). Behavior theory and the models of man. *American Psychologist*, 29(12), 859–869.

Barlow, D.H. and Durand, V.M. (1999) *Abnormal Psychology*. Pacific Grove: Brooks/Cole.

Barnes, M. and Berke, J. (1973) *Mary Barnes: Two Accounts of a Journey Through Madness*. Harmondsworth: Penguin.

Bartholomew, R.E. (1998) The medicalisation of exotic deviance: a sociological perspective on epidemic koro. *Transcultural Psychiatry*, 35, 5–38.

Bateman, A. and Fonagy, P. (1999) Effectiveness of partial hospitalisation in the treatment of borderline personality disorder: a randomised control trial. *American Journal of Psychiatry*, 156, 1563–1569.

Bateman, A. and Holmes, J. (1995) *Introduction to Psychoanalysis*. London: Routledge.

Battle, Y.L., Martin, B.C., Dorfman, J.H. and Miller, S. (1999) Seasonality and infectious disease in schizophrenia: the birth hypothesis revisted. *Journal of Psychiatric Research*, 33, 501–509.

Baxter, L., Schwartz, J. and Bergman, K. (1992) Caudate glucose metabolic rate changes with both drug and behaviour therapy for obsessive compulsive disorder. *Archives of General Psychiatry*, 49, 681–689.

Beck, A.T. (1976) *Cognitive Therapy and the Emotional Disorders*. New York: International Universities Press.

Beck, A.T., Rush, A.J., Shaw, B.F. and Emery, G. (1979) *Cognitive Therapy of Depression*. New York: Guilford.

Bentall, R., Baker, G.A. and Havers, S. (1991) Reality monitoring and psychotic hallucinations. *British Journal of Clinical Psychology*, 30, 213–222.

Bergin, A.E. and Garfield, S. (1978) *Handbook of Psychotherapy and Behaviour Change*. New York: Wiley.

Beutler, L.E. (1991) Have all won and must all have prizes: revisiting Luborsky *et al.*'s verdict. *Journal of Consulting Clinical Psychology*, 59, 226–232.

Bion, W.R. (1967) *Second Thoughts: Selected Papers on Psychoanalysis*. London: Heinneman.

Black, D., Noyes, R., Goldstein, R. and Blum, N. (1992) A family history of obsessive compulsive disorder. *Archives of General Psychiatry*, 49, 362–368.

Blakemore, C. (1988) *The Mind Machine*. London: BBC Publications.

Borkovec, T.D. and Mathews, A. (1988) Treatment of nonphobic anxiety disorders: a comparison of non-directive, cognitive and coping desensitisation therapy. *Journal of Consulting and Clinical Psychology*, 56, 877–884.

Botella, C., Villa., H., Banos, R., Perpina, C. and Garcia-Palacios, A. (1999) The treatment of claustrophobia with virtual reality: Changes in other phobic behaviours not specifically treated. *CyberPsychology and Behaviour*, 2(2), 135–141.

Bowlby, J. (1958) The nature of the child's tie to his mother. *International Journal of Psychoanalysis*, 39, 350–373.

Bowlby, J. (1969) *Attachment and Loss, Vol. I*. London: Pimlico.

Bowlby, J. (1980) *Attachment and Loss, Vol. III*. New York: Basic Books.

Bradley, B.P., Mogg, K., White, J., Groom, C. and de Bono, J. (1999) Attentional bias for emotional faces in generalised anxiety disorder. *British Journal of Clinical Psychology*, 38, 267–278.

Breslau, N., Davis, G. and Andreski, P. (1991) Traumatic events and post-traumatic stress disorder in an urban population of young adults. *Archives of General Psychiatry*, 48, 216–221.

Breuer, J. and Freud, S. (1896) *Studies on Hysteria. The Complete Works of Sigmund Freud, Vol II.* London: Hogarth.

Brewin, C.R., Dalgeish, T. and Joseph, P.H. (1996) A dual representation theory of posttraumatic stress disorder. *Psychological Review*, 103, 670–686.

Brown, D. and Pedder, J. (1991) *Introduction to Psychotherapy.* London: Routledge.

Brown, G.W. (1972) Influence of family life on the course of schizophrenic disorders: a replication. *British Journal of Psychiatry*, 121, 241–248.

Brown, G.W. and Harris, T.O. (1978) *The Social Origins of Depression: A Study of Psychiatric Disorder in Women.* London: Tavistock.

Brown, R. (1996) Life events, loss and depressive disorders. In: Heller, T. *et al* (eds) *Mental Health Matters.* Basingstoke: Macmillan.

Bruch, H. (1982) Anorexia nervosa: therapy and theory. *American Journal of Psychiatry*, 132, 1531–1538.

Burnett, P.C. (1999) Children's self-talk and academic self-concepts. *Educational Psychology in Practice*, 15, 195–200.

Burstow, B. (1996) *Radical Feminist Therapy.* New York: Sage.

Butler, A.C. and Beck, J.S. (2001) Cognitive therapy outcomes: a review of meta-analyses. *Tidsskrift for Norsk Psykologforening*, 38, 698–706.

Callanan, M. (2000) Anxiety. In: Champion, L. and Power, M. (eds) *Adult Psychological Problems.* Hove: Taylor and Francis.

Cantor-Graae, E., McNeill, T.F. and Torrey, E.F. (1994) Links between pregnancy complications and minor physical abnormalities in monozygotic twins discordant for schizophrenia. *American Journal of Psychiatry*, 151, 1188–1193.

Carson, R.C. and Butcher, J.N. (1992). *Abnormal Psychology and Modern Life*, 9th edition. New York: Harper Collins.

Cassidy, J. and Shaver, P.R. (1999) *Handbook of Attachment.* New York: Guilford Press.

Castle, D., Scott, K., Wessley, S. and Murray, R.M. (1993) Does social deprivation during gestation and early life predispose to schizophrenia? *Social Psychiatry and Psychiatric Epidemiology*, 25, 210–215.

Chadda, R.K. (1995) Dhat syndrome: is it a distinct clinical entity? A study of illness behaviour characteristics. *Acta Psychiatrica Scandinavica*, 91, 136–139.

Chadwick, P., Sambrooke, S., Rasch, S. and Davies, E. (2000) Challenging the omnipotence of voices: group cognitive behaviour therapy for voices. *Behaviour Research and Therapy*, 38, 993–1003.

Champion, L. and Power, M. (2000) *Adult Psychological Problems*. Hove: Taylor and Francis.

Chartier, M.J., Walker, J.R. and Stein, M.B. (2001) Social phobias and potential childhood risk factors in a community sample. *Psychological Medicine*, 31, 307–315.

Chowdhury, A.N. (1996) Koro: a state of sexual panic or altered physiology? *Sexual and Marital Therapy*, 11, 165–171.

Chowdhury, U. and Lark, B. (2001) Clinical implications of brain imaging in eating disorders. *Psychiatric Clinics of North America*, 24, 222–234.

Christo, G. (1997) Child sexual abuse: psychological consequences. *The Psychologist*, 10, 205–209.

Cinnerella, M. and Loewenthal, K.M. (1999) Religious and ethnic group influences on beliefs about mental illness: a qualitative interview study. *British Journal of Medical Psychology*, 72, 505–525.

Coffey, C.E. (1993) Structural brain imaging and ECT. In: Coffey, C.E. (ed.) *The Clinical Science of ECT*. Washington DC: American Psychiatric Association.

Colman, A.M. (1993) *Facts, Fallacies and Frauds in Psychology*, 2nd edition. London: Routledge.

Comer, R.J. (1992) *Abnormal Psychology*, 2nd edition. New York: W.H. Freeman.

Comer, R.J. (1995) *Abnormal Psychology*. New York: Freeman.

Cooper, M. and Turner, H. (2000) Underlying assumptions in anorexia nervosa and dieting. *British Journal of Clinical Psychology*, 39, 215–218.

Coopersmith, S. (1967) *The Antecedents of Self-esteem*. San Francisco, CA: Freeman.

Cormier, J.F. and Thelen, M.H. (1998) Professional skepticism of multiple personality disorder. *Professional Psychology*, 29, 163–167.

Corrigan, P.W., River, L.P., Lundin, R.K., Uphoff, W., Campion, J., Mathisen, J., Goldstein, H., Bergman, M., Gagnon, C. and Kubiak, M.A. (2000) Stigmatising attributions about mental illness. *Journal of Community Psychology*, 28, 91–102.

Costello, T.W., Costello, J.T. and Holmes, D. (1995). *Abnormal Psychology*, International edition. New York: Harper Collins.

Craske, M.G. Rapee, R.M. and Barlow, D.H. (1992). Cognitive-behavioural treatment of panic disorder, agoraphobia, and generalised anxiety disorder. In: Turner, S.M., Calhoun, K.S. and Adams, H.E. (eds) *Handbook of Clinical Behavior Therapy*, 2nd edition, pp. 39–65. New York: Wiley.

Crisp, A.H. and Kalucy, R.S. (1974) Aspects of perceptual disorder in anorexia nervosa. *British Journal of Medical Psychology*, 47, 349–361.

Crisp, A.H., Palmer, R.L. and Kalucy, R.S. (1976) How common is anorexia nervosa? A prevalence study. *British Journal of Psychiatry*, 128, 549–554.

Critchley, E.R.M., Denmark, J.C., Warren, F. and Wilson, K.A. (1981) Hallucinatory experiences in prelingually profoundly deaf schizophrenics. *British Journal of Psychiatry*, 138, 30–32.

Crits-Christoph, P. (1992) The efficacy of brief dynamic psychotherapy: a meta-analysis. *American Journal of Psychiatry* ,149, 151–158.

Crits-Christoph, P., Cooper, A. and Luborsky, L. (1988) The accuracy of therapists' interpretations and the outcome of dynamic psychotherapy. *Journal of Consulting and Clinical Psychology*, 56, 490–495.

Crowe, M.J. (1997) Sexual disorders. In: Murray, R., Hill, P. and McGuffin, P. (eds) *The Essentials of Postgraduate Psychiatry*. Cambridge: Cambridge University Press.

Crowe, T.J. (1980) Molecular pathology of schizophrenia: more than one disease process? *British Medical Journal*, 280, 66–88.

Crowe, T.J., Ball, J., Bloom, S.R., Brown, R., Bruton, C.J., Colter, N., Frith, C.D., Johnstone, E.C., Owens, D.G.C. and Roberts, G.W. (1989) Schizophrenia as an anomaly of development of cerebral asymmetry. *Archives of General Psychiatry*, 46, 1145–1150.

Culbertson, F.M. (1997) Depression and gender: an international review. *American Psychologist*, 52, 25–31.

Dare, L. and Eisher, I. (1997) Family therapy for anorexia nervosa In: Garner, D.M. and Garfinkel P.E. (eds) *Handbook of Treatment for Eating Disorders*. New York: Guilford.

Darton, K. (2000). What is Mind's view on psychosurgery? MIND factsheet. October 1998, updated 2000.

Davidson, J., Hughes, D., Blazer, D. and George, L. (1991) Post-traumatic stress disorder in the community: an epidemiological study. *Psychological Medicine*, 21, 713–721.

Davison, G.C. and Neale, J.M. (1994) *Abnormal Psychology*. New York: Wiley.

Davison, G.C. and Neale, J.M. (2001) *Abnormal Psychology*, 8th edition. New York: Wiley.

Davey, G.C.L. (ed.) (1997) *Phobias: A Handbook of Therapy Research and Treatment*. Chichester: Wiley.

Department of Health (1997) *The Spectrum of Care: Local Services for People With Mental Health Problems*. London: HMSO.

Depatie, L. and Lal, S. (2001) Apomorphine and dopamine hypothesis of schizophrenia: a dilemma? *Journal of Psychiatry and Neuroscience*, 26, 203–220.

de Jonghe, F., Kool, S., van Alkst, G., Dekker, J. and Peen, J. (2001) Combining psychotherapy and antidepressants in the treatment of depression. *Journal of Affective Disorders*, 64, 217–229.

Donnelly, C.L., McEvoy, J.P., Wilson, W.H. and Narasimbachari, N. (1996) A study of the potential confounding effects of diet, caffeine, nicotine and lorazepam on the stability of plasma and urinary homovanillic acid levels in patients with schizophrenia. *Biological Psychiatry*, 40, 1218–1221.

Dozier, M., Stvall, K.C. and Albus, K.E. (1999) Attachment and psychopathology in adulthood. In: Cassidy, J. and Shaver, P.R. (eds) *Handbook of Attachment*. London: Guilford Press.

Dwyer, D. and Scampion, J (1995) *Work Out A level Psychology*. Basingstoke: Macmillan.

Dwyer, D. and Scampion, J. (1996) *Mastering A-level Psychology*. Basingstoke: Macmillan.

Egeland, J.A., Gerhard, D.S., Pauls, D.L., Sussex, J.N. and Kidd, K.K. (1987) Bipolar affective disorders linked to DNA markers on chromosome 11. *Nature*, 325, 783–787.

Eley, T.C. and Stevenson, J. (2000) Specific life-events and chronic experiences differentially associated with depression and anxiety in young twins. *Journal of Abnormal Child Psychology*, 28, 383–394.

Ellis, A. (1962) *Reason and Emotion in Psychotherapy*. New York: Life Stuart.

Ellis, A. (1991) The revised ABCs of rational emotive therapy (RET). *Journal of Rational-Emotive and Cognitive-Behaviour Therapy*, 9, 139–172.

Ellison, Z., Foong, J., Howard, R., Bullmore, E., Williams, S. and Treasure, J. (1998) Functional anatomy of calorie fear in anorexia nervosa. *Lancet*, 352, 1192.

Emmelkamp, P. M. (1994). Behaviour therapy with adults. In: Bergin, A.E. and Garfiel, L. (eds) *Handbook of Psychotherapy and Behaviour Change*, 4th edition. New York: Wiley.

Engels, G.I., Garnekski, N. and Diekstra, R.R.W. (1993) Efficacy of rational-emotive therapy: a quantitative analysis. *Journal of Consulting and Clinical Psychology*, 61, 1083–1090.

Estcourt, C.S. and Goh, B.T. (1998) Koro presenting to genitourinary medicine services. *International Journal of STD and AIDS*, 9, 175–176.

Eysenck, H.J. (1952) The effects of psychotherapy: an evaluation. *Journal of Consulting Psychology*, 16, 319–324.

Eysenck, H.J. (1967) *The Biological Basis of Personality*. Springfield, IL: Charles C Thomas.

Eysenck, H.J. (1992) The tyranny of psychotherapy. In: Dryden, W. and Feltham, C. (eds) *Psychotherapy and its Discontents*. Milton Keynes: Open University Press.

Eysenck, H.J. (1997) *Anxiety and Emotion: A Unified Theory*. Hove: Psychology Press.

Eysenck, M.J. and Keane, M.T. (1995) *Cognitive Psychology: A Student's Handbook*, 3rd edition. Hove: Psychology Press.

Eysenck, M.J. and Keane, M.T. (2000) *Cognitive Psychology: A Student's Handbook*, 3rd edition. London: Psychology Press.

Fairburn, C.G. (1982) *Binge Eating and Bulimia Nervosa, Vol. 1 (4)*. Welwyn Garden City: Smith Kline & French.

Fancher, R. T. (1995) *Cultures of Healing*. New York: Freeman.

Farmer, A. and McGuffin, P. (1999) Comparing ICD-10 and DSM-IV. *British Journal of Psychiatry*, 175, 587–588.

Ferenczi, M. (1997) Seasonal depression and light therapy. http://nimnet 51.nimr.ac.uk/mhe97/sad.htm.

Ferguson, E. and Cassaday, H.J. (1999) The Gulf War and illness by association. *British Journal of Psychology*, 90, 459–475.

Fernandez, A.F., Dahme, B. and Meerman, R. (1999) Body image in eating disorders: A preliminary study. *Journal of Psychosomatic Research*, 47, 419–428.

Fichter, M.M. and Pirke, K.M. (1986) Effects of experimental and pathological weight loss on the hypothalamo-pituritary-adrenal axis. *Psychoneuroendocrinology*, 11, 295–305.

Fichter, M.M. and Pirke, K.M. (1995) Starvation models and eating disorders. In: Szmukler, G., Dare, C. and Treasure, J. (eds) *Handbook of Eating Disorders*. Chichester: Wiley.

Finkelhor, D. (1994) The international epidemiology of child sexual abuse. *Child Abuse and Neglect*, 18, 409–417.

Foa, E., and Tillmanas, A. (1980). The treatment of obsessive–compulsive neurosis. In: Goldstein, A. and Foa, E. (eds) *Handbook of Behavioural Interventions*. New York: Wiley.

Fonagy, P. (1996) *What Works with Whom? A Critical Review of Psychotherapy Research*. London: Guilford Press.

Fonagy, P., Leigh, T., Steele, M., Steele, H., Kennedy, R., Mattoon, G., Target, M. and Gerber, A. (1996) The relationship of attachment status , psychiatric classification and response to psychotherapy. *Journal of Consulting and Clinical Psychology*, 64, 22–31.

Freeman, H.L. (1984) The scientific background. In: Freeman, H.L. (ed.) *Mental Health and the Environment*. London: Churchill Livingstone.

Freeman, H.L. (1994) Schizophrenia and city residence. *British Journal of Psychiatry*, 164, 39–50.

Freud, S. (1896) The aetiology of hysteria. *Collected Papers, Vol. I*. London: Hogarth.

Freud, S. (1909) Analysis of a phobia in a five-year-old boy. *Collected Papers, Vol. III*, pp. 149–295. London: Hogarth.

Freud, S. (1912) The dynamics of transference. *Complete Works of Sigmund Freud, Vol. 12*. London: Hogarth.

Freud, S. (1917) Mourning and melancholia. *Collected Works of Sigmund Freud, Vol. 14*. London: Hogarth.

Freud, S. (1926) *Inhibitions, Symptoms and Anxiety*. London: Hogarth.

Friedman, B.H. and Thayer, J.F. (1998) Anxiety and autonomic flexibility: a cardiovascular approach. *Biological Psychology*, 49, 303–323.

Friedman, B.H., Thayer, J.F. and Borkovec, T.D. (2000) Explicit memory bias for threat words in generalised anxiety disorder. *Behaviour Therapy*, 31, 745–756.

Frith, C.D. (1987) The positive and negative symptoms of schizophrenia reflect impairments in the perception and initiation of action. *Psychological Medicine*, 17, 631–648.

Frith, C.D. (1992) *The Cognitive Neuropsychology of Schizophrenia*. Hove: Psychology Press.

Frith, C.D. and Done, D.J. (1983) Routes to action in reaction time tasks. *Psychological Medicine*, 13, 779–786.

Frith, C.D. and Done, D.J. (1986) Stereotyped responding by schizophrenics on a two-choice guessing task. *Psychological Research*, 48, 169–177.

Frith, C.D. and Done, D.J. (1989) Experiences of alien control in schizophrenia reflect a disorder in the central monitoring of action. *Psychological Medicine*, 19, 359–363.

Fromm-Reichmann, F. (1948) Notes on the development of treatment of schizophrenics by psychoanalytic psychotherapy. *Psychiatry*, 11, 263–273.

Gagne, G.G., Furman, M.J., Carpenter, L.L. and Price, L.H. (2000) Efficacy of continuation ECT and antidepressant drugs compared to long-term antidepressants alone in depressed patients. *American Journal of Psychiatry*, 157, 1960–1965.

Gaines, J. (1974) The founder of Gestalt therapy: a sketch of Fritz Perls. *Psychology Today*, 8, 117–118.

Garcia-Palacios, A., Hoffman, H.G., See, S.K., Tsai, A. and Botella, C. (2001) Redefining therapeutic successes with virtual reality exposure therapy. *CyberPsychology and Behavior. Special Issue*, 4(3) 341–348.

Garner, D.M., Garfinkel, P.E., Schwartz, D. and Thompson, M. (1980) Cultural expectation of thinness in women. *Psychological Reports*, 47, 483–491.

Geller, J.L. (1992) A historical perspective on the role of state hospitals viewed from the era of the 'revolving door'. *American Journal of Psychiatry*, 149, 1526–1533.

George, M.S., Wasserman, E.M. and Williams, W.A. (1995) Daily repetitive transcranial magnetic stimulation improves mood in depression. *Neuroreport*, 6, 1853–1856.

Gergen, K.J. (1985) The social constructionist movement in modern psychology. *American Psychologist*, 40, 266–275.

Gilbert, P. (1997) *Coping With Depression*. London: Robinsons.

Gilroy, L.J., Kirkby, K.C., Daniels, B.A., Menzies, R.G. and Montgomery, I.M. (2000) Controlled comparison of computer-aided vicarious exposure versus live exposure in the treatment of spider phobia. *Behaviour Therapy Special Issue*, 31(4), 733–744.

Glenmullen, J. (2001) *Prozac Backlash*. Touchstone Books.

Goldfried, M.R. and Davison, G.C. (1994) *Clinical and Behaviour Therapy*. New York: Holt, Rinehart and Winston.

Goldstein, J.M. *et al.* (1999) Cortical abnormalities in schizophrenia identified by structural magnetic resonance imaging. *Archives of General Psychiatry*, 56, 537–547.

Gomm, R. (1996) Mental health and inequality. In: Heller, T., Reynolds, J., Gomm, R., Muston, R. and Pattison, S. (eds) *Mental Health Matters*. Basingstoke: Macmillan.

Goodwin, F.K. and Jamison, K.R. (1990) *Manic Depressive Illness*. New York: Oxford University Press.

Gottesman, I.I. (1991) *Schizophrenia Genesis: The Origins of Madness*. New York: Freeman.

Grazioli, R. and Terry, D.J. (2000) The role of cognitive vulnerability and stress in the prediction of postpartum depressive symptomatology. *British Journal of Clinical Psychology, 39, 329–347.*

Greenberg, L.S., Elliott, R.K. and Lietaer, G. (1994) Research on experiential psychotherapies. In: Bergin, A.E. and Garfield, S. (eds) *Handbook of Psychotherapy and Behaviour Change*. New York: Wiley.

Gross, R. *et al.* (2000) *Psychology: A New Introduction*. London: Hodder and Stoughton.

Guthrie, E. (2000) Psychotherapy for patients with complex disorders and chronic symptoms: The need for a new research paradigm. *British Journal of Psychiatry*, 177, 131–137.

Guthrie, E., Kapur, N., Mackway-Jones, K., Chew-Graham, C., Moorey, J., Mendel, E., Marino-Francis, F., Sanderson, S., Turpin, C., Boddy, G. and Tomenson, B. (2001) Randomised control trial of brief psychological intervention after deliberate self-poisoning. *British Medical Journal*, 323, 7305.

Hallak, J.E.C., Crippa, J.A.S. and Zuardi, A.W. (2000) Treatment of koro with citalopram. *Journal of Clinical Psychiatry*, 61, 951.

Hammen, C. (1997) *Depression*. Hove: Psychology Press.

Harriman, E. (2001). The missing warning on a drug for desperate people: users of an antidepressant are not yet alerted to a possible suicide risk. *The Guardian*, 17 May 2001.

Harrington, R., Campbell, F., Shoebridge, P. and Whittaker, J. (1998) Meta-analysis of CBT for depression in adolescents. *Journal of the Academy of Child and Adolescent Psychiatry*. 37, 1005–1006.

Healy, D. (1993) *Psychiatric Drugs Explained*. Kings Lynn: Mosby.

Heenan, C. (1996a) Women, food and fat: Too many cooks in the kitchen? In: Burman, E., Alldred, P., Bewley, C., Goldberg, B., Heenan, C., Marks, D., Marshall, J., Taylor, K. and Ullah, S (eds) *Warner Challenging Women: Psychology's Exclusions, Feminist Possibilities*. Buckingham: Open University Press.

Heenan, C. (1996b) Feminist therapy and its discontents. In Burman, E., Aitken, G. Alldred, P., Allwood, P., Billington, T., Goldberg, B., Gordo-Lopez, A.J., Heenan, C., Marks, D. and Warner, S (eds) *Psychology Discourse Practice: From Regulation to Practice*. London: Taylor and Francis.

Heller, T. *et al.* (eds) *Mental Health Matters*. Basingstoke: Macmillan.

Henry, W.P. (1994) Psychodynamic approaches. In: Bergin, A.E. and Garfield, S. (eds) *Handbook of Psychotherapy and Behaviour Change*. New York: Wiley.

Hepworth, J. (1999) *The Social Construction of Anorexia Nervosa*. London: Sage.

Herpertz-Dahlmann, B., Hebebrand, J., Müller, B., Herpertz, S., Heussen, N. and Remschmidt, H. (2001) Propsective 10-year follow-up in adolescent anorexia nervosa: Course, outcome, psychiatric comorbidity and psycosocial adaptation. *Journal of Child Psychology and Psychiatry*, 42, 603–612.

Heston, L.L. (1966) Psychiatric disorders in foster home reared children of schizophrenic mothers. *British Journal of Psychiatry*, 112, 819–825.

Hetterna, J.M., Neale, M.C. and Kendler, K.S. (2001) A review and meta-analysis of the genetic epidemiology of anxiety disorders. *American Journal of Psychiatry*, 158, 1568–1578.

Hodgson, R.J. and Rachman, S.J. (1972) The effects of contamination and washing on obsessional patients. *Behaviour Research and Therapy*, 10, 111–117.

Hollander, E., Decaria, C. and Nitescu, A. (1992) Serotonergic function in obsessive compulsive disorder: behavioural and neuroendocrine responses to oral-M-chlorophenylpiperazine and fenfluramine in patients and healthy volunteers. *Archives of General Psychiatry*, 49, 21–28.

Hong, C.J., Du, Y.W.Y. and Lin, C.H. (2001) Association analysis for NMDA receptor subunit 2B (GRIN2B) genetic variants and psychopathology and dozapine response in schizophrenia. *Psychiatric Genetics*, 11, 219–222.

Horowitz, M.J. (1990) Psychotherapy. In: Bellack, A.S. and Hersen, M. (eds) *Handbook of Comparative Treatments for Adult Disorders*. New York: Wiley.

Hsu, L.K.G. (1990) *Eating Disorders*. New York: Guilford.

Humphrey, L.L. (1989) Observed family interactions among subtypes of eating disorders using Structured Analysis of Social Behaviour. *Journal of Counselling and Clinical Psychology*, 57, 206–214.

Hunt, L. (1997) *Trauma in Older Adults*. London: Jessica Kingsley.

Husain, M.M., Black, K.J., Doraiswamy, P.M., Shah, S.A., Rockwell, W.J.K., Ellinwood, E.H. Jr and Krishnan, K.R. (1992) Subcortical brain activity in anorexia and bulimia. *Biological Psychiatry*, 31, 735–738.

Ironbar, N. O. and Hooper, A. (1989) *Self-instruction in Mental Health Nursing*. London: Ballière-Tindall.

Jablensky, A. (1988) Schizophrenia and environment. In: Henderson, A.S. and Burrows, G.D. (eds) *Handbook of Social Psychiatry*. Amsterdam: Elsevier.

Jahoda, M. (1958) *Current Concepts of Positive Mental Health*. New York: Basic Books.

Jarvis, M. (2001) *Angles on Child Psychology*. Cheltenham: Nelson Thornes.

Jarvis, M. *Psychodynamic Psychology: Classical Theory and Contemporary Research*. London: Thomson Learning (in press).

Jarvis, M., Russell, J., Flanagan, C. and Dolan, L. (2000) *Angles on Psychology*. Cheltenham: Nelson Thornes.

Jimerson, D.C., Lesem, M.D., Kaye, W.H. and Brewerton, T.D. (1992) Low serotonin and dopamine metabolite concentrations in cerebrospinal fluid from bulimic patients with frequent binge episodes. *Archives of General Psychiatry*, 49, 132–138.

Johanson, A., Gustafson, L., Passant, U., Risberg, J., Smith, G., Warkentin, S. and Tucker, D. (1998) Brain function in spider phobia. *Psychiatry Research: Neuroimaging*, 84, 101–111.

Johnson, W.R. and Smith, E.W.L. (1997) Gestalt empty-chair dialogue versus systematic desensitisation in the treatment of a phobia. *Gestalt Review, Special Issue*, 1, 150–162.

Johnstone, E.C., Crow, T.J., Frith, C.D., Carney, M.W.P. and Price, J.S. (1978) Mechanism of the antipsychotic effects in the treatment of acute schizophrenia. *Lancet*, i, 848–851.

Joiner, T.E. (2000) A test of the hopelessness theory of depression in youth psychiatric patients. *Journal of Clinical Child Psychology*, 29, 167–176.

Jones, M.C. (1924) The elimination of children's fears. *Journal of Experimental Psychology*, 7, 382–390.

Kane, G.C., Leone, F.T. and Rowane, J. (1998) Guidelines for depot anti-psychotic treatment in schizophrenia. *European Psychopharmacology*, 8, 55–56.

Kapci, E.G. (1998) Test of the hopelessness theory of depression: drawing negative inference from negative life events. *Psychological Reports*, 82, 355–363.

Kazdin, A.E. and Weisz, J.R. (1998) Identifying and developing empirically supported child and adolescent treatments. *Journal of Consulting and Clinical Psychology*, 66, 19–36.

Kelly, J. and Murray, R.M. (2000) What risk factors tell us about the causes of schizophrenia and related psychoses. *Current Psychiatry Reports*, 2, 378–385.

Kendler, K.S., Neale, M.C., Kessler, R.C., Heath, A.C. and Eaves, L.J. (1992) Major depression and generalised anxiety disorder: same genes (partly) different environments? *Archives of General Psychiatry*, 49, 716–722.

Kim, Y. and Berrios, G.E. (2001) Impact of the term schizophrenia on the culture of ideograph: the Japanese experience. *Schizophrenia Bulletin*, 27, 181–185.

Kindt, M. and Brosschot, J.F. (1997) Phobia-related cognitive bias for pictorial and linguistic stimuli. *Journal of Abnormal Psychology*, 106, 644–648.

Kippin, T.E. (2000) Olfactory-conditioned ejaculatory preferences in the male rat: implications for the role of learning in sexual partner preferences. *Dissertation Abstracts International*, 61, 1678.

Kivlighan, D.M., Multon, K.D. and Patton, M.J. (2000) Insight and symptom reduction in time-limited psychoanalytic counselling. *Journal of Counselling Psychology*, 47, 50–58.

Klein, D.N., Riso, L.P., Donaldson, S.K., Schwartz, J.E., Anderson, R.L., Ouimette, P.C., Lizardi, H. and Aronson, T.A. (1995) Family study of early-onset dysthymia. *Archives of General Psychiatry*, 52, 487–496.

Klein, E. (2000) Magnetic brain stimulation- a new therapeutic tool in psychiatry. *Israel Journal of Psychiatry and Related Sciences*, 37(1), 1–2.

Klein, M. (1946) Notes on some schizoid mechanisms. *International Journal of Psychoanalysis*, 27, 99–110.

Klimek, V., Stockmeier, C., Overholser, J., Meltzer, H.Y., Kalka, S., Dilley, G. and Ordway, G.A. (1997) Reduced levels of norepinephrine transporters in the locus coeruleus in major depression. *Journal of Neuroscience*, 17, 8451–8458.

Kluft, R.P. (1993) *Clinical Perspectives on Multiple Personality Disorder*. Washington DC: American Psychiatric Press.

Kortegaard, L.S., Hoerder, K., Joergensen, J., Gillberg, C. and Kuvik, K.O. (2001). A preliminary population-based twin study of self-reported eating disorder. *Psychological Medicine*, 31, 361–365.

Koss, M.P., Goodman, L.A. and Browne, A. (1994) *No Safe Haven: Male Violence Against Women at Home, at Work and in the Community*. Washington DC: American Psychological Association.

Kraepelin, E. (1896) Dementia Praecox (trans.). In: Cutting, J. and Shepherd, M. (eds) (1987) *The Clinical Routes of the Schizophrenic Concept*. Cambridge: Cambridge University Press.

Kramer, P. (1997) *Listening to Prozac*. London: Penguin.

Krieg, J.C., Lauer, C., Leinsinger, G., Pahl, J., Woflgang, S., Pirke, K.M. and Moser, E.A. (1989) Brain morphology and regional cerebral blood flow in anorexia nervosa. *Biological Psychiatry*, 25, 1041–1048.

Krystal, J.H., Kosten, T.R., Southwick, S., Mason, J.W., Perry, B.D. and Giller, E.L. (1989) Neurobiological aspects of PTSD: review of clinical and preclinical studies. *Behaviour Therapy*, 20, 177–198.

Lai, K.Y.C. (2000) Anorexia nervosa in Chinese adolescents. Does culture make a difference? *Journal of Adolescence*, 23, 561–568.

Laing, R.D. (1965) *The Divided Self: An Existential Study into Sanity and Madness*. Harmondsworth: Penguin.

Laing, R.D. (1967) *The Politics of Experience and the Bird of Paradise*. Harmondsworth: Penguin.

Laing, R.D. and Esterson, A. (1964) *Sanity, Madness and the Family: Families of Schizophrenics*. London: Tavistock.

Lang, P.J. and Lazovik, D.A (1963) Experimental desensitisation of a phobia. *Journal of Abnormal and Social Psychology*, 66, 519–525.

Lau, S. and Pun, K. (1999) Parental evaluations and their agreement: relationship with children's self-concepts. *Social Behaviour and Personality*, 27, 639–650.

Lavender, T. (2000) Schizophrenia. In: Champion, L. and Power, M. (eds) *Adult Psychological Problems*. Hove: Psychology Press.

LeDoux, J. (1998) *The Emotional Brain*. London: Weidenfeld and Nicolson.

Leff, J. (1997) *Care in the Community – Illusion or Reality?* Chichester: Wiley.

Leff, J.P. and Vaughn, C.E. (1985) *Expressed Emotion in Families*. New York: Guilford Press.

Leichsenring, F. (2001) Comparative effects of short-term psychodynamic psychotherapy and cognitive-behavioural therapy in depression: a meta-analytic approach. *Clinical Psychology Review*, 21, 401–419.

Lemieux, G., Davignon, A. and Genest, J. (1965) Depressive states during rauwolfia therapy for arterial hypertension. *Canadian Medical Association Journal*, 74, 522–526.

Lemma-Wright, A. (1995) *Invitation to Psychodynamic Psychology*. London: Whurr.

Lemma-Wright, A. (1996) *Introduction to Psychopathology*. London: Sage.

Leon, G., Fulkerson, J.A., Perry, C.L., Cudeck, R. (1993) Personality and behavioural vulnerabilities associated with risk status for eating disorders in adolescent girls. *Journal of Abnormal Psychology*, 102, 438–444.

Leshner, A.I. (1992) *Outcasts on Main Street: Report of the Federal Taskforce on Homelessness and Severe Mental Illness*. Washington DC: Interagency Council on The Homeless.

Levav, I., Kohn, R., Golding, J.M. and Weissman, M.M. (1997) Vulnerability of Jews to affective disorders. *American Journal of Psychiatry*, 154, 941–947.

Lewis, D.O., Yeager, C.A., Swica, Y., Pincus, J.H. and Lewis, M. (1997) Objective documentation of child abuse and dissociation in 12 murders with dissociative identity disorder. *American Journal of Psychiatry*, 154, 1703–1710.

Lidz, T., Fleck, S. and Cornelison, A. (1965) *Schizophrenia and the Family*. New York: International Universities Press.

Lindstroem, L.H., Gefvert, O., Hagberg, G., Lundberg, T., Bergstroem, M., Hartvig, P. and Langstroem, B. (1999) Increased dopamine synthesis rate in medial prefrontal cortex and striatum in schizophrenia indivated by L (beta-sup-l-sup-lc) DOPA and PET. *Biological Psychiatry*, 46, 681–688.

Littlewood, R. and Lipsedge, M. (1997) *Aliens and Alienists: Ethnic Minorities and Psychiatry*. London: Routledge.

Lohr, J.M., Tolin, D.F. and Lilienfled, S.O. (1998) Efficacy of eye movement desensitisation and reprocessing: Implications for behaviour therapy, *Behaviour Therapy*, 29, 123–156.

Lovibond, P.F. (2001) The 'near miss' as a fourth pathway to anxiety. *Behavioural and Cognitive Psychotherapy*, 29, 35–43.

Lupien, S.J., King, S., Meaney, M.J. and McEwen, B.S. (2000) Children's stress hormone levels correlate with mothers' socioeconomic status and depressive state. *Biological Psychiatry*, 48, 976–980.

MacDonald, J. and Morley, I. (2001) Shame and non-disclosure: a study of the emotional isolation of people referred for psychotherapy. *British Journal of Psychotherapy*, 74, 1–22.

Mackewn, J. (1994) Modern gestalt – an integrative and ethical approach to counselling and psychotherapy. *Counselling,* 5, 105–108.

Macmillan, F.J. (1984) The first schizophrenic illness: presentation and short-term outcome, incorporating a trial of prophylactic neuroleptic maintenance therapy versus placebo. MD thesis, University of Edinburgh.

Magee, W.J. (1999) Effects of negative life experiences on phobia onset. *Social Psychiatry and Psychiatric Epidemiology,* 34, 343–351.

Mahon, L. and Kempler, B. (1995) Perceived effectiveness of therapeutic factors for ACOAs and non-ACOAs in heterogeneous psychotherapy groups. *Alcoholism Treatment Quarterly,* 13, 1–11.

Maier, E.H. and Lachman, M.E. (2000) Consequences of early parental loss and separation for health and well-being in mid-life. *International Journal of Behavioural Development,* 24, 183–189.

Main, M. and Solomon, J. (1986) Discovery of a disorganised disoriented attachment pattern. In: *Affective Development in Infancy.* Norwood, NJ: Ablex.

Malan, D. (1995) *Individual Psychotherapy and Science of Psychodynamics.* London: Butterworth-Heinemann.

Marder, S.R., Wirsting, W.C. and Mintz, J. (1996) Two-year outcome of social skills training and group psychotherapy for patients with schizophrenia. *American Journal of Psychiatry,* 153, 1585–1592.

Marks, I. (1986). *Behavioral Psychotherapy. Maudsley Pocket Book of Clinical Management.* Bristol: Wright.

Marks, I. (1987). *Fears, Phobias and Rituals.* New York: Oxford University Press.

Marks, I.M. (1976) The current status of behavioural psychotherapy: theory and practice. *American Journal of Psychiatry,* 133, 253–261.

Masling, J.M. and Bornstein, R.F. (1996) *Psychoanalytic Perspectives on Developmental Psychology.* Washington DC: American Psychological Association.

Masson, J. (1984) *The Assault on Truth.* New York: Harper Collins.

Masson, J. (1992) The tyranny of psychotherapy. In: Dryden, W. and Feltham, C. (eds) *Psychotherapy and its Discontents.* Milton Keynes: Open University Press.

Mayhew, J. (1996) *Psychological Change: A Practical Introduction.* Basingstoke: Macmillan.

McGlynn, F.D. (1994) Simple phobias. In: Herson, M. and Ammerman, R.T. (eds) *Handbook of Prescriptive Treatments for Adults,* pp. 179–196. New York: Plenum.

McGuffin, P., Katz, R., Watkins, S. and Rutherford, J. (1996) A hospital-based twin register of the heritability of DSM-IV unipolar depression. *Archives of General Psychiatry,* 53, 129–136.

McKeon, P. and Murray, R. (1987) Familial aspects of obsessive–compulsive neurosis. *British Journal of Psychiatry,* 151, 528–534.

McLeod, J. (1996) The humanistic paradigm. In: Woolfe, R. and Dryden, W. (eds) *Handbook of Counselling Psychology*. London: Sage.

McMullen, S. and Rosen, R.C. (1979) Self-administered masturbation training in the treatment of primary orgasmic dysfunction. *Journal of Consulting and Clinical Psychology*, 47, 912–918.

McNeal, E.T. and Cimbolic, P. (1986) Antidepressants and biochemical theories of depression. *Psychological Bulletin*, 99, 361–374.

Mearns, D. and Thorne, B. (1988) *Person-centred Counselling in Action*. London: Sage.

Menditto, A.A., Valdes, L.A. and Beck, N.C. (1994) Implementing a comprehensive social-learning program within the forensic psychiatric service of Fulton State Hospital. In: Corrigan, P.W. and Liberman, R.P. (eds) *Behavior Therapy in Psychiatric Hospitals*, pp. 61–78. New York: Springer.

Menzies, R.G. (1996) The origins of specific phobias in a mixed clinical sample: classificatory differences between two origins instruments. *Journal of Anxiety Disorders*, 10, 347–354.

Merry, T. (1995) *Invitation to Person-centred Psychology*. London: Whurr.

Merskey, H. (1992) The manufacture of personalities: the production of multiple personality disorder. *British Journal of Psychiatry*, 160, 327–340.

Meyer, V. and Chesser, E.S. (1970) *Behaviour Therapy in Clinical Psychology*. Baltimore, IL: Penguin.

Miller, E. (1999) Conversion hysteria: is it a viable concept? *Cognitive Neuropsychiatry*, 4, 181–192.

Milo, T.J., Kauffman, G.E., Barnes, W., Konopa, L.M., Crayton, J.W., Ringlestein, J.G. and Shirazi, P.H. (2001) Changes in regional blood flow after electroconvulsive therapy for depression. *Journal of ECT*, 17, 15–21.

Mineka, S., Davidson, M., Cook, M. and Keir, R. (1984) Observational conditioning of snake fear in rhesus monkeys. *Journal of Abnormal Psychology*, 93, 355–372.

Moffaert, M.V. and Dierick, M. (1999) Noradrenaline and depression: role in aetilogy and therapeutic implications. *CNS Drugs*, 12, 293–305.

Molnos, A. (1995) *A Question of Time*. London: Karnac.

Mullan, B. (1995) *Mad to be Normal: Conversations with R.D. Laing*. London: Free Association Books.

Mumford, D.B. (1996) The 'Dhat syndrome': a culturally determined symptom of depression? *Acta Psychiatrica Scandinavica*, 94, 163–167.

Mumford, D.B., Whitehouse, A.M. and Platts, M. (1991) Sociocultural correlates of eating disorders among Asian schoolgirls in Bradford. *British Journal of Psychiatry*, 158, 222–228.

Muraoka, M.Y., Carlson, J.G. and Chemtob, C.M. (1998) Twenty-four-hour ambulatory blood pressure and heart rate monitoring in combat-related posttraumatic stress disorder. *Journal of Traumatic Stress*, 11, 473–484.

Murray, R., Hill, P. and McGuffin, P. (eds) *The Essentials of Postgraduate Psychiatry*. Cambridge: Cambridge University Press.

Myers, S. (2000) Empathic listening: reports on the experience of being heard. *Journal of Humanistic Psychology*, 40, 148–173.

Nathan, D. (1994) Dividing to conquer? Women, men and the making of multiple personality disorder. *Social Text*, 40, 77–114.

Newman, L. Waller, G. and Thomas, G. (2000) Outcome of group cognitive-behaviour therapy for bulimia nervosa: The role of core beliefs. *Behaviour Research and Therapy*, 38, 145–156.

Ng, C., Schweitzer, I., Alexopoulos, P., Celi, E., Wong, L., Tuckwell, V., Sergejew, A. and Tiller, J. (2000) Efficacy and cognitive effects of right unilateral electro-convulsive therapy. *Journal of ECT*, 16, 370–379.

Nicholls, D., Chater, R. and Lask, B. (2000) Children into DSM don't go: a comparison of classification systems for eating disorders in childhood and adolescence. *International Journal of Eating Disorders*, 28, 317–324.

O'Callaghan, E., Gibson, T. and Colohan, H. (1991) Season of birth in schizophrenia: evidence for confinement of an excess of winter births, to patients, without a family history of mental disorder. *British Journal of Psychiatry*, 158, 764–769.

Oie, T.P.S. and Free, M.L. (1995) Do cognitive behaviour therapies validate cognitive models of mood disorders? A review of the empirical evidence. *International Journal of Psychology*, 30, 145–180.

Opler, L.A., Caton, C.L.M., Shrout, P., Dominguz, B. and Kass, F.I. (1994) Symptom profiles and homelessness in schizophrenia. *Journal of Nervous and Mental Disorders*, 182, 174–178.

Orbach, S. (1986) *Hunger Strike*. London: Faber & Faber.

Owen, P.R. and Laurel-Seller, E. (2000) Weight and shape ideals: thin is dangerously in. *Journal of Applied Social Psychology*, 30, 979–990.

Oyebode, F., Jamison, R., Mullaney, J. and Davison, K. (1986) Koro – a psychophysiological dysfunction. *British Journal of Psychiatry*, 148, 212–214.

Paivio, S.C. and Greenberg, L.S. (1995) Resolving unfinished business: efficacy of experiential therapy using empty-chair dialogue. *Journal of Consulting and Clinical Psychology*, 63, 419–425.

Palmer, S. and Dryden, W. (1995) *Counselling for Stress Problems*. London: Sage.

Papolos, D. (1997) *Overcoming Depression*. New York: Harper Collins.

Parker, G., Mitchell, P. and Wilhelm, K. (2000) Twelve month episodes of non-melancholic depressive subjects: refinements of subgroups by examination of trajectories. *Annals of Clinical Psychiatry*, 12, 219–225.

Parker, I., Georgaca, E., Harper, D., McLaughlin, T. and Stowell-Smith, M. (1995) *Deconstructing Psychopathology*. London: Sage.

Patrick, M., Hobson, R.P. and Castle, D. (1994) Personality disorder and the mental representation of early social experience. *Development and Psychopathology*, 6, 375–388.

Paul, G.L. and Menditto, A.A. (1992) Effectiveness of inpatient treatment programs for mentally ill adults in public facilities. *Applied and Preventative Psychology, Current Scientific Perspectives*, 1, 41–63.

Pearson, M.L. (1997) Childhood trauma, adult trauma and dissociation. *Dissociation: Progress in the Dissociative Disorders*, 10, 58–62.

Pederson, S.H., Stage, K.B., Bertelson, A., Grinstead, P., Kragh-Sorensen, P. and Sorensen, T. (2001) ICD-10 criteria for depression in general practice. *Journal of Affective Disorders*, 65, 191–194.

Perez, M.G., Rivera, R.M., Banos, F. and Amparo, B. (1999) Attentional bias and vulnerability to depression. *Spanish Journal of Psychology*, 2, 11–19.

Perkins, R.E. and Repper, J.M. (1996) *Working Alongside People with Long-term Mental Health Problems*. London: Chapman & Hall.

Perls, F., Hefferline, R.F. and Goodman, P. (1965) *Gestalt Therapy*. New York: Dell Publications.

Petkova, B. (1997) Understanding eating disorders: a perspective from feminist psychology. *Pscyhology Review* 4(1), 2–7.

Petry, N.M., Martin, B, Cooney, J.L. and Kranzler, H.R. (2000) Give them prizes, and they will come: contingency management for treatment of alcohol dependence. *Journal of Counselling and Clinical Psychology*, 68(5), 250–257.

Philo, G., Secker, J., Platt, S., Henderson, L., McLaughlin, G. and Burnside, J. (1994) The impact of mass media on public images of mental illness: media content and audience belief. *Health Education Journal*, 53, 271–281.

Pigott, T., Pato, M.T. and Bernstein, S.E. (1990) Controlled comparisons of clomipramine and fluoetine in the treatment of obsessive–compulsive disorder: behavioural and biological results. *Archives of General Psychiatry*, 47, 926–932.

Plomin, R. *et al.* (1997) *Behavioural Genetics*. New York: Freeman.

Pope, H.G., Oliva, P.S., Hudson, J.I., Bodkin, J.A. and Gruber, A.J. (1999) Attitudes towards DSM-IV dissociative disorders diagnoses among board-certified American psychiatrists. *American Journal of Psychiatry*, 156, 321–323.

Powell, R.A. and Gee, T.L. (1999) The effects of hypnosis on dissociative identity disorder: a re-examination of the evidence. *Canadian Journal of Psychiatry*, 44, 914–916.

Pridmore, S., Bruno, R., Turnier-Shea, Y., Reid, P. and Rybak, M. (2000) Comparison of unlimited numbers of rapid transcranial magnetic stimulation (rTMS) and ECT treatment sessions in major depressive episode. *International Journal of Neuropsychopharmacology*, 3(2), 129–134.

Purdon, S.E., Woodward, N.D. and Flor-Henry, P. (2001) Asymmetrical hand force persistence and neuroleptic treatment in schizophrenia. *Journal of the International Neuropsychological Society*, 7, 606–614.

Putwain, D.W. (2000) Living with schizophrenia: family, communication and expressed emotions. *Psychology Review*, 6(4), 15–18.

Putwain, D.W., Gray, M. and Emiljanowicz, C.M. (2000) Psychopathology: The social approach. *Psychology Review*, 7(2), 8–11.

Pynoos, R., Goenjian, A. and Tashjian, M. (1993) Post-traumatic stress reactions in children following the 1988 Armenian earthquake. *British Journal of Psychiatry,* 163, 239–247.

Radziszewska, B., Richardson, J.L., Dent, C.W. and Flay, B.R. (1996) Parenting style and adolescent depressive symptoms, smoking and academic achievement: ethnic, gender and SES differences. *Journal of Behavioural Medicine,* 19, 289–305.

Renfrey, G. and Spates, C.R. (1994) Eye movement desensitisation: a partial dismantling study. *Journal of Behaviour Therapy and Experimental Psychiatry,* 25, 231–239.

Richards, G. (1996) *Putting Psychology In Its Place.* London: Routledge.

Rimland, B. (1964) *Infantile Autism.* New York: Appleton-Century-Crofts.

Ritsher, J.E.B., Warner, V., Johnson, J.G. and Dohrenwend, B.P. (2001) Intergenerational longitudinal study of social class and depression: a test of social causation and social selection models. *British Journal of Psychiatry,* 178, s84–s90.

Rizzo, A.A., Buckwalter, J.G., Neumann, U., Kesselman, C. and Thieaux, M. (1998). Basic issues in the application of virtual reality for the assessment and rehabilitation of cognitive impairments and functional disabilities. *Cyberpsychology and Behavior,* 1, 59–78.

Rogers, A. and Pilgrim, D. (1996) *Mental Health Policy in Britain: A Critical Introduction.* Basingstoke: Macmillan.

Rogers, C. (1959) A theory of therapy, personality and interpersonal relationships, as developed in the client-centred framework. In: Koch, S. (ed.) *Psychology: A Study of a Science, Vol. 3.* New York: McGraw-Hill.

Rogers, C. (1961) *On Becoming a Person: A Therapist's View of Psychotherapy.* Boston, MA: Houghton-Mifflin.

Romano, S.J. and Quinn, L. (1995) Binge eating disorder: description and proposed treatment. *European Eating Disorders Review,* 3, 67–79.

Rose, D.T., Abramson, L.Y., Hodulik, C.J., Halberstadt, L. and Leff, G. (1994) Heterogeneity of cognitive style among depressed in-patients. *Journal of Abnormal Psychology,* 103, 419–429.

Rosenhack, R., Cramer, J., Allan, E. *et al.* (1999) Cost effectiveness of clozapine in patients with high and low levels of hospital use. *Archives of General Psychiatry,* 56, 565–572.

Rosenhan, D.L. (1973) On being sane in insane places. *Science,* 179, 250–258, 365–369.

Rosenstein, D.S. and Horowitz, H.A. (1996) Adolescent attachment and psychopathology. *Journal of Consulting and Clinical Psychology,* 64, 244–253.

Rothbaum, B.O., Hodges, L., Kooper, R., Opdyke, D., Williford, J. and North, M.M. (1995). Effectiveness of virtual reality graded exposure in the treatment of acrophobia. *American Journal of Psychiatry,* 152, 626–628.

Rothbaum, B.O., Hodges, L, Smith S, Lee, J.H. and Price, L. (2001) A controlled study of virtual reality exposure therapy for fear of flying. *Journal of Counselling and Clinical Psychology,* 68, 1020–1026.

Salzman, L. (1995) *Treatment of Obsessive and Compulsive Behaviours*. Northvale: Aronson.

Sandahl, C., Herlitz, K. and Ahlin, G. (1998) Time-limited group psychotherapy for moderately alcohol dependent patients: a randomised controlled clinical trial. *Psychotherapy Research*, 8, 361–378.

Sandell, R., Blomberg, J., Lazar, A., Schubert, J., Carlson, J. and Broberg, J. (1999) As time goes by: long-term outcomes of psychoanalysis and long-term psychotherapy. *Forum der Psychoanalyse*, 15, 327–347.

Sanderson, T.L., Best, J.J., Doody, G.A.; Cunningham-Owens, D.G., and Johnstone, E.C. (1999) Neuroanatomy of comorbid schizophrenia and learning disability: a controlled study. *Lancet*, 354, 1867–1870.

Sarason, I.G. and Sarason, B.R. (1998) *Abnormal Psychology: The Problem of Maladaptive Behaviour*. New York: Prentice-Hall.

Scheff, T. (1966) *Being Mentally Ill: A Sociological Theory*. Chicago, IL: Aldine.

Schmidt, U., Humfress, H. and Treasure, J. (1997) The role of family environment and sexual and physical abuse in the origins of eating disorders. *European Eating Disorders Review*, 5, 184–207.

Schofield, W. and Balian, L. (1959) A comparative study of the personal histories of schizophrenic and non-psychiatric patients. *Journal of Abnormal and Social Psychology*, 59, 216–225.

Scott, M.J. and Stradling, S.G. (1997) Client's compliance with exposure treatment for posttraumatic stress disorder. *Journal of Traumatic Stress*, 10, 523–526.

Scott, M.J. and Stradling, S.G. (2001) *Counselling for Post-Traumatic Stress Disorder*. London: Sage.

Senior, J. (2001) Eye movement desensitisation and reprocessing: a matter for serious consideration? *The Psychologist*, 14(7), 360–363.

Shallice, T. (1988) *From Neuropsychology to Mental Structure*. Cambridge: Cambridge University Press.

Sham, P.C. O'Callaghan, E. and Takis, N. (1992) Schizophrenia following prenatal exposure to influenza epidemics between 1939 and 1960. *British Journal of Psychiatry*, 160, 461–466.

Shapiro, F. (1989) Efficacy of eye movement desensitization procedure in the treatment of traumatic memories. *Journal of Traumatic Stress*, 2, 199–223.

Shapiro, F. (1995) *Eye Movement and Desensitization: Basic Principals, Protocols and Procedures*. New York: Guilford Press.

Shepherd, G. (1998) Models of community care. *Journal of Mental Health*, 7, 165–177.

Shepherd, G., Muijen, M., Dean, R. and Cooney, M. (1996) Residential care in hospital and the community – Quality of care and quality of life. *British Journal of Psychiatry*, 168, 448–456.

Siebert, A. (2000) How non-diagnostic listening led to a rapid recovery from paranoid schizophrenia: what is wrong with psychiatry? *Journal of Humanistic Psychology*, 40, 34–58.

Silberg, J. *et al.* (1999) The influence of genetic factors and life stress on depression among adolescent girls. *Archives of General Psychiatry,* 56, 225–232.

Silverman, M.S., McCarthy, M. and McGovern, T. (1992) A review of outcome studies of rational-emotive therapy from 1982 to 1989. *Journal of Rational-Emotive and Cognitive-Behaviour Therapy,* 10, 111–175.

Simmonds, M. (1914) Über Hypophysisschwund mit todlichem Ausgang. *Deutshe Medizinische Wochenschrift,* 40, 332–340.

Skinner, L., Berry, K. and Griffith, S. (1995) Generalisability and specificity of the stigma associated with the 'mental illness' label: a reconsideration 25 years later. *Journal of Community Psychology,* 23, 3–17.

Skre, I., Onstad, S., Torgersen, S. and Kringlen, E. (2000) The heritability of common phobic fear: a twin study of a clinical sample. *Journal of Anxiety Disorders,* 14, 549–562.

Slade, D.D. and Russell, G.F.M. (1973) Awareness of body dimensions in anorexia nervosa: Cross sectional and longitudinal studies. *Psychological Medicine,* 3, 188–199.

Smith, M.L., Glass, G.V., and Miller, T.I. (1980) *The Benefits of Psychotherapy.* Baltimore, MD: Johns Hopkins University Press.

Smyth, J.M. and Greenberg, M.A. (2000) Scriptotherapy: the effects of writing about traumatic events. In: Duberstein, P. R. and Masling, J.M. (eds) *Psychodynamic Perspectives on Sickness and Health.* Washington DC: American Psychological Association.

Solomon, A. and Haaga, D.A.F. (1995) Rational emotive behaviour therapy research: What we know and what we need to know. *Journal of Rational-Emotive and Cognitive-Behaviour Therapy,* 13, 179–191.

Spanos, N.P. (1996) *Multiple Identities and False Memories: A Sociocognitive Perspective.* Washington DC: American Psychological Association.

Spitzer, R.L., Yanovski, S. Z. and Wadden, T. (1993) Binge eating disorder: its further validation in a multisite study. *International Journal of Eating Disorders,* 13, 137–153.

Stampfl, T.G. (1975) Implosive therapy: staring down your nightmares. *Psychology Today,* 8(9), 66–68, 72–73.

Stoppard, J. (2000) *Understanding Depression: Feminist Social Constructionist Approaches.* London: Routledge.

Stowell-Smith, M. and McKeown, M. (1999) Race, psychopathy and the self: a discourse analytic study. *British Journal of Medical Psychology,* 72, 459–470.

Sue, D. and Sue, S. (1990) *Understanding Abnormal Behaviour,* 3rd edition. Boston, MA: Houghton Miffin.

Swaffer, T. and Hollin, C. (2001) Anger and general health in young offenders. *Journal of Forensic Psychiatry,* 12, 90–103.

Sweet, R.A., Mulsant, B.H., Gupta, B. *et al.* (1995) Duration of neuroleptic treatment and prevalence of tardive dyskinesia in late life. *Archives of General Psychiatry,* 52, 478–486.

Szmukler, G., Dare, C. and Treasure, J. (1995) *Handbook of Eating Disorders*. Chichester: Wiley.

Thigpen, C.H. and Cleckley, H.M. (1957) *The Three Faces of Eve*. London: Secker and Warburg.

Thorne, B. (1992) *Carl Rogers*. London: Sage.

Thorndike, E.L. (1911) *Animal Intelligence: Experimental Studies*. New York: MacMillan.

Thornicroft, G. and Sartorius, N. (1993) The course and outcome of depression in different cultures: a 10 year follow-up of the WHO collaborative study on the assessment of depressive disorders. *Psychological Medicine*, 23, 1023–1032.

Tienari, P. (1992) Implications of adoption studies on schizophrenia. *British Journal of Psychiatry*, 161, 52–58.

Trauer, T., Farhall, J., Newton, R. and Cheung, P. (2001) From long-stay psychiatric hospital to Community Care Unit: evaluation at 1 year. *Social Psychiatry and Psychiatric Epidemiology*, 36, 416–419.

True, W., Rice, J. and Eisen, S. (1993) A twin study of genetic and environmental contributions to laibility for post-traumatic stress symptoms. *Archives of General Psychiatry*, 50, 257–264.

Tyrrell, C. and Dozier, M. (1997) The role of attachment in therapeutic process and outcome in adults with serious psychiatric disorders. *Paper presented at the biennial meeting of the Society for Research in Child Development, Washington DC*.

Vaughn, C.E. and Leff, J.P. (1976) The influence of family and social factors on the course of psychiatric illness. *British Journal of Psychiatry*, 129, 125–137.

Venable, V.L., Carlson, C.R. and Wilson, J. (2001) The role of anger and depression in recurrent headache. *Headache*, 41, 21–30.

Vitousek, K. and Manke, F. (1994) Personality variables and disorders in anorexia nervosa and bulimia nervosa. *Journal of Abnormal Psychology*, 103, 137–147.

Warner, R. (2000) *The Environment of Schizophrenia*. Hove: Taylor and Francis.

Wahlberg, K.E., Wynne, L.C., Oja, H., Keskitalo, P., Pykalainen, L., Lahti, I., Moring, J., Naarala, A., Sorin, S., Seitamaa, M., Laksy, K., Kolassa, J. and Tienari, P. (1997) Gene–environment interaction in vulnerability to schizophrenia: findings from the Finnish Adoptive Family Study of schizophrenia. *American Journal of Psychiatry*, 154, 355–362.

Watson, J.B. and Rayner, R. (1920) Conditioned emotional responses. *Journal of Experimental Psychology*, 3, 1–14.

Weinberger, D.R. (1988) Premorbid neuropathology in schizophrenia. *Lancet*, ii, 959–960.

Weissman, M.M. (1984) Depression and anxiety disorders in parents and children: results from the Yale family study. *Archives of General Psychiatry*, 41, 845–852.

Weissman, M.M. and Olfson, M. (1995) Depression in women: implications for health care research. *Science*, 269, 799–801.

Wiederhold, B.K. and Wiederhold, M.D. (1999). Clinical observations during virtual reality therapy for specific phobias. *CyberPsychology and Behavior*, 2(2), 161–168.

Wilson, D.L., Silver, S.M., Covi, W.G. and Foster, S. (1996) Eye movement desensitisation and reprocessing: Effectiveness and autonomic correlates. *Journal of Behaviour Therapy and Experimental Psychiatry*, 27, 219–229.

Wolfe, R. and Dryden, W. (1996) *Handbook of Counselling Psychology*. London: Sage.

Wolpe, J. (1958) *Psychotherapy by Reciprocal Inhibition*. Stanford CA: Stanford University Press.

Wolpe, J. (1973) My philosophy of psychotherapy. *Journal of Contemporary Psychotherapy*, 6, 59–62.

Yehouda, R. (ed). (1998) Neuroendocrinology of trauma and PTSD. In: *Psychological Trauma*. Washington DC: American Psychiatric Press.

Youssef, H.A. and Youssef, F.A. (1999). Time to abandon electroconvulsion as a treatment in modern psychiatry. *Advances in Therapy*, 16 (1).

# index

Page references in italics indicate figures.